The Time of the Sign

Advances in Semiotics

General Editor, Thomas A. Sebeok

THE TIME
OF THE SIGN

A Semiotic Interpretation
of Modern Culture

Dean MacCannell and
Juliet Flower MacCannell

 INDIANA UNIVERSITY PRESS
BLOOMINGTON

Copyright © 1982 by Dean MacCannell and Juliet Flower MacCannell

All rights reserved

No part of this book may be reproduced or utilized in any form or by any means, electronic or mechanical, including photocopying and recording, or by any information storage and retrieval system, without permission in writing from the publisher. The Association of American University Presses' Resolution on Permissions constitutes the only exception to this prohibition.

Manufactured in the United States of America

Library of Congress Cataloging in Publication Data

MacCannell, Dean.
    The time of the sign.

    (Advances in semiotics)
    Bibliography: p.
    Includes index.
    1. Culture. 2. Civilization, Modern—20th century.
3. Semiotics. I. MacCannell, Juliet Flower, 1943–
II. Title. III. Series.
HM101.M19 1982   306   81-47960
ISBN 0:253-36021-8   AACR2
1 2 3 4 5 86 85 84 83 82

While Government and Laws provide for the safety and well-being of assembled men, the sciences, letters and arts, less despotic and perhaps more powerful, spread garlands of flowers over the iron chains that bind them, stifle in them the sense of that original liberty for which they seem to have been born, make them love their slavery and turn them into what is called civilized peoples.

—JEAN-JACQUES ROUSSEAU, *The Discourse on the Sciences and the Arts*

Contents

Acknowledgments

Versions of some chapters in this book either have already been published in *Semiotica* or are about to be. Chapter 1 will appear as "The Semiotic of Modern Culture"; chapter 3 was published as "The Past and Future of Symbolic Interactionism" (1976); chapter 4 appeared under its current name, "Ethnosemiotics" (1979); and chapter 2 is in press also under its current title, "Phallacious Theories of the Subject." Most of this material has been extensively revised for incorporation in this book and is republished here in its current form with permission. We owe a tremendous debt of gratitude to the editor-in-chief of *Semiotica,* Professor Thomas A. Sebeok, for his many helpful suggestions over the years. This book would not be were it not for him.

Chapter 1 was originally written for the Fifth Annual Conference on Sociology and the Arts, 1976, at the invitation of Professor Bruce Jennings. Chapter 4 was originally written at the request of Professor D. Jean Umiker-Sebeok for presentation at a special session on the semiotics of culture at the American Anthropological Association meetings, Houston, 1977. Chapter 5, "The Second Ethnomethodology," was first drafted in 1971 and has been continuously read and revised over the years, first at the 1975 meetings of the Southern Section of the American Sociological Association, later at various universities. While it is published here for the first time, it was given in its current form as a Horizons of Knowledge Lecture at Indiana University, sponsored by the Departments of Sociology, Anthropology, and Linguistics and the Research Center for Language and Semiotic Studies. Chapter 6, "On the Nature of the Literary Sign," was prepared (together with chapter 7) as a seminar paper for the 1980 meetings of the International Association for Philosophy and Literature, University of Maine, Orono. We wish to thank Professor Robert C. Carroll of that institution for commissioning the paper and the other seminar participants for helpful commentary.

We have received support in writing this book from the Office of the Vice Chancellor for Academic Affairs, University of California, Davis; the Program in American Studies, University of California, Davis; and the Macrosocial Accounting Project of the College of Agricultural and Environmental Sciences, University of California, Davis. Additional support came via a grant from the National Endowment for the Humanities which sponsored the IC^4: Interdisciplinary Consortium for a Comparative Cultures Curriculum under the directorship of Professor Jay Mechling, University of California, Davis. We have benefited in numerous ways from lively discussions in the IC^4 group, and support is gratefully acknowledged. We also wish to thank our fellow members in the Northern California branch of the "Chicago Seminar in Symbolic Anthropology." Our gratitude also extends to our students in several official and unofficial seminars on semiotics offered by us in Davis.

Preface

This book is about the recent rapid development of semiotics as a body of ideas and techniques for the social sciences and humanities. It is equally a response to some changes which are happening in the "real world." We think the two are related. A quick scan of current popular entertainments reveals an obsession with alien things and sensations—monstrous creatures and emotions squeezing humanity from without and within. A decade ago, we might have borrowed some ideas from Herbert Marcuse and easily dismissed such a trend as the commercial exploitation of alienation, i.e., as a logical progression of a particular socio-economic system. Now it appears that we are up to something more basic than making profits from our own alienation. We are in the process of re-drawing the lines around humanity. *Alienation* is not even a technical term in post-structural thought. Political questions and positions which were unthinkable even in the halcyon radicalism of ten years ago are now routine: Are you for or against the United States using nuclear weapons on Europe as a historical object lesson and a way of avoiding a direct confrontation with the Soviet Union? Are you pro- or anti-life?

Certainly the current condition of the collective conscience is deplorable. But equally deplorable are corrections that are based on a return to the earlier values consensus: e.g., men are superior to women; no underdeveloped country could ever win a war with the United States; we are better than they are; etc. It was the easy falsifiability of these "truths" that led to the current historical moment. By now it should be clear that the 1970s tendency for everyone to split off into thousands of little groups, each one built around a controversial attitude, was less a solution than a psychological retreat from modernity.

Today it is commonplace for individuals and groups, via words and deeds, to question *structure*, to question, that is, the validity of previously unchallenged associations, oppositions, and hierarchies. When we hear someone say "government policies are the best available example of modern fiction," or "whales are us," or "God is returning and boy is She pissed," we can safely assume that the world itself is becoming post-structural. Everything that was once thought to be a "fact," or a "self-evident truth," or a belief that could exist beyond question is now seen as a social expression or a *sign*. Even if no one had raised the technical specter of semiotics, the current epoch would still be the time of the sign.

And, we think that even if no one had participated in the development of semiotics, the current radical questioning of the ultimate value of Western arts and sciences would still have occurred. After Marx's analysis of class conflict it was only a matter of time before some bright student would see that Cartesian rationalism follows the same violent pattern of dominance and submission in playing out the subject/object relationship in the bourgeois disciplines. At which point everyone else, being non-Marxist, would become anti-Marxist by definition.

Since the stage on which these dramas are occurring is our culture and its reflection in the social sciences and humanities, we are proposing here a closer look at culture, specifically at complex modern cultures and the mechanisms of cultural change. We will suggest that it is only at this point that semiotics becomes indispensable. We might sloganize this beginning as a kind of mid-game substitution: in the place of the subject/object split we are sending in the *sign,* a unification of subject and object or things and their meanings or values.

The following critical essays, analyses of culture and institutions and modest attempts at theory construction, are *interdisciplinary,* just as the humanities and culture are "interdisciplinary." In this regard we have been favored by an excellent marriage as a basis for a working partnership of the social sciences (Dean's background) and humanities (Juliet's). No doubt some will complain that we have exceeded our interdisciplinary license. Perhaps. But there are compelling reasons for pressing these limits in the social sciences and humanities today, reasons that have already been expressed (better than we can here) in the editorial stance of such journals as *Semiotica*, *Diacritics*, *Signs*, *Sémiotext(e)*, *Sub-stance*, *Glyph*, *Social Text*, *Critical Inquiry*, *Poetique*, etc.

The first part of the book, "The Semiotic Mechanism of Cultural Production," presents a modified Saussurian model of the sign we have devised as a minimally adequate framework for both literary and sociocultural analysis of culture. The other parts of the book build and expand upon this model. Part Two, "Socio-Cultural Applications," explores the implications of the general model for the social sciences. Chapter 3, "The Deconstruction of Social Reality," is intended to be theoretically and methodologically programmatic in that it provides a semiotic model of behavior. The remaining chapters in Part Two are critical. Each contains a re-reading of some recent tendencies in the social sciences from a semiotic perspective: the new anthropology ("ethnosemiotics"), "ethnomethodology," etc. Part Three of the book addresses literary and cultural criticism. Chapter 6, "On the Nature of the Literary Sign," is analogous to chapter 3, "The Deconstruction of Social Reality," in that it provides a model for reading literary texts that is a version of the model presented in chapter 3 for "reading" behavior, Chapter 7, "On the Discriminations of Signs," sorts out the recent intellectual historical evolution from phenomenology through existentialism, structuralism, post-structuralism, and semiotics, viewing this evolution from the standpoint of the successive transformations of our understanding of the *sign* that have taken place during this history. The last chapter, "A Community without Definite Limits," is a critique of counterrevolutionary tendencies that have recently surfaced within semiotics.

The fact that our collaboration has been both productive and, for us, genuinely enjoyable has not had a rational institutional result: we are both on the faculty of the same university but on campuses five hundred miles apart.

D. MacC.
University of California, Davis

J.F. MacC.
University of California, Irvine

December, 1981

The Time of the Sign

Introduction
The Semiotic Revolution

A SEMIOTIC APPROACH TO CULTURE

When we use the term "post-disciplinary" in this book, we are refer-ring to the paradigms in the social sciences and humanities that have undergone recent rapid development: phenomenology, structuralism, and semiotics. Each of these three frameworks has exhibited a capacity to cross disciplinary boundary lines and stimulate discussion that goes beyond the concerns, as traditionally defined, of any single discipline. We know that the term "post-disciplinary" can also convey a belief that the disciplines are dead. We do not want to imply that. But some of the most pressing problems, the study of modern culture among them, are beyond the grasp of the theories and methods of any one discipline, such as anthropology, sociology, literary criticism, philosophy, history, etc. We are using "post-disciplinary" to mean that we have tried to extend our models of culture beyond those found in the academic disciplines, and we have built our models always on the base of more than one discipline. In other words, we approached the boundaries of our individual disciplines as thresholds, not as the ultimate horizons, of knowledge.

Our main purpose in writing this book is a positive one: we wanted to contribute to the development of an approach to the description and analysis of cultural forms, of drama, language, behavior, ritual, litera-ture, and so forth. But the book also contains a double critique. We criticize the academic disciplines for carving up the study of culture into many exclusive, circumscribed, closely defended domains, thus foster-ing confusion and stagnation at precisely the historical moment when what is most needed is the leadership they could provide if they were willing to work with and learn from one another in their common enter-prise. And we criticize structuralism and phenomenology for often fail-ing to incorporate an adequate base of hard-won disciplinary knowledge into their formulations. This latter tendency leads to the

1

creation of naive models of culture presented in unwieldy, overelaborate terminology.

We assume, then, that any scholar/researcher will base his or her study of culture on a core of disciplinary knowledge, which includes knowing the history of the particular discipline's ideas and basic concepts, knowing how they are applied, having a trained ability to criticize and develop the basic conceptions, and being experienced in using the discipline's methods of research and analysis on concrete materials (plot outlines, the ethnographic record, famous case studies of neuroses, etc.) Far from denying the importance of discipline competence, we assume it as a starting point for the work that follows. And we also assume that the scholar/researcher will show a certain degree of flexibility, will be interested in what can be learned from the various perspectives and skills developed within the other disciplines. Literary critics know, among other things, that when they are analyzing a text, they must discover what meanings of the words were current when the text was written. Anthropologists know that much behavior once thought to be biologically "innate" occurs only in certain cultures. This kind of basic discipline knowledge is a prerequisite for the study of culture but, we shall argue, it should not be pursued as an end in itself. When it is pursued as an end in itself, it does not contribute to our understanding of culture so much as to the institutional fiction of "disciplines," where lines are drawn mainly as a matter of administrative convenience, that is, for political and organizational, not scholarly, reasons.

Some social scientists, literary scholars, designers, and others have already opted to locate their creative activities beyond the boundaries of their disciplines. Our book is for these students and scholars and others seeking to understand the intellectual base of such work. We think it is already possible to discern some interesting overall features of the semiotic movement. (1) It transcends national boundaries. (2) It transcends major political divisions, for example, that between Communist and capitalist nations. We find open and lively dialogue between Lévi-Strauss, Roman Jakobson, Juri Lotman, Umberto Eco, Hans Gadamer, Décio Pignatari, and others representing North and South America, eastern and western Europe and the Soviet Union. After Marx, none of the intellectual movements in the humanities and social sciences, not even existentialism and psychoanalysis, have shown the capacity for such wide extension. (3) Underlying this trans-national dialogue there is a common intellectual base, which can be found in the writings of the American philosopher Charles S. Peirce and the Swiss linguist Ferdinand de Saussure. (4) Most of the research and scholarship that makes up the semiotic core is also technically post-rational in that it refuses to accept uncritically any form of subject/object dualism. (5) Finally, this work is increasingly organized around the explication of *signs*.

In addressing our own disciplines, comparative literature, sociology and anthropology, we have adopted the stance that comparative cultural studies cannot make sense except as a contribution to a general semiotics of culture.

Even though it has not been carefully thought through, and some would prefer not to think it through, the continued development of semiotic perspectives is having a profound impact on the organization of the social sciences and humanities. As a minority of scholars from the diverse disciplines join the semiotic revolution or one of its precursor movements (phenomenology, structuralism), we must be cautious not to produce new and counter-productive oppositions between the new approaches and the old. There is already sufficient discomfort in the humanities and social sciences with new problems and frameworks. Some critics, for example, apply their insight beyond the confines of the literary text to film, advertising, propaganda, even to the writings of other critics, but not without stirring debate about the propriety of abandoning the "great book" tradition.[1] Sociology splits into several factions. One adheres to the "scientific" sociology tradition based on survey methods and functional theory, while others have branched into ethnomethodology, symbolic structuralism, and Marxist analysis. Historians searching for new approaches to universal history have found the key to understanding to be rhetorical tropes as often as "material conditions" or "great ideas." Some anthropologists now make observations of modern society, agricultural systems, tourism, etc., topics that are in conflict with anthropology's traditional and continuing concern with "primitives." These changes are not occurring in an orderly series, the way the progress of a discipline is presented in one of its introductory textbooks. Rather, they are proliferating simultaneously like Protestant sects after the Reformation.

This disorganization is distressing to some scholars and scientists, but we think attempts at restoring order, the order of older cultural disciplines, would impose unnecessary and intolerable restrictions on the development of cultural knowledge and is, in fact, impossible except as an artificial reaction. We are referring to the limits implicit in the design of boundaries around existing disciplines and subspecialties in the traditional social sciences and humanities. Cultural anthropology divides the world into "culture areas": South America, Oceania, Africa south of the Sahara, etc. It makes of these the general areas of expertise of individual scholars. Scholarly *specialties* are the whole bundle of cultural practices of a single group in the area: Bororo, Tipokia, Ndembu, etc. Western cultural studies by contrast, are internally differentiated by genre (music, literature, drama, etc.) and further subdivided internally by time period and language (nineteenth-century English fiction, etc.). Taken together, these systems, which at first appear to be based on a simple logic of efficiency, are far from innocent. They reinforce the separation of our Western, or "high," culture from the cultures of other peoples. They assure that non-Western ideas, insofar as they are incorporated into the academic curriculum, will be assigned to ethnic ghettoes separate from the departments that guard the sacred cultural traditions of the West. And they subdivide our understanding of our own cultural development to the point where our culture ceases to exist as a subject of systematic study in its own right.

In short, as we have already suggested, the liberal arts became the victim of their own criticism of society at just the moment when their leadership was most needed. They taught us that there has been a crisis of communication and reason; that there was no longer a rigorous philosophical basis for what is *good, true,* or *beautiful.* The center did not hold. Things fell apart. Meaning, in the sense of a meaning for life that can be conveyed via a good liberal arts education, disappeared. By their own account, the old social science and humanistic disciplines are no longer useful for holding our moral/aesthetic universe together. Is it not natural, then, that the disciplines degenerate into merely technical exercises with no unifying spirit? Is it not understandable that a good humanist would just sit around waiting for the apocalypse?

We think not. And in this book we attempt to show that semiotics has the power to transform criticism into a progressive intellectual movement.[2] The crisis of communication and reason necessarily occurred at exactly the same moment when central human concerns were coming to be understood as problems of *language.* As the disciplines became increasingly self-conscious about the importance of language and their use of it, they lost confidence in the universality of their truths. We think that this is deeply ironic, for the interpretative and critical liberal arts have a better handle on the kinds of issues the world faces today than the positivistic sciences have. The very old humanistic tradition of questioning our *being* might reclaim the territory that it has lost to moralistic cant: writers and social philosophers have, after all, had a great deal to say about the way one can face chaos, misunderstanding, error, and the disappearance of the divine.

If it is true, as we suggest, that the liberal arts disciplines faltered when they realized that they are only another form of language, a discourse, a myth, a "metalanguage" in Barthes's terms, they could fruitfully use this insight for a renewal of spirit and direction. The techniques, vocabulary, and critical philosophy of semiotics are available for examining the specifically linguistic nature of the disciplines.

If we continue to work within the disciplines without recognizing their linguistic and figurative underpinnings, then the disciplines will fall short of comprehending culture. Descartes himself, father of rational science, attempted to minimize the role language played in conception, but his *Discourse on Method* and his *Meditations* are inevitably entangled with language.

Merely demonstrating that the Cartesian *cogito* is a 'myth' accomplishes little, however. If we continue to work within the discourse of the disciplines in opposition to the Cartesian *cogito,* we always arrive at an impasse. We can show that the *cogito* is a myth, but in so doing we are also demonstrating that only language can attack language and we are caught in our own trap. We are forced to side with the neo-idealists and existentialists (perhaps against our own scholarly programs) in the erroneous belief that we have the power to transform society through our philosophizing. There is another way to arrive at the same impasse. Still working within language, we might advance the claim that not all reality is language, that language has a separate order of its own that is opposed to the 'natural' order. This is the neo-rational position, in which language occupies the position once held by scientific thought: that is, the only legitimate subjectivity.

Here is precisely the point at which a different metalanguage—semiotics—is necessary to get beyond the impasse. A semiotic framework can and must account for the different and often opposing meanings the sign has in various fields. Consider the status of the *sign* in idealism on the one hand and rationalism on the other. In idealism and existentialism, the sign is always a *metaphor* (a relationship between signifier and signified), a means of inscribing all of human culture into the "poetic," "imaginative," tropic, or rhetorical side of being. The *critic,* literary or social, who demystifies metaphors by showing their arbitrariness acts as censor for the idealist sign as it tends to exceed its imaginary limits and become reality. In a rational framework, the sign is totally arbitrary; the merely conventional sign, like the notation in music or the systems used in mathematics, is the basic sign-unit. The rational sign is opposed by the unconventional (the 'irrational') attitude that censors the rational sign's arbitrariness, and demands latitude for disorder, free-play, and the recognition of elements that exceed reason. Framed in another metalanguage, idealism is Oedipal and rationalism is schizoid.

We are suggesting, then, that language is not the only reality, as idealists and neo-idealists would have it, nor is it an epiphenomenon, as the materialists would have it. It participates in a structuring process that occurs at all levels of the organization of matter and spirit. In this book we want to develop a method for explication of this structuring process by moving from the *word* to the *sign* as our basic analytical term. And following Peirce, Husserl, Saussure, and Derrida, we might find ourselves once more able to return to "thought": not because it dominates and masters speech, but because it, like speech, is steeped in *signs.*

We know that most of the problems we discuss here have already been solved by Edmund Husserl and his followers. Husserl's radical critique of science and culture is indispensable to the semiotic work that followed it through existentialism and structuralism to post-structuralism. And, of course, Husserl's work foreshadowed the current loss of faith in the ultimate wisdom of science. Still we feel that there are important matters of method and domain, as well as some concrete problems that must be solved in the analysis of culture, which have so far been assessed in only a partial fashion by phenomenologists. Much of what we have written is a re-assessment of these matters. We have tried to present these debates in such a way that the issues are clear and can be understood without resort to special knowledge.

Comment on Some Recent Changes in Our Social Institutions and Culture

The central hypothesis of this book is that continued adherence to pre-semiotic modes of understanding is one reason colleges of arts and sciences in American universities have become separated from the mainstream of American life during the last ten years. The cultural disciplines as they are currently constituted can be used against themselves to sacralize and rigidify genre boundaries and ethnic "identities." A semiotic approach emphasizes the mechanisms in the production of culture, and cultural values, in the interactions between genres and groups. During the last decade, public recognition of national and international differences became an essential internal element of American culture. We think that the growth of this recognition has sometimes outstripped our academic capacity to define and articulate cultural differences. In spite of heroic efforts in programs of international studies and ethnic studies and among other post-disciplinary elements of the liberal arts disciplines, the recent pace of cultural semiosis in American society is outrunning academic understanding.

Consider the recent rapid evolution of the image of the black American in the popular consciousness. Intelligent blacks are now a normal component of television series. Contrast this not only with the Step-N-Fetchits of the nineteen thirties and forties, but with the Sidney Poitier and Harry Belafonte roles of the fifties and sixties: wooden heroes whose most important act was to exhibit hostility on appropriate cue. Middle America is in the process of revising its stereotypes. But why? A case can be made that there has been little concomitant shift in the economic relations between blacks and whites: for example, the unemployment rate for black youths continues to be disproportionately high. From a practical, political, or functional standpoint, the revision of stereotypes that now affects all ethnicities in American society makes very little sense. It often appears as the simple pendulum-swinging of a confused propaganda machine. Consider the Chinese. Ten years ago, the then Secretary of State, Dean Rusk, could conjure the image of a half-billion yellow demons "each with an H-bomb under his arm." Today, that image has receded. Mexican Americans were once working class by definition. Now they are also bourgeois. Ten years ago the Japanese were everyone's favorite ethnic group; now they are seen as capable, once again, of violence and political extremism.

A semiotics of culture accepts as one of its central tasks the responsibility to account for these changes intellectually and to accommodate them institutionally. Note that the fundamentals of the Western view of the Chinese have actually remained quite stable. Now they are friendly, intelligent, cultured, clever; before they were wily, decadently overcivilized, and devious—all the same traits under a negative rather than a positive sign. Similarly, though our estimation of the Russians keeps cycling, the Russians continue to have "soul." But the case of the blacks is not a simple sign reversal. Less than ten years ago, our most highly educated liberal intellectuals were frightened by intelligent blacks (perhaps some still are). We recall the remarks of one of our Ivy League professors about a young National Urban Fellow, "He's so intelligent he's frightening." Blacks now have intellect even in Middle American eyes. It is interesting that even though women also developed a national political base during the same period, they did not gain "intellect" in the process: they are still believed to be incapable of abstract, theoretical thought.

The semiotics of culture enables us not only to talk about, but to perceive and, we think, to eventually control the nonverbal expressions of heterogeneous groups and entities, *and* to comprehend them in terms of their *structured relationships with other groups and entities.* Semiotics undoes the white myth of the *isolate,* which has spilled over from our ethnopolitics into the discipline cultural sciences as the (false) idea that we can study and understand groups, texts, and/or genres in and of themselves without reference to their *relations* to other groups, texts, and genres.

Cultural Semiosis Does Not Stop at the Last Ethnic Frontier

The simultaneous appearance of "It" motion pictures about alien creatures and the re-birth of interest in Freud's "Id" (the alien creature within) signals on both the popular and intellectual fronts a growing uneasiness with all the divisions and distinctions by which we have lived, a (potentially unfortunate) search for new and absolute oppositions. One now urges the American public to be either pro- or anti-life and calls on the Supreme Court to finalize a definition of death. Not only can we not assume that "we" are better than "they" are on a cultural plane, our other most sacred moral and philosophical divisions have come into question: self/other, mind/matter, form/content, male/female, West/East, subject/object. The aim of general semiotics is to illustrate concretely the ways in which these oppositions are necessary fictions from the standpoint of our culture as we once knew it and are also merely arbitrary and replaceable. Here is the point of greatest disagreement between semiotics and conventional Western science and philosophy: according to conventional wisdom, values and meanings, on some level, must be accepted without question if they are to exist in the first place. They must appear to have a basis *in reality* or the 'facts' or the 'data' that goes beyond their status as mere meanings. In its division of all meanings into signifiers and signifieds, however, semiotics necessarily throws the integrity of our values into question and exposes the collective unconscious motives behind what is taken to be 'reality.' In other words, in addressing the problem of *how we know* and *how things mean* from a non-abstract standpoint, semiotics transforms all science into political action.

A SEMIOTIC MANIFESTO

Now we want to make explicit what we have so far only implied, that there is a concrete and living link between the semiotic revolution and the current rapid pace of change of values and behavior in modern social life. Semiotics is the study of the *means of the production* of meaning. "*How* do, *how* can, we know?" is a serious question, not merely philosophically but also at the level of everyday existence. The question, as we have asked it, averts definitions and responses in terms of ultimate, original and/or authentic being. There are no naive beginnings in semiotics and, as Max Fisch has said, "no inference-terminating conclusions." By deferring the problem of defining *what* things mean, semiotics may be less than philosophically authoritative, but all the more adept at describing cultural existences. Philosophical framing makes pure definitions seem to be set off from other definitions that have been provided. But the differentiations of things owes as much to the peculiar history of meanings that have already been ascribed to them—consciously or not—as to any pristine or pure definitions. Rousseau wrote of the autobiography he was then planning to write that its *style* would be a part of his story, as much a part as the narrative succession of 'facts.' We can say the same of our social institutions: their style too is "significant" and the official definitions of them are always, as Freud, Goffman, and Derrida have so nicely shown, eroded by their "underlife."

The current alternative to a semiotics of culture and institutions is rationalism and positivism. Rationalism contains the idea that any social or human problem can be solved by development and application of analytical models refined always in the direction of increasingly truthful representations of the 'real-world.' Though he saw it as too massive an undertaking, Descartes was able to conceive of a total reconstruction of the house of culture. Eventually, positivism, in its role as the political arm of rationalism, would accept Descartes's challenge and make the social sciences and humanities the engines of 'progress' in the development of our Western cultural institutions and the domination of Western values over the rest of the world. Descartes wrote:

> I was convinced that a private individual should not seek to reform a nation by changing all its customs and destroying it to construct it anew, nor to reform the body of knowledge or the system of education. . . . For public affairs are on a large scale, and large edifices are too difficult to set up again once they have been thrown down, too difficult even to preserve once they have been shaken, and their fall is necessarily catastrophic. [Descartes 1965:9]

Only one century later, such thinking found its response, as Rousseau labored at deconstructing the "purity" of origins, showing how they are contaminated by time and history (see Derrida 1967a). And in the following century, Saussure (1966:71–72) did the same for language:

> No society in fact has ever known language other than as a product inherited from preceding generations, and one to be accepted as such. . . . [S]ucceeding generations are not superimposed on each other like the drawers of a piece of furniture, but fuse and interpenetrate, each generation embracing individuals of all ages—with the result that modifications of language are not tied to the succession of generations.

(Saussure assumes that language is analogous to other social institutions.)

Saussure's work brought forth the revolution in Western cultural understanding called "structuralism" whose historic import and impact have yet to be fully assessed. From Piaget and Lévi-Strauss to Lacan and Bateson, structuralism provides one of the first examples of a pan-disciplinary intellectual movement that saw alliances between technology, language, and culture. The *Zeitgeist* of the nineteen fifties and sixties to which structuralism responded has passed, of course, but the current epoch, still groping toward self-consciousness, must come to terms with structural insights in nearly every aspect of Western science, natural or cultural.[3] It may well be that these insights will be modified or radically re-written by confrontation with altered social conditions, but the idea of "structure" (zero change) in itself provides all the necessary impetus for our attempt to conceive of change or "revolution" properly so-called. It is the confrontation of structure and post-structural (semiotic) perspectives on change and revolution that prompted our second reading of Rousseau, Saussure, and Peirce, and Descartes, and much of this book is based on that second reading.

No one knew better than Rousseau, Saussure, and Peirce that our institutions—linguistic and otherwise—are subject to mutability, to change. Tradition, the multiplicity of their signs, collective inertia, and the overcomplexity of institutional systems operate against change. But because they have no basis other than arbitrariness, signs can *change their meanings.* "Change" is very strictly defined by Saussure (1966:75) as a "shift in the relationship of signifier and signified." The meaning of an institution can change—even without its being destroyed or renewed—like the linguistic sign, it can be "transvalued," losing whatever "meaning" it had had for its community. This kind of revolution—the semiotic revolution—is unlike other conceptions of revolution as put forth by puritans and Marxists: it is neither a cyclical return to a prior historical state nor the arrival in a brave new world without future history.

Semiotics, like Rousseau's *supplement* (see Derrida 1967a), is the 'appropriate technology' for a philosophy that confines itself to the peculiarities, hazards, and bizarreries of existence. Some semioticians will be more interested in the traditional institutions than in the moment of change (the 'originary' moment); there is not only room for both kinds of emphasis in semiotics, they are mutually determinant and inescapable. We may finally, we think, be ready to get beyond oscillation in our cultural methods: literary history collapses of boredom without the excitement of regenerated meanings and values that various movements, from New Criticism to Deconstructionism, have fortunately provided; the primitive world is tearing away from anthropology's grasp while the modern world demands better descriptions of its own structure and consciousness. Semiotics makes possible the transvaluation of disciplines by permitting both aspects, history and tradition, to work together, not just as forced associates or antagonists, but as necessary partners in the study of culture.

Semiotics—indeed the very definition of the sign—includes the interpreter (perceiver, addressee) as a constitutive component of meaning. Merely by asking the semiotic question, "Who is speaking and to whom?" (as Freud once demanded of his patients' fragmentary phrases) one comes to view cultural forms in a new light, a light that puts the working intellect back at the center of thought, 'figuring things out'. Semiotics offers the alternative to the great schisms (schizms?) that have always attended Western science by bringing the active communicative aspect of culture into any analysis. Even though there is within semiotics itself some retreat from the semiotic question (see the recent work by some writers on the concept of subjectivity)[4] the semiotic question will persistently demand to be answered.

Our starting point is the assumption that culture is not a rational structure, that it cannot be understood from the standpoint of either *arché* or *telos,* origin or aim, but must be understood as it unfolds, develops, changes, erases itself, and rewrites itself. Culture is neither fantastic nor unordered, neither historical nor ahistorical. And we shall not understand enough about culture until we can accept its postrational expressions as such.

We want to make it clear from the beginning that we do not wish to join in the creation of a new set of oppositions between semiotic cultural sciences and our cultural traditions. Rather, we want to advance the semiotic revolution and the cultural sciences by a critical review of some major semiotic and proto-semiotic insights about culture and its products. To a semiotician trained in prognosis and diagnosis (trained, that is, in the reading of signs) the confrontations between culture and the various analyses of culture are archetypes: they are moments in the evolution of a semiotic system when the boundaries are redrawn and there is a shift in the relationship between the signifiers and the signifieds. Ferdinand de Saussure (1966:74) wrote of the structure of language and its bizarre quality of being both perfectly immutable and perfectly mutable: "Because the sign is arbitrary it follows no other law than that of tradition, and because it is based on tradition it is arbitrary. Time, which insures the continuity of language wields another influence apparently contradictory to the first: the more or less rapid change of linguistic signs." Compare Saussure's vision with that of rational science and traditional morality which, in order to function properly, must be taken in by their own fictions of stability and order. At the structural level, the level of all meaning, the semiotic revolution is a total shift in the relationship of ideas and signs. The current effort to redraw academic boundaries and the production of new differentiations of culture are visible manifestations of a semiotic revolution.

Language, Thought, and Signs

> There are no men, not even the insane, so dull and stupid that they cannot put words together in a manner to convey their thoughts. On the contrary, there is no other animal, however perfect and fortunately situated it may be that can do the same. . . . And this proves not only that animals have less reason than men, but that they have none at all. . . . Note that we should not confuse speech with the natural movements that indicate passions, and can be imitated by machines as well as by animals; nor should we think, like some of the ancients, that animals speak although we do not understand their language. [Descartes (1637, *Discourse on Method*) 1965:37]

Descartes asks us to believe in a complete separation between ourselves and the other animals and that this separation is based on uniquely human faculties, *language* and *reason*. His formulation is innocent enough as a claim for what is human and as the base for the monuments we have constructed to reason and language—our modern sciences and humanities. But it also perpetuates an assumption that has lost all its authority in the twentieth century; namely, that the thinking human subject is the sole owner of logic and reason. In effect, Descartes rules out the possibility of a trans-subjective logic or system that emerges from and goes beyond any of its individual manifestations, which leads the thinking subject along the path of insight. Already in the nineteenth century, Charles Darwin had described one such system: the process of natural selection, an emergent logic, complex and elegant, had been producing species each uniquely adapted to an ecological niche, while eluding the scientific *cogito.* It is all the more remarkable from a Cartesian standpoint that this collective work is done so intelligently by plants and animals without the intervention of either God or science—indeed, when science gets involved it often breeds maladaptive monstrosities.

Today, any "Cartesian" science or philosophy that establishes boundaries around its subject matter and claims exclusive control over what constitutes the truth therein, is suspect and open to challenge. We note that not all of these challenges produce felicitous results. Analytical atrocities are routinely committed in the name of post-rational thought. First among these, and perfectly predictable, is the recent (heavily supported) research designed to demonstrate that apes can be taught English.[5] There are other examples, much less clear-cut. Parapsychology openly challenged theoretical physics at a recent forum of the national meetings of the American Association for the Advancement of Science. Midwifery and "natural healing" confront the American Medical Association, sometimes from within.

The current confrontation of rational and post-rational thinking is sharply defined in scientific communities but not confined to them. Satanic cults demand responses from organized religion to questions concerning the ultimate value of life, and the answers are not forthcoming.[6] Natural "sciences of the concrete," to borrow Lévi-Strauss's term, such as astrology, folk medicine, and primitive agricultural practices are being revived and studied avidly. Similarly, in the realm of everyday morality, liberal common sense, which once supplied quick answers to any question no matter how outlandish the question, now equivocates on every question concerning human sexuality. On homosexuality, for example, there is tolerance and also the sense that full acceptance undermines natural reproduction and social relationships. So we take an Ann Landersish stand, "It's all right for them, perhaps they should seek therapy, but we have no right to call them 'sick'," etc.

While 'Cartesian' logic no longer holds, it is also evident that the quality of insight based on a mere denial of rationalism is not necessarily superior. The intellectual *avant-garde* has never been so volatile as it is at the present moment. When everything goes right, someone 'pulls off' a major breakthrough into the inner workings of a transsubjective system: for example, Chomsky's critique of what he called "Cartesian linguistics" and his subsequent development of "generative grammar," which carried us from the deadend notion that thought produces language to the logic of creation within language itself. When everything goes wrong, the exhausted Cartesian *cogito* ends up opposed to a modern weirdo, undisciplined and irrational, masquerading as post-rational and post-disciplinary.

In the last ten years semiotics has been revived (as it was on several other similar occasions in the past) for use as a kind of all-terrain vehicle conveying these issues across the various scientific and humanistic fields. In a sense this is an unfair burden thrust upon semiotics by disciplines that have faltered in their own philosophical and theoretical development. The semiotic movement contains within itself the full range of strengths and weaknesses associated with post-rational thought. In this book, we have attempted to restrict ourselves to the positive side, to a progressive general semiotics that does not abdicate its revolutionary responsibilities.

Descartes told us that our humanity is conditional upon our ability to use words to convey thoughts. And he warned us "that we should not confuse speech with the natural movements that indicate passions, and can be imitated by machines as well as by animals; nor should we think, like some of the ancients, that animals speak although we do not understand their language." As we have suggested, the seeds of the semiotic revolution (and perhaps some others) were already planted in the writings of Jean-Jacques Rousseau:

> What the ancients said in the liveliest way, they did not express in words, but by signs. They did not say it, they showed it. [Rousseau (1754?, *Essay on the Origin of Language*) 1966:6]

We know that so long as semiotics functions only as a partner to modern structural linguistics it cannot be called revolutionary. The revolution that empowered language and speech above other human activities and made the forms of language—its rules and its beauties—the universal "human substance" was begun as early as the seventeenth and eighteenth centuries. Language was esteemed by rationalism be- cause it pictured *thought,* although thought remained elevated over its representative. Philosophical expression of this is found in Descartes, who dismissed communication as a means of defining the human; other animals communicate but only we can think. Yet his dismissal gener- ated perhaps more partisans *for* language as the arbiter of human destiny than the seventeenth century rationalist could ever have imag- ined. Any involvement with language—as with sex—seems to generate endless interest in it, and the controlled and orderly rationalist entry into the linguistic arena (the search for universal grammar) spawned the eighteenth century's startling and sprawling insight reversing Des- cartes: thought is the product of associated (linguistic) images.[7]

We think that the Cartesian *cogito* has achieved its abundance of technological miracles and disasters, has played out the wealth it pro- duced, and is exhausted. Again *language,* as in the eighteenth century, asserts its claims to define humanity. In an ironic reversal of priority of the ancient seven liberal arts (the trivium gaining the upper hand over the quadrivium) speculation about grammar, rhetoric, and logic have re-emerged to suggest once more that language is the key and the riddle of humanity. Continental and Anglo-American philosophers, lin- guists and poets, psychoanalysts and sociologists, historians and social theorists, even the last hold-outs in the practical arts, economists and medical doctors, are assimilating and even accepting a linguistic defini- tion of their discipline tasks. One could recite a very long list of the scholars and thinkers[8] engaged in, entangled in, language and agreeing upon the linguistic horizon of nearly every field of knowledge: we have genetic *codes,* computer *languages,* the retrieval of socio-cultural knowledge from fragments of conversation, personality and character construction in psychoanalysis as well as in literary texts—even physi- cists cheerfully adopt Lewis Carroll's freeplay in naming the subatomic particles that they hold to be the base of physical reality.

The cultural sciences have tended to use the grammatical and rhetor- ical aspects of language for their models. As *rhetoric,* language denies *order* to reality outside its controlled formation by tropes (for example, metaphor, metonymy, hyperbole, chiasmus, synecdoche, analogy, irony, etc.). As *grammar,* language controls the creation of meaning through sets of rules that regulate "creativity." It seems that we now find ourselves on the verge of being able to tie up the loose ends of cultural life in the linguistic package, ratifying, as it were, the modernity of our culture in the reflexive act of honoring language.

The contribution semiotics has made to this situation should not be underestimated. Semiotics and linguistics are empirically linked in the works of the influential Swiss linguist Ferdinand de Saussure, who claimed that linguistics was only a subfield of a larger and more general science of signs yet to be developed. Following Saussure (although the studies did not always agree with the details of his theory), there was an explosion of semiolinguistic studies in Western and Eastern Europe and America. These studies in aggregate constitute the most developed practical working-out of the structure of language and languages that we have ever witnessed. While there are those who object to the inflation of language—its being overworked as the model of creation—it is nonetheless the case that we are, for the moment at least, enmeshed in it, and it is our duty to comprehend it. Semiotics has provided the most fruitful source of insight into the nature, structure, and development of language yet devised. In the semiotic mirror, language at last acquires a self-image.

Semiotics honors and mirrors language, restoring its centrality in culture. But it also transcends language, going beyond it as the final cause of meaningful existence. By the continuous and always subversive intrusion of the question of the *sign,* in which subject, object, and interpretation are fused, semiotics can liberate meaning from language, and vice versa, relieving language of some of its overheavy cultural burdens. The semiotic question, the search for the sign-character in any meaningful event or structure (that is, the question *how,* not *what,* does this mean?), keeps the primary linguistic model, with its tendency toward idealism, pinned down, in context, and capable of self-reflection. Semiotic analysis insists on uncovering all the sign-components in meaning: subject/object/interpretant; signifier/signified/language community; sender/referent/receiver; writer/text/reader; etc. In other words, semiotics is the method that *reflects on* linguistic structures— even those structures already purported to be reflection on language. One role of semiotics is to keep these reflections honest and open. Rhetorical analysis, for example, can become one-sided. The subjectivist will-to-power seems all too easily legitimated when, as with Foucault, the world is seen as a series of tropes, whose aesthetic and emotional meanings are unimportant. Yet when rhetoric is seen as ornamental or purely aesthetic, the analysis loses sight of the communicative intent and/or function of the trope (e.g., persuasion, appeal, seduction). Semiotics demands of rhetoric that it reveal both its aspects eventually if not simultaneously.

Semiotics embodies within itself the same analytic flexibility by which all cultural systems (such as "language" and "humanity") live, including the radical oppositions found at the very heart of cultural systems. This is the reason that semiotics has the capacity both to center and decenter the linguistic primacy (discussed above), not from a hostile or mute stance, but from within. It should come as only a mild surprise, when viewed from this perspective, as a paradox we might have expected, that one of the greatest masters of semiotic analysis in our century, Roland Barthes, should have asked that semiotics subordinate itself to linguistics (1975).

Here is the crucial decision for cultural studies: do we use the actual terminology devised linguistically for the analysis of language and apply it to other sign systems, discovering the tropic nature of history, for example, or the grammar of the *Decameron*? Or do we assume that one of the pleasures of the text arises from its offering, as language does, the matter *and* the form of/for analysis? Our study of culture is based on the second option.

Conclusion

Recent social change and corresponding shifts in intellectual paradigms in the social sciences and humanities have been so rapid that many scholars are being asked to reject a system of ideas they never accepted in the first place. This is producing hopeless confusion in the academy. We have suggested that the linguistic critique of logocentric or rational science only went so far as to set up grammar and rhetoric in the place of the Cartesian *cogito*. Even the linguistic critique is unacceptable from the standpoint of conventional discipline wisdom, and yet we are already demanding that it be set aside in favor of a still more radical general semiotics of culture. It is quite natural under these circumstances that semiotics would appear to some as a useless surplus of activity and reconstructing of domains—language, art, science, politics, medicine, etc.—that have seemed adequate and valid till now. Even some so-called semioticians think of it as a useless surplus of activity and are attracted to it mainly because it provides them with the latest set of fashionable buzzwords from Paris or Germany or Tel Aviv or Mexico City, a jargon that serves as the status marker for a few self-styled intellectual elites. Sometimes we suspect that semiotics has established itself on American soil by means of gestures hostile to that soil: through the efforts of foreign language teachers who can do 'semiospeak' and who consciously reserve its 'mysteries' for their initiates.

It appears most often as a kind of cult, rather than as part of a partnership between a maturing American intellectual life and a serious European attraction for American materials. This integration is in fact growing; it is real on both the theoretical and the practical planes, as a survey of professional exchanges and/or bibliographies reveals; and competency at 'home' and 'abroad' may soon be a minimal requirement for academic life even outside the 'foreign language' orientation. Thus, despite its initial image as a 'foreign import' competing with more sensible American products and despite the fear of job displacement by 'foreign workers' (scholars whose work and interests cross national and/or discipline boundaries), semiotics is growing and extending its appeal.[9] We think that the growth of semiotics under such adverse institutional circumstances is based on its power as method: it offers the best, if not the only, way of responding to important changes that have occurred in us and in the world.

Not only in academia but in all walks of life each of us must play different roles and meet a diversity of challenges, and each is required to excel in more than one area. In fact, one might make a case that the academy, with its tenure system and organization of specializations into departments, is less responsive to the changes in modern values than any other area of society. A medical doctor we know has just earned a law degree. And we know of others who are considering the same move as a "matter of necessity." The actor Paul Newman has recently placed in the grueling twenty-four-hour automobile race at Le Mans. Former Harvard professor Timothy Leary now works as a stand-up comic in Los Angeles nightclubs.

These new patterns and combinations are signs that the cultural oppositions that formerly organized life in modern society are no longer valid. And the erosion of the validity of former cultural oppositions operates not merely on the level of individual careers but on the total system: for example, witness our recent difficulty in distinguishing between art and pornography. Modernity has promoted the erotic to the point where its denial leads to the death of culture. But while the liberation of eros is complete, or almost complete, on a legal level, there remains a strange alignment of official morality and aesthetic judgment that continues to suppress the erotic by defining it as "pornography." Not only does this suppression skew both "straight" art and "porn," it assures that advances on one of our most important new frontiers occur outside the context of critical discussion and evaluation. And this is not the only area in which the un-thought-through popular consciousness has seized the initiative from academic, disciplined thought. Sociology is haunted by the spectre of journalism. In fact, "journalism" competes with many of the fields of cultural studies and sometimes, like fiction, outruns them.

Even on the personal and psychological level, the former oppositions are no longer certain. It used to be that one was either a career woman *or* a mother: one was a capitalist *or* a communist; a businessman *or* a professor; scientist *or* aesthete; even American *or* foreigner. There were no in-betweens. You could not be a blonde movie actress *and* be smart; you could not be young *and* wise or old *and* healthy; you could not be a hard-driving success *and* a good father. These fundamental oppositions, like any syntagm, are losing their grip on the structure of life in modern society; and while they have not been replaced, we are in that provisional situation in which instead of either/or we all have to be both/and. This is one of the reasons the woman has become a central figure during the last few years. Women have traditionally been permitted to represent authority only if they truncated their other roles —wife, mother, etc. And so, over time, they became adepts at masking their authority and balancing multiple, overlapping, and seemingly contradictory roles. They have developed some expert solutions to a problem men are only now beginning to face.

The revolution makes demands on everyone, not merely on those who have consciously joined it. Once everyone has doubled and redoubled their roles, positions, and points of view, revolution occurs not by a multiplication of effort but by a reduction of effort. For example, an entire 'class' might disappear in a relatively short period of time by the simple expedient of mass rejection of one role in favor of others that are already in place. And the process might even go unnoticed. We think that we have already witnessed the quiet undoing of a human type, actually a decent figure, the *liberal* who was once the pillar of the liberal arts. Liberals believed in the dignity and equality of individuals, the trustworthiness of persons in positions of authority, the infallibility of our society and its institutions, detachment and objectivity as the basis for scientific progress, the principle of a direct relationship between effort and reward, and the openness of our institutions to new ideas and talents. There is considerable liberal backlash in the liberal arts today, and great nostalgia for the image, but no one seriously accepts the assumption of a rational social system on which this particular set of values is based, and most liberals have simply given up being liberals.

At the level of our actual existence, the semiotic revolution has begun, and it will complete itself as everyone gets tired of their schizoid performances and concentrates their efforts on the roles and perspectives they favor above the others. We are reminded of Rousseau's description of France before the revolution that he predicted but did not live to see:

> Although everyone preaches with zeal the maxims of his profession, each prides himself on having the tone of another. The magistrate takes on a Cavalier air, the financier acts like a Lord, the Bishop makes gallant proposals; the Courtier speaks of philosophy; the Statesman of wit and letters; down to the simple artisan, who, unable to assume a different tone, dresses in black Sundays in order to look like a man of the Palace. [1964b: II:235]

Apparently, most of these eighteenth-century "drugstore cowboys" were striving for intellectual recognition or upward social mobility. And it was their revolutionary spirit that Marx gave ultimate and radical formulation as consciousness-for-itself and seizure of the means of production. We do not think there is any reason to believe that the revolution of modernity is located so unambiguously under a positive sign, that it will inevitably produce upward social mobility and self-improvement. We do believe, however, that it is the historical task of semiotics to figure out what sign it is under.

Part I

The Semiotic Mechanism of Cultural Production

1

A General Semiotic of Cultural Change

Toute sémiologie d'un système non-linguistique doit
emprunter le truchement de la langue, ne peut donc
exister que par et dans la sémiologie de la langue. . . .
La langue est l'interprétant de tous les autres
systèmes, linguistiques et non-linguistiques.

—Emile Benveniste, "Sémiologie de la langue"

No language in the full sense of the word can exist
unless it is steeped in the context of culture.

—Juri Lotman and Boris Uspensky, "On the Semiotic
Mechanism of Culture"

Semiotics cannot develop except as a critique of
semiotics.

—Julia Kristeva, *Sémiotikè*

In this chapter, we want to present the general framework that serves
as the base for the special analyses that follow. The most elementary
questions in the study of culture involve morals and values and the ways
that morality and values are organized vis-à-vis aesthetics and utility.
One version of the difference between so-called primitives and ourselves is that our values and morals change while those of primitives
do not. Lévi-Strauss (1967:46–47) writes:

> Although they exist in history, these ["primitive"] societies seem to
> have elaborated or retained a particular wisdom which incites them to
> resist desperately any structural modification which would afford his-
> tory a point of entry into their lives. . . . In a word, these societies, which
> we might define as "cold" in that their internal environment neighbors
> on the zero of historical temperature, are . . . distinguished from the
> "hot" societies which appeared in different parts of the world following
> the Neolithic revolution.

We cannot agree that primitive societies are unchanging, but we accept
the implicit challenge that any systematic approach to modern culture

necessarily awaits the construction of a general model of socio-cultural change.*

When we approach morals and values as signs, certain widely held conceptions about culture are overturned. For example, within conventional frameworks, it is commonplace to assume the stability of cultural forms, that change requires effort. In this chapter we find, on the contrary, that culture is originally and essentially pure change, and it achieves stability and order only as a kind of death which it attempts to prolong. As we have already suggested, however, the sort of model we are proposing requires additional development of a second semiotic that takes us beyond linguistic models of the sign.

From Linguistic to Semiotic Models of Cultural Change

Semiotic interpretation of cultural production currently operates within a limiting framework of opposing assumptions, having to do with the relationship of "natural language" to other cultural systems. On the one side is Benveniste's (1969:130) seemingly radical semiotic assertion that "natural language" is the ultimate interpretant for all other aspects (departments) of culture. On the other is the Tartu school's more recent opening (Lotman and Uspensky 1978) of Benveniste's position: the suggestion that language is dependent, at least in part, on the existence of other cultural forms. According to Lotman and Uspensky, cultural productions act as models, as the 'semiotic mechanism', of cultural *evolution.* Tzvetan Todorov came to much the same conclusion when he advanced the claim (1977:19–20), that literature, while secondary, is also the form of semiotic system that serves as a model *for* language as well. One would thus have to question (as Roland Barthes has; see our chapter 7) the traditional view of the imaginative arts, especially literature, as having a primarily semantic (meaning-bearing) function in relationship to 'natural language,' as Benveniste would have it. Yet it is undeniable that at least these arts feed upon 'naturalized' cultural systems, such as language, as their source: and 'natural' codes have been most successfully applied to their analysis by structural semiology.

This 'natural language vs. all other sign systems' formulation is not a helpful polarization of the semiotics of cultural production. The Tartu group has moved to liberate art from the primacy of language but we

---

*Roland Barthes's "Myth Today" (1972:15lff.) judges the anti-historical bias of mythic thought to be pathological in a modern context.

think they have not moved far enough to the 'semiotic mechanism' that operates throughout the realm of modern culture on language, art, social movements, morality, ritual, propaganda. We want to continue to open the question of the semiotics of culture in directions that would clarify the ways in which cultural images in all spheres exert both conservative and radical influences on total cultural development.

The Lotman/Uspensky thesis has the effect of introducing a dynamic —specifically an evolutionary element into the semiotic investigation of cultural forms (1978:223 and 1974:302–3): "Man is included in a more mobile world than all the rest of nature." This responds not only to an intuitive sense that the semiotics of culture must necessarily include a dynamic mechanism, but it also responds to the conservative literary criticisms of semiotic inquiry as to the 'mythic' and synchronic in relation to literature (De Man 1971: 10–11). In the essay on the "Semiotic Mechanism of Culture" and elsewhere, Lotman's terms curiously repeat those of Sigmund Freud in *Beyond the Pleasure Principle* and alert us to the tendency of culture to prevent its own development except as a perpetuation of a synchronic illusion of pure contemporaneity (repetition, an ally of the death instinct). Questions of 'pure change' recur in the Lotman/Uspensky theses which raise for discussion the very categories of the semiology of language itself—synchronic and diachronic.

The approach we propose aims to liberate signifying systems from the matrix ('natural language') to vie for primacy as the semiotic mechanism of cultural production and they are limited only insofar as one would use conventionally defined 'Cultural Productions' as a model for cultural production in general. Lotman/Uspensky limit the generative, productive power to conventionally conceived 'artistic acts'. But the potential is there to go beyond these, to expand semiotic inquiry about the development of cultural change into the heart of other forms of cultural production—into "the heart of social life" as de Saussure wanted—into those cultural productions usually studied by anthropologists.

Interestingly, Lévi-Strauss (1967:49) reserved such an investigation of self-reproductive culture for a cybernetic future:

[A]dvances in information theory and electronics give us at least a glimpse [of] the conversion of a type of civilization which inaugurated historical development at the price of the transformation of men into machines into an ideal civilization which would succeed in turning machines into men. Then culture having entirely taken over the burden of manufacturing progress, society would be freed from the millennial curse which has compelled it to enslave men in order that there be progress. Henceforth history would make itself by itself.

Such a 'future' is, of course, already at hand; and we need only bring the practitioners of its analysis together with Lotman/Uspensky's theses to make this clear. In modern culture, manners (Erving Goffman, Lévi-Strauss himself), morals (Dean MacCannell), passions (Freud), social movements (Durkheim, Frank Young), and those great modern fictions—governmental policies—have all been demonstrated to be local systems to semiosis that equally have the empirical potential, the power, to serve as models for any and/or every other facet of culture. Attempts to reserve primacy (ontological or otherwise) for a particular semiotic system—be it 'natural language' or 'Art'—is an evident error.[1] Even everyday life proliferates cultural productions that serve as meta-systems of interpretation: from below the level of the individual to the self and beyond, to class, and to any human system, we engage in a drama of interpretations that *is* the mechanism (secondary modeling systems) of cultural development. Before we did, Emile Durkheim (1965a:24) recognized in everyday cultural arrangements a pre-figurative (pre-conceptual/inspirational) model for cultural conceptions even of the highest type:

> There are societies in Australia and North America where space is conceived in the form of an immense circle, because the camp has a circular form.[2]

In other words, everyday 'natural' cultural arrangements function as sign systems by virtue of the fact that they call forth other sign systems, or in Peirce's terms (1955:99), "signs give birth to other signs, and especially one thought calls forth another." (See also Lotman 1974:303.)[3]

The sender-receiver model applies here in a curious way: culture sends a message to itself (the sign, as Peirce often wrote, is always 'addressed' to someone), but the receiver's reading of this message (culture's reading itself) will always be a more developed sign than that originally addressed to it.[4] It is not merely a gesture or a sign, it is one that has been read or interpreted. And even when that interpretation is less skilled than it need be, or more skilled, as when a student fails to understand an assignment, or understands it better than its author, the original sign plus its reading constitutes an expanded structure. The expanded structure is composed of the sign and some form of response to it. This is the heart of cultural evolution. It begins with a production and proceeds to a reproduction that is not a simple doubling but a reflection at a higher power. This progress is called "pure rhetoric" by Peirce.

Now it is possible to map two different directions to cultural evolution. The mechanism of the self-reading of culture can spiral ever upwards until all sense of the 'natural cultural' source is forgotten. The model for this is the toy Freud called a magic tablet, on which the child may write or draw, then erase clear by lifting the surface sheet off the underlying gelatin base. Each erasure appears to provide a new beginning, a clean start, but the impression of each previous use remains embedded in the base. Lotman/Uspensky (1978:216) speak, in an unconscious echo of Freud's *magic tablet* and all true philosophical *tabulae rasae,* of cultures' having an apparent periodic need of "forgetting," at which point one must, as Husserl insisted, return to the "things themselves." The essence of culture may reside in an interplay between its mnemonic function (memory, recording, writing) and resistance to such remembering.

The other possibility is that the reflection of the sign can begin to assert its own stability and deny birthright to other signs. It can act prospectively; the sign can declare itself the anti-revolution. In this case, the sign is structured as an attempt to stabilize 'natural' cultural arrangements so as not to have to progress or change. An example would be the touristic image of an 'authentic' ethnic identity. Following this direction, the realization of the true destiny is to promote unchangeability. Lotman/Uspensky (1978:227) write:

> In order to fulfill its social function, culture has to appear as a structure subject to unified constructive principles. . . . There comes a moment when it becomes conscious of itself, when it creates a model of itself. This model defines the unified, the artificially schematized image that is raised to the level of a structural unity.
>
> When imposed onto the reality of this or that culture, it exerts a powerful regulating influence, preordaining the construction of culture, introducing order and eliminating contradiction.

This form of cultural "reproduction" and production, like Oscar Wilde's "life imitates art," is the classical mimesis (the imitation of nature) in reverse. Everyday cultural arrangements become merely a representative, or sign, of reflected images. Some ethnomethodologists (see chapter 5) base their understanding of everyday life entirely on this one-sided view of cultural "evolution." They have concentrated all their analysis on those aspects of culture that contain the seeds of its own destruction. The mimetic attitude is sterile and conservative and leads inevitably to the death of culture (the death, that is, of culture in the sense of an evolutionary striving, of thought and action that give rise to other thoughts and actions.) The anti-revolutionary cultural sign is trapped in a specular stasis of the narcissistic type best described by Lacan's "stade du miroir."

Culture that reproduces itself as a series of endless mirrorings, yet adds nothing either to the original 'natural' culture or to the original 'image' of it, is literally the death of culture—it conserves itself as is. Art becomes 'regulative' or propaganda; everyday life is merely a matter of impression-management, ethnic groups attempt to construct, then operate within, quasi-official 'authentic' versions of themselves.

The current attack in France on 'the self' (the mirrored image) in the name of 'the subject' is a desperate attempt to sabotage this mechanism and to inspire some cultural mobility (in the form of *the* personal motive, 'desire').[5] This attempt is hardly new in the history of Western thought: one need only read of Gérard de Nerval's maddening impotence at seeing *his* Sylvie, self-conscious after reading Rousseau, unable to be a peasant—she can only act at being one.

SEMIOSIS AND THE MORAL ORDER—COMMENT
ON ROUSSEAU

As has been suggested above, these issues were originally framed in their distinctively modern form by J. J. Rousseau with an insight that is far from being exhausted. Rousseau made his critique of contemporary modern culture precisely in terms of the question of development, or progress.

His first major work was *The Discourse on the Sciences and the Arts* (1749 and 1964a), the prize-winning essay that answered the Académie de Dijon's question whether the advancement of culture in modern times had helped to improve our mores (*moeurs,* morals, manners, customs). Rousseau relates that the structure of the *Discourse,* which he repeatedly referred to as the fatal and unlucky piece of writing that opened his unhappy literary career, appeared to him in an almost visionary way while en route to visit his fellow radical *philosophe* Diderot, imprisoned at Vincennes.

The *Discourse* stunned a cosmopolitan and culturally smug Europe with its negative response (the advancement of modern culture, according to Rousseau, had *not* helped to perfect our mores). It brought Rousseau instant notoriety, as well as rejoinders from such unlikely figures as King Stanislaus of Poland. Advanced civilization—arts and sciences—had become second nature to the sophisticated eighteenth-century upper classes. The "mind of the Enlightenment," as Cassirer (1955:305 and 93ff.) calls it, was at the height of its powers, relishing its own prowess. How, then, could an upstart dare to find culture potentially flawed in terms of its consequences for morals, manners, and customs?

Rousseau first contrasts the culture of his day with the images of past cultures—Sparta, early Rome—as counter-proof of progress: there, laws and conduct, rules and rule-governed behavior were in virtually perfect accord. Any subsequent developments that claim to desire the meshing of Law with Public Order could never be seen as a 'progress', but only as a degeneration. Such a 'degeneration' obviously must have occurred, in the Roman instance, at least, for by the time of Rome's greatest expansion, law and order, art and life, sign and meaning had obviously radically diverged. In the voice of Fabricius, transported in time from early to late Rome, Rousseau cries, "What is the meaning of these statues, these paintings, these buildings? Madmen, what have you done? . . . Do rhetoricians govern you?" (1964:45).

What has intervened, as the complaint makes clear, is the advent of the *sign*, with its merely arbitrary relation to meaning. Semiosis is exhibited in the Roman case first in concrete 'natural' cultural forms, forms such as buildings, temples, and houses (1964:54) wherein front and back regions have no necessary semantic relationship to each other. And semiosis extends even and especially to manners, morals, and passions today:

> An Inhabitant of some faraway lands who wanted to form a notion of European morals [*moeurs*] on the basis of the state of the sciences among us, from the perfection of our arts, from the decency [*bien-séance*] of our entertainments, the politeness of our manners. . . . and the tumultuous competition of men of all ages and conditions who seem anxious to oblige one another from dawn to dark: this [*foreigner*], I say would guess our morals to be exactly the opposite of what they are. [1964a:39]

Man seems to be freed via culture from all necessary meaning. This liberation occurs by the process of culture's having reflected upon its 'natural' cultural arrangements and its having entered into the realm of speculative semiosis. The implicit political program of cultural anthropology with its claims for the coherence of primitive culture is in part the anthropologists' way of attempting to correct for the failings of our own culture by showing us that real cultures are not contaminated by uncontrolled semiosis.

At this point, most readings of Rousseau equivocate: does he then want a primitivist return to a 'nature' that would pre-exist all culture? Or does he, with Hegel, wish to use culture to heal the wound (the scandalous gap between sign and meaning) that he has uncovered? It is clear that Rousseau's discursive mode is highly ambiguous at this point, for while one might assume that he wishes for a return to a pre-semiotic state,[6] he is in fact doing something else.

He is demonstrating the liberation from nature that semiosis brings, on the one hand, and, on the other, the fear of its own freedom on the part of culture. So far from being used to effect a supreme liberation, Rousseau finds, signs are now used repressively, as a way of maintaining social order.[7] Even in the *absence* of any transcendental standard or 'meaning' to which signs would adhere, men have managed to use signs against themselves. They find principles, rules for meaning, competency, interaction even in the very mechanism of semiosis. They now *know* sign and meaning will diverge and *expect* it or are at least resigned to it.

The first reflections on 'natural' cultural arrangements are what we call 'arts and sciences'. It is the arts and sciences that have introduced a stable orderliness into the otherwise purely mobile world of semiosis. This orderliness goes so far as to include even the most intimate intersubjective *relations* among men. Anticipating the work, though not necessarily the cool neutral attitude of twentieth-century ethnomethodologists, including especially Harold Garfinkel and Erving Goffman, Rousseau wrote:

> Today when subtler researches and a more refined taste [*esprit*] have reduced the art of pleasing to set rules, a base and deceptive uniformity prevails in our customs, and all minds seem to have been cast in the same mould. Incessantly politeness requires, propriety [*bienséance*/decorum] demands: incessantly usage is followed. . . . [1964a:38]

Even the most 'personal' of relationships are codified, not because of a priori prescriptions, but because semiosis has introduced the possibility of acting merely for pleasure rather than out of necessity. Yet men have now made of pleasure itself an art with its own poetics. The very possibility of *intending* to please depends upon a variable ratio between sign and meaning. Only if one can adjust one's projected image (message, sign given) to suit what one presumes the receiver expects or prefers can we attempt consciously to please (see D. MacCannell 1976a:108). Every aspect of culture becomes accommodation: men anticipate the response of the other before acting; cultural productions become commodities as they tailor themselves more and more to the marketplace and try to please the audience.

At the end of his now classic study, *The Presentation of Self in Everyday Life,* Erving Goffman (1959:251) reflects:

> [I]ndividuals who are performers dwell more than we might think in a moral world. . . . As performers we are merchants of morality. Our day is given over to intimate contact with the goods we display and our minds are filled with intimate understandings of them, but it may well be that the more attention we give to these goods, then the more distant we feel from them and from those who are believing enough to buy them. To use a different imagery, the very obligation and profitability of appearing always in a steady moral light, of being a socialized character, forces one to be the sort of person who is practiced in the ways of the stage.

Going beyond everyday social performances, sacred painting (re)-becomes pornography, sculpture (re)becomes idolatry, art pleases and it does not guide. Yet its sway is all the more potent since it binds men with art to their own self-satisfaction, their present felicities (Rousseau 1964a:53).

Pleasure, now a principle, becomes in turn a principle of self-preservation, a regulation for repetition. Ironically, it will now serve the death of culture, the repression of semiosis. Well before Freud, Rousseau saw that cultural man has the capacity to generate a norm out of the most norm-free of situations and to serve, in the name of maintaining itself, the "death instinct." In short, 'culture' seems always to tend to rebecome 'nature', i.e., an *ordered* set of principled, fixed behaviors and structures. It can only 'progress', then, if resubjected to the radical reflection on 'natural' cultural arrangements by which semiosis originates.

Rousseau's *First Discourse* fulfills this reflective function for the modern culture of the European Enlightenment, the cultural situation in which we still exist, the one in which we do our humanist and social scientific work. It not only reopened to speculation what had seemed a closed question as to the assured progress of contemporary culture; it also served as a volatile point of departure for subsequent cultural history. The developments of Romanticism and modern thought have used Rousseau's writings as a mobilizing force, both in the political and personal senses.

The radical question thus put to culture is: how do we generate unfreedom and a 'natural' order out of the freedom from nature provided by culture-as-semiosis? The most cogent answers to this question lie in the fields of linguistics, cultural anthropology, ethnomethodology, and Durkheimian sociology, whose goal is to specify the systems of norms which 'free' and arbitrary acts of association generate.[8]

But there is another side to the question: Rousseau demonstrated that the pragmatic Horatian maxim that cultural productions must 'please' has become a fixed standard and a rule for order. How do we generate freedom (cultural progress, semiotic evolution) out of the unfreedom of principled or rule-governed activity? Especially when these norms do not exist as "fixed or external criteria," in Saussure's terms (Rousseau coined the word *criterion* [1964a:48]) but seem to arise spontaneously, inexorably. This is the question that interested Peirce.

Prefiguring de Saussure (1966:115–22), Rousseau has uncovered the structuring mechanism, that which 'naturalizes' culture, fixes 'meanings', rigidifies signs, and stabilizes patterns in the way in which *values* are created in the void, in the semiotic absence of any fixed or external criteria. The demobilization occurs by means of creating evaluative scales by which one can compare one sign to another or exchange one sign against the other to determine at least a relative value, meaning or worth: money, status, power, progress. These values originate in an 'arbitrary' act of *association** (one could call it pre-metaphoric thought); but this fluid, open possibility soon finds closure and the values appear to be fixed and firm (syntagmatic-chained-oppositions).

Value can only arise through speculative association or the reading of one cultural production in the light of another, that is, through reflection. It is the original relationship, the conceptual act, or figuring. But it is a thoroughly mobile act, like thought, capable of endless deconstructive generation if not stabilized in some form or figure. Like the metaphor, it is entirely too transportable and generates its own antithesis, a

*This doing and undoing process is discussed in detail in our later chapter on the literary sign.

desire for self-preservation and stability. Thus semiosis, the divergence between sign and meaning, fosters a semiotic system of evaluation that operates as a counter to pure changeability. As de Saussure showed, the structure of 'natural language' operates despite its arbitrary basis (the sign):

1) by creation of an *exchange value,* or the means of measuring cultural products of dissimilar nature
2) or by creation of a *comparative value* in which cultural productions (chief among them 'man') of a similar nature are measured.

In short, according to Saussure (and Rousseau) the basis for the structure of values is metonymy (exchange) and metaphor (comparison).

Semiosis and Social Values—Economy, Metonymy, and Metaphor

Once all cultural items have found their relative values and 'principles' have been generated therefrom, social organization is fixed and culture appears 'natural'. Men are seen as equals by an original act of metaphor/evaluation, a transfer of identity. Their association begins as a free one, based upon pleasure; they become fixed in a social hierarchy according to their use value; similarly commodities are originally designed for utility; they become revalued by a metaphoric transfer to the pleasure scale. Marx saw metaphorization as the basic act of evaluation, one which is not restricted to language, but to all systems of cultural production.

> Value ... does not stalk about with a label describing what it is. It is value, rather, that converts every product into a social hieroglyphic. Later on we try to decipher the hieroglyphic to get behind the secret of our social products. For to stamp an object of utility as a value is just as much a social product as a language. [1965:74, discussed in D. MacCannell 1976a:19–22]

We repress the origin of values by forgetting the sign mechanisms (first, association, and then, comparison/exchange) by which they arise.[9] It is only this repression which makes possible the automatism, ease (Rousseau's word is *commodité,* p.54), and perpetuation of modern culture. Modern culture is the new Eden, a second nature. Cultural development and proliferation reassure us, man's 'art' can impose 'order over chaos', or 'give existence meaning'. But in forgetting its semiotic or figurative origin culture fails to 'progress', and self-satisfaction, the death of culture, ensues.

How then does change occur? Must it arise from a violence to the social order, from a willful act or transgression against 'natural' arrangements? Many have assumed this to be the only exit from the present, and the current fashion for 'violence' stems in part from the feeling of being trapped in what Nietzsche called 'the prison-house of language'. Rousseau, however, had a much less hopeful view of the will than such a notion would suppose. For him, change just as much as fixity arises from the heart of social life, from the semiotic mechanism. The *scales* of value, based upon an original metaphorization, tend to rotate ninety degrees around an axis, and to be applied metonymically to other aspects of culture: items that should only be compared (e.g., persons) are exchanged, and items that should be exchanged (e.g., goods) become compared:

> Ancient politicians spoke incessantly about morals and virtue, those of our time talk only of business and money. One will tell you that in a given country a man is worth the price he would fetch in Algiers; another, following this calculation will discover some countries where a man is worth nothing and others where he is worth less than nothing. They evaluate men like herds of cattle. [1964a:51]

Luxuries are examples of the second transfer, the conversion of dissimilar items into comparative equalization along the aesthetic dimension of 'pleasing' (p. 50). In each case, what had been an item in a scale with an assignable value, meaning, or worth, suddenly loses its 'properties' by a transfer to the other scale. It acquires (or re-acquires) the mode of being of the *sign:* in the case of man, he becomes a mathematical figure/a measure of his labor or use-value; and in the case of commodities, they become aesthetic objects, decorative, ornamental, useless.[10]

To recapitulate: each scale of value, hierarchical/vertical/numerical or lateral/temporal/aesthetic originates through *figuration,* the placement together of two signs in juxtaposition. From there, value judgments of either superiority/inferiority or primary/secondary are made. From then on, the scale (or syntagmatic chain) is assumed to be fixed, principles or regulative inferences are drawn from it, and the originally arbitrary act of association or positioning is forgotten or repressed: "Men are born free . . . and everywhere they are in chains." Only a revolution[11] can re-metaphorize this now 'natural' arrangement and bring out the original semiotic mechanism by means of which the value system arises. This revolution re-institutes the sign as value-free and arbitrary, as a pure metaphor (concept/figure), but this in turn will also produce a new distribution of values along a scale and generate new principles.

Many thinkers after Rousseau also attempted to separate and sort these confused value scales into proper order, for selected local areas of culture: Kant, for example, tried to divest the aesthetic judgment, or 'delight',[12] of its confusion with utility principles. And several novelists and poets, such as Stendhal (J. MacCannell 1978b), Nerval, and Baudelaire, not to mention Nietzsche, show an overt but sometimes impotent hostility toward figures—of speech, of language, and of geometry as these become fixed figures. The most recent development in this opposition can be seen in the deconstructionist movement and the interest in open tropes, or the freeing of metaphor/metonymy from their place (see Derrida 1974 and 1979). It remained for de Saussure to make especially clear the basic value axes in any semiotic system. Only the sign (figure) can generate culture, and only the sign (figure) can institute the death of culture, its 'naturalization'.

Conclusion

The dialectic of enlightenment has often appeared as an impasse for pragmatic, modern culture: we are either trapped in culture's artificiality, or we go 'primitive' and join the barbarian attack on culture. The writings of Jean-Jacques Rousseau have often been presumed to be paradigmatic of this enlightenment dilemma. What we are suggesting here is an alternative reading of Rousseau. Clearly there are moments, interstitial gaps, in which cultural change occurs—meaning is lost; things are revalued—and ever since Rousseau we have been avid in our attempts to prolong these 'acultural' periods. Thus we have Deleuze and Guattari (1977) railing against the Oedipal (repressive) generation of cultural figures that Freud revealed; we have neo-Marxists and literary critics "unable to write poetry (or about it) after Auschwitz," just as we have the spokesman of Hitler's Imperial Chamber of Culture saying, "When I hear the word 'culture', I reach for my gun" (quoted in Adorno 1967:26). And, of course, we have the various romanticisms with their love-hate for culture that were so well discriminated by A. O. Lovejoy (1948:228–53).

We are suggesting a reformulation of questions of either/or, for or against culture. By scrutinizing culture as a production not *of* but *like* social and economic relations, semiotics can begin to comprehend the importance that cultural productions have assumed alongside of mechanical, industrial, financial, biological, and social productions. The "purity" of high art, the nineteenth-century era of the ivory tower wherein aesthetic pleasure came to be known as "work" has been succeeded by an era in which work is supposed to be pleasure (D. MacCannell 1976a): this is a reversal of a fundamental binary opposition no semiotician can ignore.

2

Phallacious Theories
of the Subject
On the Freudian Marxist Synthesis

> All the philosophies of subjectivity are. . . . at the bottom
> only two ideas of subjectivity—that of empty, unfettered
> and universal subjectivity, and that of full subjectivity
> sucked down into the world—and it is the same idea.
>
> —Merleau-Ponty, *Signs* (154)

Freud is being "read" these days, in groups much like those who gathered to "read" Marx in the early sixties: groups composed of intellectuals who are interested in areas of thought marginal to purist academic definitions of their interests. Freud lifts barriers, becomes the intersection of intellectual pulsions and drives, and operates transversally between codes: such are the roles we currently assign him, although they are roles he would hardly have sought. Perhaps this conspiratorial aura is a necessary artifact of the way Freudian theory connects to culture studies outside the medical fields—a replay of the Lacanian French adventure.[1] Where we once discovered, in the wake of Marx, *economic* motivations in our cultural productions, we now find *unconsious* ones: wishes disguised as symbols, desires mut(il)ated into false loves, lifeless forms, frustrations; Freud as liberator, Freud as key, Freud as master text.

In our apparently endless quest to decode culture, Marx has been revised and collated with Freud in order to give his work credibility as a cultural interpreter. Everyone in the semiotic revolution participates in this revision, seeing in Lacan's work the theory that brings to Freud a *social structure* (the Symbolic Order) and to Marx a *subject* that he lacks and needs. In this chapter, we show some difficulties in this endeavor from a theoretical point of view. These difficulties center on a particular existential definition of "material" (subject, presence, subject matter) that does not adequately give play to its alternative: within the existential frame, "matter" is an event that is prefigured not by a symbolic order but by an imaginary order. And within this frame, the "thetic" (positioned) subject can become the synthetic (composed) ego or a hypothetical (fictional) psyche. We think that Freud was trying to show that matter and form, biology and semiology, primary and second-ary processes, subject and ego each have the uncanny capacity to become the other.[2] (Laplanche 1976:64–65 and the appendix gives an eerily persuasive account of this.) Binary oppositions that do not them-selves stay fixed seem incapable of "fixing" concatenations, signifying chains and hierarchies with any degree of authority.

In other words, we are suggesting that the self-appointed intellectual avant garde has become uncertain about its recent genealogy, about its foundational binary oppositions: public and private, inner and outer man, with Marx the patron of the first and Freud the second.[3] What value can the two authors retain for us if they have lost their "place" in our bourgeois history? Why read them?

Our answer can only be that culture itself has already reinterpreted them, changing their places, that the intellectuals are playing catch-up. Just as the hippiedom of the sixties and the schizopolitics of first Laing and then Guattari and Deleuze showed us the vast apersonal face— the "desiring machine"—of phenomenological 'authenticity,' so too has sexual liberation made of Freud a socio-cultural theoretician and of Marx a source of individual freedom. Now we can read Marx and Freud as texts, not as books, with all that the former concept has of pure contradiction.

Freud and Marx After Semiotics

What are the chief discoveries of Freud and Marx in the light of semiotics? In this question, let us state from the outset, that we do not intend to read Saussure or Peirce as a 'key' or 'master' text. That approach has already (for Freud and Saussure at least) been taken by Lacan. Rather, one must read all three sets of cultural productions— Freudian, Marxist, and semiotic—in a relation of equality to each other. These are the most important texts of our late modern era—and by 'text' we mean the body of writings and their followers and -isms as well —which constantly reinterpret each other.

The semiotization of Freud was the signal accomplishment of the sixties and we are beginning to comprehend Marx's semiotic as well. Saussure and his linguistic/literary ancestors and descendants (Plato/ Rousseau/Roland Barthes et al.) have, conversely, undergone a mate-rialist critique.[4] Working this triadic configuration out in all its significant ramifications—from biology to theology—is probably the chief task of the coming decade.

The state of the synthesis at the present moment is utter confusion: the reader is constantly besieged with such a variety of strange bedfellows that the bed, semiology, must be suspected of Procrusteanism. Mao and Chomsky, Althusser and Heidegger, Marx and Saussure all cohabit in this contiguous stream of partial similarities, local parallels. This is a very model of association, each of the thinkers making his or her modest (metonymic) contribution to the corpus. One wonders at first what can indeed be the purpose of such an assemblage, which has neither diachronic and historical nor synchronic and paradigmatic value.

A deep reading of this confusion suggests a marshalling of allies for an assault upon the *enemy:* ideas of 'fixed and uniform subjectivity', bourgeois illusions of subjective identity, autonomy, and freedom. It is these illusions that act as a barrier to social renewal.

In their recent study, *Language and Materialism,* Rosalind Coward and John Ellis (1977:68–75 and 114ff.) refer to Barthes's (1974) reading of Balzac's *Sarrasine. Sarrasine* is the story of a man who obtains a night with a beautiful woman on the condition that he tell the tale of another man who fell in love with a "woman" who was really a eunuch, a *castrato.* Coward and Ellis make the story into an analytical model designed to attack the foundation, the bedrock, of bourgeois society: sexual identity. Whether in Balzac, Lacan, Barthes, or Lévi-Strauss, in *Sarrasine,* in the theory of the castration complex, or in the arbitrary nature of symbolic classification, the central task of the Freudian-Marxist convergence has been the demystification of *sexual* (and therefore subjective) identification. It is the breakdown of this classificatory system that Coward and Ellis and others believe will lead to the semiotic revolution.[5]

We are suggesting that there is a still more basic issue at stake in the current attack on the subject. If we follow Derrida and Foucault through and beyond the disturbance of sexual identity, we find the death of the subject occurring at the level of the ego, imagination, rhetoric, the self, and forms (figures). The Freudian-Marxist thinkers of the sixties (and after) do not have a philosophical or a theoretical-conceptual goal. Their goal is religious and redemptive. "The subject has to be destroyed," we read, but this is immediately followed by the subtle reassurance, "and remade in the signifier" (Coward and Ellis 1977:130). Other examples of this effort to displace the subject by means of its death and resurrection proliferate in the writings of the Freudian Marxists, structuralists, and post-structuralists. We would not be disturbed if we could classify these lapses as classical instances of the millennial mentality common to participants in a social movement behind a new paradigm.[6]

But what would happen if the paradigm itself become contaminated by this redemptive theology?

Let us turn away from this disquieting possibility and go back to Lacan for a new beginning. Lacan's existentialism and semiotization of Freud contains both possibilities: a semiotic redemption of the individual and a radical disconnection of the ego, self, subject, and imagination, etc., from their overdetermination by socio-historical process. Friend to and intellectual affiliate of the existentialists, Heideggerian in his outlook, Lacan could see in structuralism a logical development beyond existentialism but in need of the subjective theses he could bring to it. Structuralism had become an idealism, the sign too much inscribed in hypostasized sets of oppositions (signifier/signified) that had quickly become hierarchies of privileged meaning over mere *signifiants*. Lacan's 'materialist critique of the sign' (actually quite distinct from Derrida's) was to bring to an arid and static structuralism the central and clearly existential question of the "subject" (as material presence, speaker) in spirit and in the flesh. Language, the taking up of a position which is already pre-formed by linguistic categories,[7] offers the means of linking symbolic (fixed) structures to their source and vice versa. Continuity out of the discontinuity of experience is the goal. Structural order becomes pliable under the force of the *drives*. But they also liberate the subject from the oppressive weighty Symbolic Order into which it is thrown. (We are referring to the Symbolic Order as discovered by Heidegger as *Gerede* and Lévi-Strauss as 'myth,' or network. [See Wilden 1968:130]). Lacan (168:42) writes in his *Discours de Rome:*

> Symbols . . . envelop the life of man in a network so total that they join together before he comes into the world, those who are going to engender him *'par l'os et par la chair,'* so total that they bring to his birth, along with the gifts of the stars, if not with the gifts of the fairy spirits, the design of his destiny; so total that they give the words that will make him faithful or renegade, the law of the acts which will follow him right to the very place where he *is* not yet and beyond his death itself; and so total that through them his end finds its meaning in the last judgment where the *verbe* absolves his being or condemns it—

except he attain the subjective bringing to realization of being-for-death.

Servitude and grandeur in which the living would be annihilated, if desire did not preserve its part in the interferences and pulsations which the cycles of the Language cause to converge on him, when the confusion of tongues takes a hand, and when the orders interfere with each other in the tearing apart of the Universal work.

As Merleau-Ponty might have put it, corporeal desire, desire incarnate, material desire, reveals the pretensions of the *Universe* to be only that of a *world,* when seen from the point of view of subjective experience or the present moment. The Heideggerian vocabulary is unmistakable, and although it was in vogue at the time (recall that the *Discours* took place in 1953), the schema does permeate Lacan's work. The subject is thrown into everyday life's network of symbols that are apparently fixed; but these are meaningless in themselves, lack Being, and are really only signifiers dependent upon other such signifiers for any meaning at all. Weak and fallen, Heidegger's subject can yet have some moments in which the particular mode of Being of *Dasein* (time) can be experienced with intensity; similarly, in Lacan, within the finite diction-ary-totality of signifiers certain signifiers achieve a kind of fleeting supe-riority of status, as *"points de capiton,"* (privileged signifier, or symbols), nodal points[8] that have the prestige of generating chains of *signification* (Coward and Ellis 1977:97).

It is difficult to sort out Lacan from his commentators, not because of problems of translation, but because he has arbitrarily excluded his own readings of Freud from his (belated) published *Ecrits.*[9] It is often unclear whether Lacan is basically being interpreted in the hermeneutic way (the hermeneutics we just learned, only to have it attacked by post-structural rhetoric) or whether he is in fact ironizing hermeneutics. But there is little doubt that his version of the subject is both that of a personal experience of fragmentation and that of a Symbolic Order, the appearance of a meaningful totality that is in fact ungrounded —an 'it', a "they say" (Discourse of the Other), an unconscious, or an "id"—a dictionary whose meanings only exist by dint of the existence of the totality of signifiers.[10] The subject-as-Universal-Symbolic-Order both oppresses and sustains the personal subject.

The intricacies of this system are produced by its link with existential-ism, which link is the greatest difficulty in the Freud-Marx-Saussure triad. Can Marx be articulated to the redemptive notion of the subject in post-structural thought? Not unless he is disfigured. We must try to push these ideas beyond the idea of redemption, which is based on a myth of innocent origins of the subject, of consciousness. It is on precisely this point that Marx cannot be dragged into a premature Marxist "synthesis." All oppositions and contradictions within Marx's project are essentially and originally repressive. And consciousness that emerges from opposition cannot have an innocent beginning. Sartre and Merleau-Ponty crashed on the same rocks, Sartre when he attempted a synthesis of existentialism and Marxism (especially in the *Critique de la Raison dialectique*);[11] Merleau-Ponty when he took a stand of purely personal commitment for which he did not adequately account intellectually. The two -isms cohabit but with discomfort in the postwar period, in what is technically a pre-semiotic comprehension of Husserl and possibly Heidegger.[12]

Marx resists incorporation in a redemptive post-structural paradigm. But there seems some room for movement in a radical reconfiguration of the question of the subject that has not been designed in the first place to keep the old subject alive in the new paradigm. We have already suggested the potential for a Marxist semiotic (chapter 1) and the work of applying key Freudian concepts to Marx's analysis has been begun by Louis Althusser. Let us move on to the more interesting matters.

Consider the difference between the 'subject' of the Heideggerian Lacan and the 'subject' of psychoanalysis, i.e., the experiential one. Imagine for a moment that entire Symbolic Order as absent or as bearing no evident signs of relationships, no support networks, nor even interconnected lines or channels through which communication with their subjective grounding could ever be possible. Imagine an Unconscious that is *not full* of the archaeologic ruins, that is *not composed* of fragments and marks of an earlier subjectivity and desire that have been temporarily alienated from its prior intentions.[13] Imagine an Unconscious that is not structured like a grammar fixing the symbolic order and identifying the personal subject but is instead structured as a rhetoric (Derrida 1967b: 310 and Charles 1977:116), in which order fails at every step and at every stage and requires one to take a position. Imagine a non-Hegelian subject.

Think of Emma Bovary—all the Emmas (or Flauberts) like her suffering from Yonneville to San Jose (in all the yawn villes)—precisely because the "Symbolic Order" has yet to be invented. Getting the symbolic order together is not the most 'revolutionary' act of the modern subject, as Coward and Ellis suggest: it is in fact the sole source of continuity, this ongoing manufacture of 'tradition'. Emma, expectant at every upcoming 'stage' of life, finds quite simply that no fixed institutions await her. A minimal investment of libido, informing and forming her relationships with love, interest, or merely attention, is precisely the gesture she will not make: she fails, literally, to take a position and thereby to participate actively in the 'social construction of reality'. And *she,* not the 'revolutionary', becomes the disruptive, asocial force, albeit not in the mode of a willed gesture. She does not know why "everything I touch turns rotten," as she says on finding her garden loveseat in decay. Her failure to invest disfigures all social roles, institutions, and rites: a more spiritless wife, mother, and mistress it would be hard to find.[14]

The "Symbolic Order" is a vast network that has been produced by rhetorical positions that have forgotten their origin in desire or are, rather, a perversion of these desires. Lacan (1970:189) once said the manifestation of the unconscious as a Symbolic Order is like "Baltimore in the morning." The anonymous structures seem to stand as testimony to the impossibility of desire's being named as such or ever manifesting itself except in a completely ruined form.[15] This has been how many of Lacan's interpreters understand the unconscious. We shall follow these later developments now to show a current impasse in their thinking.

How does one rescue desire, which, as Lacan wrote in the *Discours de Rome*, is the only human force to counter the elaboration of the network and revitalize it? Two directions have been proposed within post-Lacanian semiotics, one by Julia Kristeva, the other by Deleuze and Guattari. Neither is necessarily satisfactory because each finally avoids confronting the question of the subject.

We shall see in chapter 7 Kristeva's equation of "the semiotic" with desires that escape symbolic repression, in the pre-linguistic form of partial articulations or signifiers without signifieds. In her version the semiotic acts as a force because it is in contradiction to the order of men and things; it becomes a productive force by virtue of being a disruptive force.

Kristeva's almost Hegelian vision is quite distinct from that of another branch of neo-Lacanians, the group around Deleuze and Guattari. Here the ultimate absence of repression seems to be possible—desire, the final signified, can be manifested in its essence. The Unconscious-as-a Symbolic-Network is a labyrinth that has been created by dammings or repressions.[16] Liberation is tantamount to facilitating freeflow of libido, to "transversing" (Guattari's term) the line separating conscious and unconscious. The aim would be to allow desire to circulate freely, to allow it to display itself openly. Guattari's impatience (like Emma's) is clear: "The real question is whether the production of desire, a dream, a passion, a concrete Utopia, will finally acquire the same existential dignity in social life as the manufacturing of cars or fads" (Guattari 1977:79). There is an ultimate homology between the individual body and the socio-symbolic order, a homology between individual desire and Kapital,[17] and it is this homology that makes all of the socioeconomic system open to liberation. The alternative to liberation—in the case of terminal disorder—is the decision like Emma's not to invest, to divert desire and (libidinal) capital to alternative areas. The final revolution is dropping out.

The poles of the thesis of the "Symbolic Order" as the blockages of unconscious desire produced by the mechanism of repression, the mechanism that also authors the self and the consciousness, seen in Kristeva on the left and Guattari on the right (or is it the reverse?), are of course part of the larger movement that has difficulty with the question of the restrictions posed by *form,* which we have begun to sketch. It is still form, in the psychoanalytic case, the ego, that seems to us to require a Marxist rethinking before it can be so easily bypassed. Freud stresses in *Beyond the Pleasure Principle* and in his writing on crowd behavior how central repression is to his theory (Freud 1929:91 and 1948:84–97). We can take this concept seriously not as another word for oppression or subjugation as many of the neo-Freudian/neo-Marxists of the sixties did, and we can also make more explicit a Freudian link to Marx's analytic through their common semiotic of form/and/matter.

THE SEMIOTIC OF THE SELF

The self or ego is that form (figure) which is itself a secondary interpretation of subjective existence. In Freud's own terms it is an institution or a composition that is totally dependent upon an investment of desire and love (Freud 1936:24–25). We do have some current readings of Freud that confine themselves to the level of the self, or figurative aspect of the subject. Philippe Lacoue-Labarthe's (1977) brilliant analyses of mimesis and his recent attack on the problem of representation (1978:19) in Freud is an example of this analytic, which relegates the unconscious to Sartrean nothingness. This theoretical move allows one to interpret the manifestations of consciousness, its figures, as the totality of its subject matter. By denying the reality of deep structures or of backs behind fronts, we can study the self as a kind of reverse sign: it is a presentation that masquerades as a representation. Saying "I" is a theatrical pretense that there is a subject to one's enunciation, a subject that is actually a mere hypothesis (see J. MacCannell 1974 and 1975).

Restricting one's semiotic to the level of sign as manifestation allows one to deal with the self or with the ego as that which, to use Nietzsche's phrase, "performs I," yet it does not really do justice to the contribution and honest complexity of Freud's semiotic. It seems to us that it is the very notion of *subject* that Freud meant to revise, by situating the ego and id as constant rivals, each capable of pyrrhic "victories" over the other, and persisting always by a fiction of having reduced or bested the other. Like signifier and signified in Saussure's terms, ego and id, consciousness and the unconscious, are mutually determinant, and defined by their difference. This difference is repression, and it is this difference, like a semi-permeable membrane, that allows for the intense involvements of each in the other. Reinscribing this structure in the language of subjectivity before taking account of the drama, the *agon,* that is the essence of psychic life in Freud, is premature and leads to distortions. Freud's basically conflictual model would include all the other meanings the term 'subject' can have, primarily its implication in being defeated, in subjection, thrown under. There are 'loyal subjects' and 'subjects of experiments', and the surplus meanings of 'subject' reveal the desire for dominance that resides in subjective life, and which it was Freud's special talent to be able to demystify. Lacan's playful attempt to restrict analysis to the level of the signifier (the real subject is the barred subject, $, or that which does not cross the barrier of repression) is consistent with discourse analysis and yet not fully semiotic, as is Freud. Let us detour by way of Jacques Derrida's (1972:10) double science to read a Freud who fits into a post-structural version of the sign: Signs that always have "other meanings" that erode the "first" meaning from within and attack it as the id attacks the ego.

The French Freud of Jacques Derrida (1967a and b) and Jean Laplanche (1976) exposed the latency or "unthought" of Lacan's rereading of Freud and provided the occasional cause for their rewriting. Although *De la Grammatologie* for example refers overtly to these categories as they appear in Heidegger, there can be little doubt that Lacan's vocabulary is also in view: the concepts Derrida analyzes, such as subject, speech, voice, presence, and symbol, are fully as privileged in Lacan as in Heidegger. Using Freud's theory of *Nachträglichkeit* (which feeds into Derrida's *différance*), secondarity or retardation, Derrida revises Lacan's semiotization of Freud by criticizing the implicit value of the key concepts of material presence and the primacy of the signifier, corporeality, and sound. Laplanche, whose book is conceptually very close to Derrida's (1967b) essay, provides us with extremely lucid expositions of Freud that read Freud semiotically and without the subjective vocabulary often dominant in Lacan. (Laplanche and his colleague J. B. Pontalis have collaborated to offer a useful dictionary of psychoanalytic terms.) Let us now turn to this version of Freud, which does not view the fall from desire into semiosis as a subjective crisis, for ill or for good.

Freud could only view the achievement of rewriting nature, the capacity for the mind to affect the body, for semiology to (re)direct biology, as a two-edged accomplishment. As Laplanche has so ably shown us, this rewriting begins, according to Freud, in the very first situations of anaclisis: Here the "drives" (the idea of natural forces) are "propped" on the "instincts" (natural forces). Need, for example, would manifest itself earliest as a 'natural' need—physical hunger. Other needs would be analogized to be structurally similar to hunger and its manner of satisfaction, and ideational needs would be assumed to be physical needs.[18] Sexuality is the chief example: Laplanche cites Freud's repeated assertion that the psyche's interpretation that sexuality is (like) a physical need acts as much the part of a *force* in affecting behavior as any 'purely' physical forces (if there are such.)[19]

The capacity for interpreting thus exhibited by the psyche is, at both the micro and macro levels, a process of semiosis: anticipating by foresight and interpreting by hindsight experiences as signs of other experiences. There is therefore a gap in experience, moments or periods when experience—in all senses of the term—simply fails. In the derivation of psychic entities from natural entities what is most important for us to understand is the absence of any direct, primary experience of the meaning of an event. Present meanings are precluded for the peculiar construction that the psyche is because for it, meaning is only after-the-fact. The retardation, first of maturity (the prolonged helplessness of the infant), then of sexuality (the retardation of puberty), opens the breach into which semiosis (sign production) and semiotic (sign interpretation) flow. These delays promote psychic life (Freud 1936:100).

It is the failure of meaning of an experience or event to be present or embodied or located in the event that has most intrigued Derrida with

Freud's theses. Meaning is always deferred, *nachträglich,* a part of the process of reading signs: they can be read only in relation to other signs that equally fail to capture or embody meaning. The process has been interpreted by Jameson (1972:172) as the relay of meaning from signifier to signifier: but we intend here to read meaning-for-the-psyche as occurring by signs, that is signs that call to mind (consciously or not) something other than themselves. What becomes most important in this case is to look at the particular kind of representation involved in the work of the psyche. For these are signs that while they cannot be said to have an accessible concept or signified, yet *appear* to have one, and their power lies in their *seeming to be charged with meaning.* The analyst will hesitate before s/he easily makes the neo-existential gesture demystifying the signified in the name of the signifier, or vice versa.

Observe the way Freud handles the hysterical symbol as the archetypal sign in the Saussurian sense (whose referent is arbitrary). The ordinary symbol such as a flag stands, we believe, for something present, or at least recalled in the mode of re*present*ation. On the other hand in the hysterical symbol, such as flag-waving, "what is symbolized ... is entirely forgotten and has evacuated its entire charge and the whole of its affect into what symbolizes it" (Laplanche 1976:36–37; from Freud's *Project for a Scientific Psychology*). The unconscious is the indication of the lack of motivation of the symbol, the arbitrariness of the sign.

To illustrate, Freud uses the case of a young hysteric who could never enter a shop. In analysis she remembered an incident at age twelve when she had entered a shop and had fled in fright when she thought she saw a clerk laughing at her clothes. The shop, the clothes had obviously symbolized something for her, but the referent was lost. The symptom, intense, clearly charged with affect, carried the entire weight of a meaning without having one. Further probing revealed a couple of prior incidents in a shop wherein the child had possibly been the victim of a sexual assault. Yet the first incident lay fallow for it had *no meaning at the time it occurred.* It was only at adolescence, when the girl had acquired sexual ideas, that she could interpret or give a construction to the earlier scene. In the 'normal' psyche this naming of the prior experience accommodates and attenuates it; literally gives it to the 'Symbolic Order', or *langue.* But for the hysteric the 'normal' process of symbolic naming—the (repressive) construction of language—becomes a positive, unconscious misnaming ("laughing at the clothes"): one is left with a lie, the *proton pseudos.* It is the misrepresentation that intensifies the affective power, that indeed (and this is the radical point) gives the sole power to affect: without the misnaming, or metaphorization, we would have only 'memory traces without affect' (Laplanche 1976:57).[20] This deferred affect in fact mimics an original, i.e., pre-ego, emotional subjective response: as Freud writes, "the retardation of puberty makes possible the occurrence of posthumous primary experiences." The 'event' is not an 'event' until after it has already passed: Freud writes, "We never manage to fix the traumatic event historically" (cited in Laplanche 1976:43, 41).

This is enough to illustrate how different the emphasis is when Freud's analytic is to be seen as a classical semiotic, (re)discovering in the lack of motivation of the symbol (in hysteria) the arbitrary relation between symptom and disease, and the necessity for interpretation. But interpretation, reading signs, is *the* work of the psyche, not just of intellectuals. The psyche never finds its meanings ready-made in a dictionary or symbolic order, but tracks them through pathways already unconsciously traced by an experience which, while remembered at some level, has never had a proper name given it. The psychic process of misrepresentation is both idiomatic and also generic to humanity. It is the movement between the idiosyncratic process of 'creating' meaning and the collective accretion of these (mis)represented meanings that constitutes Freud's version of the subject and condemns it to exist forever between blindness and insight.

To use these two terms recalls Heidegger, and it is vis-à-vis a Heideggerian reading of Freud that Derrida's and Laplanche's can be measured. In Derrida's version there can be no 'forgetting' of the symbolic order since by definition the symbol is a remembering of something forgotten only we cannot quite remember what. Institutions are not caught in the dilemma of being either oppressive or tolerant; they are simply the meanings (conscious or unconscious) a nonmeaningful existence acquires for us. In this version the gesture of "uncovering" foundational binary oppositions that institute or fix a social hierarchy, or chain of significations—such as male/female in the castration complex fixation—can never be innocent or neutral if it indulgently accepts the particular sort of opposition it uncovers as being the way of all flesh— and of all meaning. This acceptance is itself an interpretation in the mode of agreement with the structured opposition and could never be revolutionary.

The primacy of the signifier, the prime signifier, the phallus, institutes our culture of domination and subjection: and so we find Derrida chiding

Lacan for his 'phallogocentrism' (1975:96–98), for his complicity in the *primacy* of the phallus as signifier of the first domination of nature:

> Phallogocentrism is neither an accident nor a speculative mistake which may be imputed to this or that theoretician. It is an enormous and old root which must be accounted for. It may then be described, as an object or a course are described without this description taking part in what it operates the recognition of. But this hypothesis, which would then have to extend to all the texts of the tradition, encounters in these latter, as in Freud . . . a very strictly determinable limit; the description is a 'recipient' when it induces a practice, an ethics and an education, hence a politics assuring the tradition of its truth. The point then is not simply to know, to show, to explain, but to stay in it and reproduce: the ethico-educational purpose is declared by Lacan: the motif of authenticity, of the full word, of the pledged faith, and of the 'signifying convention' showed this sufficiently.

Lacan, whose perspective is ultimately that of social reintegration in a living present of the speech act (speech being the first social institution, as the eighteenth century taught us) is an operative force in continuing this institution. Note that we must abandon Lacan and look elsewhere for a theory of a "female sexuality not organized to reproductive ends" (Coward and Ellis 1977: 156). Derrida writes:

> As to the system-link between the logic of the signifier and phallogo-centrism, everything in the Lacanian discourse responds here—in-deed—to the question he poses in 'Propos directifs pour un Congrès sur la sexualité féminine': "Is it then the privilege of the signifier which Freud aims at in suggesting that there is perhaps only one libido, and that is marked by the male sign?" [1975:98]

The phallus, the symbol not of the male organ, but of the socio-cultural counterpart to natural power (the primacy over nature) would be, in the Lacanian interpretation, an *illusion* of autonomy (desire is always dependent on its object), but a (socially) necessary mystification. In the Derridean version the mystification is an "enormous old root which must be accounted for" as perhaps above all a misrepresenta-tion. Lacan's version of the signifier-as-phallus ultimately equates de-sire with the consciousness of a lack. Derrida's version of the signifier-as-hymen (in his essay "Spurs" [1979]) links desire with the border that differentiates consciousness and the unconscious. Con-sider the possibility that the phallus is not a sign of power, but a sign of failure of desire (love) and a loss of its object (anxiety). In this alternative version, phallic primacy can be retraced to the primacy of a (feminine?) gap, a gap not in being but in existence,[21] a gap between signifier and signified.

Lacan is not philosophical enough nor radical enough to get us beyond this moment. Lacan's discovery of the phallogocentric roots of our subjectivity (like Balzac's) has the effect of perpetuating it, and not, as Coward and Ellis so ardently hope (1978:116–20), of overthrowing it to renew it in a more perfect condition. Until the political implications of the subject's (phallic) involvement in power and domination are fully explored we cannot hope to see a fundamental revision of social, culturally derived inequities. At the same time that the castration-complex and Oedipal anxiety over the phallus is assumed to be the master-pattern for organizing subjective life and culture as a whole it is being challenged by questions about the (sexual) source of the subject's existence. Deleuze and Guattari's anti-Oedipal stance is not necessarily endorsed by us, nor is Laplanche's attack on the primacy of Oedipus (Laplanche takes account of siblings, not just of parents); but these challenges to Oedipus are signs of rebellion within psychoanalysis, and they are correlated with criticism of basic cultural institutions.

Indeed the fundamental questioning of the phallic roots of our institutions may be far-reaching in its effects: one might recall Diderot's remark that there is "a little bit of testicle at the foundation of all our sentiments" to remind oneself of the powers of change that resided in some earlier questions. It is indeed ironic that literary *criticism* will be (even has been) both the source of and the object of the critical examination of its phallic roots. Literary *history* defends its established tradition of (male-created) literature, sometimes in quite harsh terms, against revisions (of which works may be 'canonized'). But already Harold Bloom's (ironic) exaggeration of the prevalence of father-killing as the basis of literary and cultural tradition shows both that the explanatory power of the Oedipal paradigm is diminishing and that tradition has origins that are not innocent. The subjective 'origin' or 'beginning' of culture is now at least again an open question. This opening of the question is due not only to the theoretical narrowness of Oedipal explanation, but also to the growing (though still disproportionately small) presence of women and minorities in academic disciplines concerned with cultural studies.

The Oedipus myth is the story of continuity through change.[22] It is a charter for traditionalism. But a traditionalism untempered by the desire for new departures is not really a part of the literary spirit (see de Man

1971:142–65). Nor is it, despite Lacan and the importation of semiotics into literature through Lacan, semiotic in spirit either. Although the underlying conservatism of Lacan's emphasis on the phallus-as-signifier appeals to Americans and has led to many critiques of Derrida (see Jameson 1978a:374–75) we will eventually have to rethink this particular enthusiastic reception, or we may find ourselves foreclosing 'modernity' (as opposed to 'history') as a literary option. Derrida's reading, which does not tolerate the indulgence ('boys will be boys') toward social mystification that he detects in Lacan, clearly threatens the male primacy (including its homosexual variants) that in theory (phallogocentrism) and in practice (the composition of "quality" French departments in the American university) leaves the *woman* out of the system.

Conclusion

There is another story, like *Sarrasine,* of a false love, a story in which the drama of the blockage of desire relates not only to social structure but to the structure of the self. It is the story of Narcissus cheated of his object by the dissolution of form into matter, self into subject. It is the story that locates the founding binary opposition not in the interpersonal realm, but in the heart of the relationship between self and subject, ego and id: what is the reflection which represents nothing? The comparison here is Rousseau's play *Narcisse* versus Balzac's *Sarrasine.*

The subtleties of self as an *imaginary* construct have apparently been overemphasized in the last two decades. But in our weariness with images we are beginning to overstate the psychoanalytic preference for the "Symbolic Order" as opposed to the "Imaginary." In conclusion, it is worthwhile to recall that Lacan, like Freud, has *both* foundation myths (Oedipus and Narcissus) in his system (castration and mirror-fixation), and it may be that they cancel each other out to produce the Real. Perhaps—this is the most radical construction one can put on it—the Real has its own founding myth, or rather, *story.* It is the story of the lapse of binary oppositions; the story of love's becoming desire and desire love; it is a story with a *feminine* hero: that of Psyche and Eros. Recall that it is this story that intrigued late antiquity (Apuleius) and European Romanticism from Rousseau's Julie and Hölderlin's Diotima to Stendhal's Clélia in *La Chartreuse de Parme.* Stendhal's great work is a post-Greek and also a post-Christian rewriting of the story of Psyche and Eros, a *realist* novel.

We owe Lacan an immense debt for his discovery of Freud's semiotic insight that the unconscious is structured like a language. But we have not yet decided whether this language is *matter* or *form*. Coward and Ellis and others suggest that the unconscious *(langue)* and the conscious *(parole)* are continuous with each other and together they position the subject. Derrida, Laplanche, and others read Freud and Saussure as saying that the unconscious, like language, having no reasonable basis, *is* sheer discontinuity.

Derrida's Freud is not intent upon humbling the subject in the name of the wider order, in the service of perpetuating the structure of domination in society. It is precisely this subject that Derrida's Freud "decenters" in a much less reassuring mode than we have seen it decentered in Lacan (or in Lévi-Strauss's "engineer" or in Merleau-Ponty's [1964:147ff] "classical reason"). The impulse in this radical reading of Freud is toward an understanding of how consciousness comes to be: in the face of Hegel and all his heirs, we still find Freud asking about that which is never yet incorporated by consciousness, assimilated, interpreted, and affected—the unconscious. Clearly, this is not the reassuring schema of an all-too-facile opposition between a desiring subject and an inhibiting ego (we could call it content *versus* form or primary *versus* secondary process). Clearly we have gotten to the point, and beyond, of questioning the male primacy instituted by the interpretation that, once the sexual binary opposition is established, it structures our symbolic order, our hierarchies, our faith, our reason, our redemption, and even our attempts (via homosexuality) to escape it. Instead in the post-structural version of Freud we have a drama of (mis)representations that views the unconscious as an empty set of only potentially meaningful markings, not as a "pool of signifiers" (a dictionary) through which social communication is assured (Brenkman 1978:438).

The unconscious is a fiction of a *material,* heterogeneous to the ego, just as the ego is the fiction of a *form* heterogeneous to the subject (matter): Freud's analytic method shows how each of these is constantly rewritten as the other. It is not easy to assimilate these theses on the endless supplementarity of psychic life nor to describe in practice the manner in which subject becomes self and self again a subject. Freud is our current master in this description; Rousseau was also adept at it. So although we feel the necessity to restore perspective by bringing the "subject" back "in"[23] we must be aware that this can never be done by fiat or by preaching its necessity: it can only be by the concrete analysis of the process of semiosis—the metaphorization of experience (condensation) and its companionate process of the experience of metaphor (displacement). The process can be analyzed in all cultural forms, individual or collective.

The Marxist and Freudian economies move towards a confusion of tongues. And it is the disappearance of the subject that is responsible: who (collective or individual) and what (form or content) is the subject of analysis, of revolutionary praxis? "Who is speaking and to whom" in our cultural practices, our social institutions: urgent questions demanding answers. This urgency has given impetus to the rhetorical, social turn in cultural analysis. (The most advanced equation of Marx and Saussure—that of Voloshinov [Bakhtin]—proceeds as rhetorical analysis.)

As the once seemingly stable categories of self, person, class, state, race, interest, etc., destabilize to reveal themselves capable of being twisted into other shapes, of being both the means of and the matter of knowledge—of being, that is, merely signs—we are less and less able to justify invoking either of these powerful theorists, Marx or Freud, in the absence of the other. Yet what is needed is not so much a *synthesis* of the two (such as appeared in the sixties) as it is a willingness

1) to admit that in the face of culture we must remain open both to Marxist and Freudian analytic tools for any specific applications, and

2) to apply pressure to both analytics in the form of a continually open semiotic questioning. As subjects transform themselves before our very eyes into signs of themselves we cannot do otherwise without risking losing even this much of a grasp of our "subject matter."

Part II

Socio-cultural Applications

3

The Deconstruction
of Social Reality

Sociology and the other sciences of culture use a consensus model of
social values and meanings which sidesteps the questions of the origin
of values and of subjectivity raised in the previous chapters. According
to disciplinary perspectives, orderly social life is based on everyone (or
a majority, or those in authority) acting out an unquestioned agreement,
upholding a consensus and maintaining the system of social norms that
is the collective masterwork of modern man. The semiotic approach we
have proposed seriously undermines the taken-for-granted quality of
social values and the authority of individual subjectivity. How do we
continue to do sociology if the base of social life is a *myth* of subjective
consensus, if all social norms are acts of self-repression? We think the
answer to this question can only be found in detailed studies of the
sign-character of actual social agreements. This chapter provides a
preliminary framework for such research which might advance sociology beyond the consensus model into the very mechanisms of social
reality construction.

It is necessary at the outset to disengage conventional morality from
sociological theory: specifically we must neutralize our approach to
agreement and stop seeing consensus in a uniformly positive light. We
are losing our capacity to deal with deceit, misunderstanding and misrepresentation except within the negative moral framework of "devi-
ance." American sociology, in particular, has aligned itself with the
moral imperative to please others: one ought to understand the other,
to be open and truthful, to construe the other's meaning in a positive
way. Anything else is allied with deceit, bad faith, and lying, and its
scientific credibility is undermined by association. Erving Goffman, because he is consistently and simply faithful to the materials he describes, makes his sociological colleagues uneasy: Whose side is
Goffman on? Is he with the goody-goodies or the con men?

We automatically get beyond alignments of everyday morality and
discipline thought when we approach the social agreement between
persons from a different angle, from the semiotic perspective. Semiot-

ics gives renewed force and importance to the idea that we all wear masks and construct our identities for others. But semiotics does not fit the construction of social reality into simple moral frameworks (see Goffman 1959, D. MacCannell 1973, and J. MacCannell 1975). Masks are worn to hide behind but also to be seen through; even, or especially, the most straightforward person is open to interpretation. The cardinal moral peccadillo, as Goffman has so often pointed out, is not lying so much as it is expressing disbelief in the other's *persona* (see also J. MacCannell 1977). We think that we have arrived at the point where we can advance no further by continuing to develop theories of social consensus. What is needed in their place is a deconstructive effort aimed at undoing the fictional consensus that supports common sense and currently repressive notions of 'social reality'. Persons are signs, and as signs we can, if we wish, obtain new powers from the splitting of the signifier from the signified which is the great potential residing in any sign. But the semiotic fission and release of interpersonal energy is blocked at every turn because the originally arbitrary link between the signifier and signified has become the template for the modern network of moral linkages, which are perverse variations on the theme of arbitrariness: they are arbitrary, but they demand to be treated as essential and binding.

Toward a Post-Moralistic Model of Social Reality

Semiotics deals with the problem of meaning by using taxonomy as its basic tool (see, for example, Barthes 1967, Morris 1964). Charles Peirce (1955:98–119), in his important early studies, claims that some signifiers are *congruent* with that which they signify (as when a mule is used to signify obstinacy), and he calls this type of sign an *icon.* An *index,* in Peirce's taxonomic system, is a type of sign that has been produced by the direct action of that which it signifies—as Friday was first represented to Robinson by his footprint in the sand.

Two principles underlie taxonomies of signs. Peirce's system is based on differences in the form of the relationship between signifier and signified (mule and obstinacy, footprint and Friday). These are *semantic* differences. The sociological symbolic interactionists' distinction between symbol and 'sign' ('sign' is proximal, and symbol is separated from its contextual meaning) is based on differences in the relationship between signs, or *syntactical* differences.

A semiotic of meaning consists of a semantic component and a syntactic component.

Taxonomies of signs that lack either component are restricted to discrete meanings based on a single observation: "a mule is a sign of obstinacy," the other meanings of 'mule' are eliminated. The meanings so described are, therefore, artificially rigidified because the taxonomy, when it lacks a syntactic component, does not permit a movement between sign and sign; and when a semantic component is lacking, there is no movement possible between the signifier and the signified. On the basis of this discussion, it is possible to rewrite the definition of symbol:

(1) (i)   A 'symbol' is a sign that lacks a syntactic component so its meaning seems constant.

Similarly 'sign' can be rewritten:

(2) (i)   A 'sign' is a sign that lacks a semantic component so its meaning seems restricted to the situation in which it occurs.

Now observe that common sense, social psychology, and taxonomies of social structural elements that lack formulations of general principles are theoretically equivalent positions. For example, the notion that some things *are* 'symbols' and some things *are* 'signs' is a dogmatic psychological assertion to the effect that subjectively experienced, meaningful reality need not be analyzed to determine its underlying structure. Common sense understanding is restricted in the same way. That is, within common sense, the limits on understanding are usually indirectly described as being products of an individual and his psyche. This locates the individual at the center of the investigation and makes social matters residual. It should be possible, however, to describe limits on understanding *directly* as alterations and interruptions in the situational syntax and semantics.

Consider this situation. A couple approaches a multi-track railroad crossing on foot. The light is green and no trains are in sight or hearing. A man on the other side of the tracks is shouting something indistinct and waving his arm. The couple

(1) (ii)   goes over to the man to find out what he is saying. A fast train runs them down.

(2) (ii)   watches the man as they cross the tracks trying to figure out what is wrong with him. A fast train runs them down.

(These accounts are adapted from news articles.) If we set aside the remote possibility that the couple committed suicide, in (1) (ii) they err syntactically, that is, fail to connect the behavior of the man with the faulty signal light and the man-light combination with the oncoming train. In (2) (ii) they err semantically, that is, they believe the man's behavior signifies a problem of his instead of a problem with the light.

THE ILLUSION OF THE IMMANENCE OF MEANING

When a person makes a mistake about meaning [(1) (ii), (2) (ii)], it is sometimes because he or she has quite another meaning in mind, one that seems to him or her to be the only possible one. In everyday life, especially, meanings are often intuitively obvious in this way. We shall refer to this intuitively obvious quality of meaning as the 'illusion of immanence'. (For a related discussion see Sartre 1940:187ff., esp. 200). The illusion of immanence refers to the individual's dogmatic belief in a meaning. It does not refer to the truth or nontruth of that meaning. The illusion of immanence is the result of a semantic or a syntactic restriction of a sign.

Berger and Luckmann (1966:22) have provided a series of helpful descriptions of the confident but mystified 'everyday' subjectivity that has the capacity to restrict its own meanings: "The reality of everyday life is organized around the 'here' of my body and the 'now' of my present." A conclusion to be drawn from their study (although not one intended by them) is that the more limited the subjective viewpoint, the more immanent (that is, 'real') the situation seems to the subject.

A definition of the illusion of immanence can be stated as a rule.
(3)   The illusion of immanence of meaning: the fewer the observations of the structure of a situation, the more its component signs lack syntactic and/or semantic elements and the more individual subjectivity is promoted to a position of theoretical and/or practical centrality.

It is now possible to consolidate these observations and move to the descriptive level of analysis.

TOWARD A DESCRIPTIVE SEMIOTIC OF SOCIAL SITUATIONS

Social situations considered naturalistically consist of differentiated material: utterances, individuals, glances, groups, gestures, and equipment such as jewelry, weapons, etc. These do not appear randomly as we have presented them. Rather, when encountered in a social situation they are associated with ideas or values.
(4) (a)   The relationship of an aspect of a social situation and its associated idea can be called a 'meaning'.
    (b)   A sign is any naturally occurring unit ('sign vehicle') that has the capacity to carry meaning.

David Sudnow (1972:260) has convincingly argued that "for many activities a single glance is a maximally appropriate unit of interpersonal observation." Perhaps Ray Birdwhistell (1952) has gone the furthest in isolating signs (following Mead he calls them "significant symbols") generated by micromotions. Sign expands into macrostructure when this operates as a totality as, for example, the revolution operates in history. It can also be noted that Sudnow's glance is only an approach to the microstructural limits of the sign. It would be possible to cut the glance in half and conduct a study of the first or the second 'take' of a doubletake.

(5) Any idea-observation relationship can be called a sign no matter how narrow or wide the social circle of its meaning.

Under conditions where the idea that is linked to an observation is the same for everyone, it is possible to speak of the observation's common sense meaning, and of everyone's shared knowledge. Glaser and Strauss (1964) have provided an analysis of the limits of shared knowledge. (For a helpful model of shared knowledge, see Labov 1972:124 and Voloshinov 1976:98–106.) At the opposite extreme from shared knowledge are ideas that are exclusively possessed by a madman or some other individual who is more individualistic than any individual need be. But the structure of the sign remains the same at both extremes.

At a descriptive level, symbol (1) and 'sign' (2) are not existentially separate entities. They are two aspects of meaning anything can have for anyone. That is, any observation can have situated significance, and most can have an initial symbolic meaning. This was Leslie White's great insight in his classic (1949:22–36) essay on the subject.

Consider the following illustration. The conventional use of the color red in warning signs meaning 'stop' is symbolic, that is, it represents a collective agreement to let red stand for danger, just as we let an octagon, cross-bars, or the image of a policeman's palm stand for 'stop'. This agreement only holds up to the point of accurate description of the social situation of symbolism. That is, the coordination of multiple viewpoints in a consensus requires a suspension of syntactical considerations and insures the collective illusion of the immanence of meaning (3). Additional detail completes the illustration on the descriptive level. An automobile stops at an empty railroad crossing where a sign is flashing red. The flashing red sign means:

(6) (i) Stop. A train is coming.

After a brief period of time has elapsed the sign means:

(6)   (ii)   The train is very far away, but the light is activated well in advance because this train travels very fast.

(iii)   The train is very slow.

(iv)   The train activated the red light before coming into view and then stopped for repairs.

(v)   The train passed by just before the automobile came to the crossing, but the light has not shut off yet.

(vi)   The light is on all the time because its switch is stuck; however, quite by accident, on this particular occasion, a train is approaching very fast.

In this actual situation, the initial symbolic meaning of the sign (i) expands into six possible alternate meanings and then contracts back to a smaller number as the automobile continues to wait (ii); or moves against the light (iii), (iv), and (v); or turns around and goes back in the direction from which it came (vi). For the duration of the situation, any observation that is made can qualitatively change the total structure of meaning or establish one meaning while negating all others. The sound of a whistle generates (ii); a repairman looking at the sign, (vi); a tendency on the part of the automobile to hesitate and die just after starting off, (vi); etc.

(7)   Changes in the meaning of a sign are produced by the introduction or deletion of another sign or signs.

It should be noted here that even the initial symbolic meaning that seems to be fixed at the group level is, in fact, built up according to (7) from a combination of signs at the level of the situation. Of course, there may be some individuals so nicely socialized that they will stop at red lights no matter what, even when there is no possibility of cross traffic. However, in most instances, the reason the motorist stops is not the light itself, but the *relationship* of the light to the track, or the light to a nearby policeman. Even though a track without a light may be just as dangerous, the light combines with the track to mean 'danger' or 'stop'.

Actual behavior in this situation is initially motivated by the illusion of immanence (3), or the symbolic meaning (1) of the sign. At the level of description, (1) and (3) are equivalent. As the situation develops, tending at each instant toward its own meaning, the 'direct reaction' to the sign is motivated by its situated significance (or insignificance), which is determined by its relationship to other signs in the situation (7). Eventually the meaning of the sign derives from the operation of the total society including, for example, the destination of the motorist, the social importance of a timely arrival at the occasion, etc. In short, the collective agreement to stop at red lights dissolves in an interplay of *signs.*

Sociologists have traditionally emphasized symbolic meanings, but these are not more important than situated meaning, or significance. Continued promotion of the importance of symbolic meaning is of no utility for semiotic description. The promotion of the symbol to a position of theoretical importance, which seems a paradoxical and stubborn aspect of symbolic interactionist thought, derives from George H. Mead's (1934:15–20) critique of Charles Darwin's (1965) theory of expression. Darwin's discovery of emotions in animals set Mead in search of a distinctively *human* quality. He discovered this quality in our ability to read symbols, something he thought animals cannot do. The important differentiation of the human from the animal world is probably not along this dimension, however. Instead, our capacity to do something that all animals do (i.e., read signs) so much better than animals is what radically separates us from them. The ability to read symbols merely distinguishes men from animals. Skill at reading signs separates the quick from the dead.

Happily, the resolution of this philosophical issue is not necessary to the continued development of a semiotic of social meaning. It is now possible to consolidate these descriptive statements and move to the explanatory level.

TOWARD A SEMIOTIC EXPLANATION OF SOCIAL MEANING

According to Saussure (1966:65ff), a sign is not the name for a thing —its status in the common sense model of meaning. Rather, it is a *bond* between an 'image' and a 'concept'. Saussure's own example is

(8) (a)   Saussure's sign (adapted):

$$\frac{\text{concept}}{\text{image}}$$

According to Saussure's definition, the *image* can be a phonetic or graphic expression or a conventionalized gesture such as those used by deaf-mutes or flagmen. For example:
(8) (b)

$$\frac{\star}{\text{``star''}}$$

The similarity between Saussure's sign (8) and the definition of symbol (1) is evident. Both depend on an ideal-typical two-person communication model (sometimes called in linguistics an 'ideal speaker-listener relationship'), wherein one sign can be passed from one individual to another individual without changing its meaning because the exchange value of the sign remains constant in the same language 'community'. On first examination, this model does not appear to be different from the consensus or common sense models of meaning. In other words, as has often been pointed out by Derrida (1967a:77–79), Chomsky (1968:17), and others, Saussure's sign is really a symbol, for it lacks a syntactic component.

Because of the greater elaboration of the linguistic sign, however, it is possible to expand this model in ways that are foreclosed by conventional sociological approaches to meaning that are based on consensus or common sense. The aspect of the linguistic sign that has received the most attention from specialists is its *arbitrariness*. For example, in (8)(b) the relationship of the signifying image "star" to the signified idea ★ is arbitrary: there is no natural link between star and ★. In another language the signifier of ★ is *sidus,* but this shift of signifier cannot change the meaning of the sign.

The arbitrariness of the sign has been preserved at great cost in complex codes (language, myth, religion, science, history), requiring as cipher not merely animal or machine intelligence but a human mind. Humankind has subordinated itself to the task of knowing purely conventional meanings only in order that these meanings can be replaced without notice or justification as the occasion demands. It is like a genetic code that does not have to wait for sexual reproduction. When a symbol is syntactically transformed into a sign with a new meaning, its first meaning is understood to have been 'merely' conventional, or 'arbitrary' in the pejorative sense. Social meaning is generated by the supplemental addition of imagery to whatever was there in the first place. If, as Saussure has suggested, an image is an essential element of a sign, "reality" has no meaning *in-itself.* Reality, in both its empirical and ideal forms, has meaning when it is re-presented in cultural systems that are, themselves, constantly destroyed and re-built in concrete social situations, ceremonies, and rituals. The pre-Romantic and Romantic stress on the indispensability of the imagination for social life and as a supplement to rational concept formation should be re-evaluated in the light of Saussure's conflation of image and concept in the sign.

It would seem, then, that even though Saussure did not spell it out in exactly this way, his sign is not technically comparable with consensus or common sense models. That is, it does have a hidden syntactic component. Implicit in the idea of the image is a duality of representation (the image *and* its referent), that is, there is a syntactic component 'built-in' to the definition.

The model of the sign we propose here is derived from the others discussed.

(9) (i)   Sign is a relation between (a), (b), and (c):
- (a) image
- (b) observation
- (c) idea

(Note that once again we have arrived at Augustine's and Peirce's definition.) The closest description of the full sign (9) (a+b+c) that is available in American sociological literature is Mead's (1934) description of what he called 'significant symbol'. According to Mead, a significant symbol is a *gesture* (a) that completes its *meaning* (c) in the *response* (b) of another. It is evident that from a technical-theoretical standpoint, most symbolic interactionism is in a pre-Meadian phase of development.

Interestingly, the semantic connection of the signifying gesture and the signified response in Mead's description is identical with the syntactical connection of the gesture and its response. This unification of semantics and syntactics at the level of explanation is a general characteristic of signs that can be formulated:

(9) (ii)   The semantic relationship between the signifier and the signified is equivalent to the syntactic relationship between signs.

In Merleau-Ponty's (1963:121–22) words: "The true sign represents the signified, not according to an empirical association, but inasmuch as its relation to other signs is the same as the relation of the object signified by it to other objects."

To use Mead's work in this way is, in a sense, to go beyond his theory. For Mead, behavior was an *exchange* of meanings. In constructing an explanation around Mead's description of the significant symbol, it is necessary to transform behavior into an *aspect* of meaning, and not a privileged aspect at that. Correlatively, the self is displaced from the center of the system, and personal identity is put into question: it becomes a matter for 'negotiation', to use the modern term. As Mead's significant symbol is extended in the way suggested here, what passes for personal *identity* is revealed to be a multiplication of meanings. Identity, like the sign, is based on a division, that is, it repeats itself in the response of the other. This is implicit in post-Meadian sociologies, including Mead's own. It is natural that the individual should complain that he has a 'true self' or that he is really something more (or less) than what he appears to be. The divided self cannot be found at the center of the empirical action; it must always complete itself elsewhere. This hint of the proximity of unity and truth is a basic characteristic of all signs that is expressed, as such, by the person, the only 'sign' that knows how to talk.

The false centrality of the self in Mead's system derives from his comment that the meaning of a gesture returns to its author as his perception of the other's response to it. (This is the famous 'feedback' equation. See the discussion in Buckley 1967:96). After s/he has served his purpose, the 'other' is gotten rid of, and Mead's model begins to drift toward individual-level reductionism in spite of the better intentions of its builder. It should be noted here that the removal of the individual from the center of Mead's system is not, technically, a radical move. The individual was not logically central in the first place. Mead and, it might be added, Saussure also, seem to have accorded the individual a privileged status, congruent with his status in consensus-based systems, before working through the full implications of their own studies. Perhaps this is the reason they did not themselves publish their own material. (Like Saussure's, Mead's *Course* was re-assembled by his students). Mead and Saussure apparently believed that the two interactants locked in permanent conversation in their systems could actually be two individuals when, in fact, the only existential status they could possibly have is two *meanings* or *values* which are trapped, after the fashion of all meanings, in their mutual determination. (For a critical comment on the 'circularity' of Mead's system, see Burke 1957:308.)

We are suggesting that social meaning has a structure of its own which is not much related to what we know, so far, about the individual, his psyche and mind. This may be less a paradox than a reflection of deficiencies in our social psychologies. From the standpoint of the model of meaning presented here, the individual appears both more and less 'human' than in other sociological systems. His or her understanding is but a reflex of the social system of meaning, but this system is composed of semantic and syntactic connections between his or her collective acts.

Implications

Semiotics displaces intentions and motives out of the individual actor and into culture. The literary critic Kenneth Burke has laid the groundwork for a semiotic of motives that might be developed within the symbolic interactionist perspective. Burke (1965:29–31) suggests "words for motives are in reality words for situations. . . . A man informs us that he 'glanced back in suspicion'. Thus suspicion was his motivation. But suspicion is a word for designating a complex set of signs, meanings, or stimuli not wholly in consonance with one another." It is worthwhile to build upon Burke's definition.

A man glances back in suspicion. He is out alone late at night in a strange dark street dappled at intervals with dim lamplight. In the dark places he walks a little faster. He is motivated by the darkness. The man is experiencing fear, and he himself may believe that it is his fear that is motivating him to walk faster. In situations that generate powerful emotions, motives *seem* to originate on a psychic plane, especially toward the end as the situation resolves itself or degenerates. Our biology is nicely geared to our cultural situation. The idea of a pre-reflective origin of motives in the individual, however, is a convenient illusion. It indicates a high level of socio-cultural organization of 'signs, meanings, and stimuli'. Meaning emerges more or less automatically from the combination of the individual's backward glance as he disappears into the shadows and the quickening of his pace. The speed-up of his heartbeat, his fear, is an aspect of the meaning of the darkening situation, but not one with the independent, or causal, status the individual may ascribe to it as his entire being is overcome by the desire to escape.

It is the cultural alignment of dramatic differentiation (light/dark) and moral differentiation (good/evil) that generates the subjective experience of fear. Note that should a man reverse the procedure of the fearful one and dash through the light spots while slowing down or lurking in the shadows, he will appear to be a cause of fear: evil. Interestingly, it is he, not the man who glances back in suspicion, who is given the name 'suspicious character'. Suspicion is motivated by this arrangement of the differentiation of light and darkness.

Note that in the generation of social meanings, norms operate on each aspect of the sign as it is described here (9)(i). *Images* (8)(a) are governed by norms, as in cosmetic and clothing styles and propagandistic art. There are norms governing *observations* (9)(i)(b), such as a rule against staring at someone who is out of place or the requirement that conversants attend one another's faces in 'face-to-face' interaction. And there are entire normative systems of *ideas* (9)(i)(c), such as religious and political beliefs. In social life each avenue to the free interplay of signs and arbitrary assemblies of meaning is blocked by norms. The only sociologically permitted exception to this rule is a negative condition: *anomie.*

Durkheim taught us that human differences as between normals and deviants are not the result of flaws in communication and socialization. They are, rather, natural structural divisions. The next logical step for the human sciences is to look at these normative differences as the original grounds of social meaning itself. In this chapter, we have tried to take this step and have arrived at the conclusion that:

(10) (a)   Social meaning is generated when the differentiations of consciousness follow the differentiations of the social world.

    (b)   Social meaning originates in social structural differentiation. In short, meaning is based on the opposite of consensus, i.e., difference.

While we have drawn much of our illustrative material from relatively bounded social situations, the relationship of differentiation to meaning retains its integrity at both micro- and macro-structural levels. For example, in Frank Young's macrostructural model of Third World development, *differentiation* is defined as "the system's capacity to process a diversity of information types, or to emphasize the mechanism by which such information is handled, it is the diversity of meaning areas in a symbolic structure." (F. W. Young 1966:47). Our suggestion that social meaning originates in structural differentiation can be read as a radicalization of Young's definition. It can also be read as a radicalization of Mead's microstructural formulation. Mead's central idea is that among humans, the meaning of an act motivates it. Or, the act is motivated by the Other's response to it. The same elements are present here as in the above macrostructural illustration: differentiation (self/other)→ meaning. (For further elaboration of this equation and its connection to the writings of Peirce and Rousseau, see chapter 4, "Ethnosemiotics.")

Some social structural differentiations, such as select groups and classes and nationalities, seem heavy and deterministic, or external and coercive, as Durkheim is supposed to have said. Other differentiations, those at the situational level, seem more manageable. The norms are there, but they can be broken after all, and the penalties are relatively light. There is one differentiation of social structure—the one that Simmel was most interested in—the secret, which seems to be almost fully under the control of the individual, a place where a person might stash his truth. Erving Goffman (1971:38–40) has named this interesting differentiation the 'information preserve' and classified it with the other divisions of territoriality and personal space. Harold Garfinkel (1967:54ff.) studies the norms that protect information preserves in the same way that the United States Air Force checks Chinese radar, by making systematic intrusions and mapping responses to them. By applying this inverted Meadian formula, Garfinkel has found that individuals are held responsible for meaning only on their own side of the line around an information preserve. For example, when an ethnomethodologist asks an individual what s/he means just after the individual has said hello, s/he may reply, "What do you mean, 'What do you mean?' you know what I mean!" The norms surrounding social structural differentiations, including the important differentiation called the 'individual ', operate like a safety net, not so much to restrain the animal in man, but to stop him from falling into the semiotic mechanism of culture.

4

Ethnosemiotics
Beyond Structural Anthropology

Discipline cultural scientists never seem to tire of writing about the problem of imposing our analytical categories on the things we study and thereby failing to understand the things in themselves. This warning places ethnographers and critics under great pressure to tell stories of authentic cultural experiences, to testify that they did not fail to understand the "true" existence, the "essence" of "their" people, "their" historical period, "their" text. We are not trying to deny the possibility of caring about and getting to know cultural productions other than one's own. But we have taken an opposite position, on the side of the cultural productions themselves, which we see as originating as addresses to cultural others. Further, we are suggesting that the pressure to get to the heart of culture has introduced into the discipline humanities and social sciences a division that propels them ever further away from one another and from their subject matter areas. This fragmenting division separates cultural studies into conservative, particularistic versions of culture on the one hand and studies of the creative activities that occur on the fringes of culture on the other. By a perverse logic that is typical of disciplined thought, when we are discussing our own cultural achievements, we refer to the creative energies on the fringes as the avant-garde or the "cutting edge." Referring to cultural others we speak of inauthenticity, disorganization, co-optation, absorption, and ruin.

We have thus far discussed the question of immanence and self-deception from an abstract and theoretical standpoint, showing in chapter 1 how the appearance of the sign vitiates disciplined attempts to get "to the things themselves" (see also D. MacCannell 1973). In chapter 3 we noted the theoretically illusory quality of immanence of meaning and the way it establishes a mythical base for modern social relations. In this chapter we want to discuss some of the consequences the quest for immanence has had on our disciplines and suggest some new working styles that are produced by an alternate, semiotic approach to the same materials.

Comment on Anthropology

Anthropology is a dialectical tension of center and periphery. During the most recent phase of anthropology's development, the center has been the positive pole of the dialectic. The system of Western values, of which anthropology is a part, reached its full expansion, and at the same time, our ethnographic descriptions of non-Western peoples attained their highest refinement.[1] These two developments would seem to cancel each other out. We know this is the hope of some anthropologists, whose entry into the field is motivated as much by a desire to question their own culture as to learn the secrets of another. But the hoped-for mutual cancellation has not happened in fact. Once relocated in an alien culture at the edge of their own world, anthropologists are required by their discipline to make a textual preservation of the core of cultural values, key symbols, and central themes they find there. Operating in this way, anthropology has built a bulwark around our civilization, a cultural equivalent to the Maginot Line or the Great Wall, a frame of tightly described, "unchanging" little societies that mark the limits of our "Western" world.

We do not wish to be read as suggesting that this structural sublimation of the rest by the West was intentionally produced by anthropologists. It was the result of a larger movement of history. At the level of individual research and writing, it appears as an accident involving the entire community of scholars who inadvertently defined their own culture not by ethnographic observation but by opposition to the "primitive" world. Now anthropologists are beginning to see themselves as agents of the Western system and to read their own acts as signs of a disturbed political consciousness.[2] But this kind of reflexive self-understanding remains limited to a few anomalous reports and journals that oppose themselves to the mainstream. This particular binary opposition generates liberal assessments like Charles de Gaulle's comment that the only real issue in the world is the global conflict of European whites versus the colored peoples. Interestingly, this opposition is always resolved hierarchically and rationally ($a/b \rightarrow \frac{a}{b}$ or $\frac{b}{a}$) rather than mythically ($a/b \rightarrow c$).

In the former headquarters of anthropological thought, in Cambridge, Columbia, Chicago, and Berkeley, one finds little review of anthropological symbols and themes as applications of modern values.[3] Once again, the center is set above the periphery by transference of creative energies to the front lines, while holding controlling techniques and assumptions above critical examination.[4]

For several decades, then, anthropology has "stabilized" the perimeter of our world, at least on paper, by constructing models of the bordering cultures, models that are subject to our scientific manipulation.[5] On assuming the Chair of Social Anthropology at the Collège de France, Lévi-Strauss remarked:

> One of the peculiarities of the small societies which we study is that each constitutes, as it were, a ready-made experiment, because of its relative simplicity and the limited number of variables required to explain its functioning. . . . By comparison with the natural sciences, we benefit from an advantage and suffer an inconvenience; we find our experiments already prepared but they are uncontrollable. It is therefore understandable that we attempt to replace them with models, systems of symbols which preserve the characteristic properties of the experiment, but which we can manipulate. [1967:25–26]

In other words, anthropological research paralleled and extended on a symbolic level the real historical campaign to stabilize the Third World by linking Western political and economic thought to manipulate foreign policy and eventually to military intervention.[6] Of course, the lesson of the last decade is that we can no longer assume that the center automatically dominates the periphery in any area of social life. The reversals suffered by the West in South East Asia and the Middle East are only the most visible signs of a total reorganization of modern life that is changing everything from communities and domestic relations to academic disciplines.[7]

ETHNOSEMIOTIC THEORY AND THE "NEW ETHNOGRAPHY"

In the current confrontation of the "rest vs. the West," the structures that are emerging on a multi-cultural plane—such as the movements within the Western middle class to adopt traits from remote cultures—seem to us to be the most complex and interesting. In this chapter, we argue that the aesthetic, moral, and other interpretative codes that are necessary for communication between cultures in multi-cultural systems are the growing historical base for a new anthropology we are calling *ethnosemiotics.*[8] The name is less important than the new form of inquiry and understanding designated by it: specifically a reversed polarity for anthropology which aims in the direction of a synthesis of center and periphery. We see in this synthesis, if accomplished on a historical and concrete cultural level, not merely the possibility for adaptation and survival but for transcendence, that is, the potential to develop new forms of society.

Ethnosemiotic studies include (1) research on the production of culture as interpretation motivated by social differences;[9] (2) turning existing anthropological insight derived from the study of remote groups back onto our own social life; and (3) continued discovery of new perspectives on "Third" and "Fourth World" peoples which have developed alongside of, often in opposition to, the official anthropological version.[10] This type of anthropology is establishing itself, not always in the traditionally strong graduate departments, as a sometimes unruly, always energetic new force.

During the same period of the initial appearance of the New Ethnography, semiotics invaded anthropology as a series of reports written in a formidable, self-conscious, technical language.[11] Semiotic discourse with anthropology hid, or rather it did not disclose, its revolutionary program at least to the extent that the theoretical, historical, and logical relations between semiotics and the New Ethnography have gone unnoticed. By now, it should be clear even to intellectual bystanders that semiotics has seized and secured the *periphery*. It is not, however, readying itself to take over the center of anthropology or the center of culture as its domain. Rather, it is designating the periphery as the positive pole of the anthropological dialectic, and it is developing in the interstices between cultures and between disciplines.

There are theoretical as well as political reasons for the precise form of the recent rapid development of semiotic anthropology, or ethnosemiotics. Consider Charles S. Peirce's (1955:88–89) search for meaning in differentiation, movements, ambiguity, and tension:

> [T]hat which particularly characterizes sudden changes of perception is a *shock*. . . . Now this shock is quite unmistakable. It is more particularly to changes and contrasts of perception that we apply the word 'experience'. We experience vicissitudes, especially. We cannot experience the vicissitude without experiencing the perception which undergoes the change. . . . It is the compulsion, the absolute constraint upon us to think otherwise than we have been thinking that constitutes experience. . . . This is present in even such a rudimentary fragment of experience as a simple feeling. For such a feeling always has a degree of vividness, high or low; and this vividness is a sense of commotion, an action and reaction, between our soul and the stimulus. [I]n the endeavour to find some idea which does not involve the element of struggle, we imagine a universe that consists of a single quality that never changes. . . .

Note that Peirce's negative characterization of an "unchanging universe consisting of a single quality" corresponds to a pre-semiotic ideal of "primitive" societies as discrete, undifferentiated, and timeless.

Without apologizing for the historical distortion, we have suggested that Jean-Jacques Rousseau provided us with the clearest post-structural vision.[12] Rousseau asserts that one of our highest cultural achievements, language, and poetic language in particular, originates in absolute human difference. All the elements of Peirce's analytic of meaning (shock, difference, a new experience, commotion of feelings, emergence of ideas) are found in this famous passage in Rousseau's (1966:13) *Essay on the Origin of Language:*

> Upon meeting others, a savage man will initially be frightened. Because of his fear he sees the others as bigger and stronger than himself. He calls them *giants.* After many experiences, he recognizes that these so-called giants are neither bigger nor stronger than he. Their stature does not approach the idea he had initially attached to the word giant. So he invents another name common to them and to him, such as the name *man,* for example, and leaves *giant* to the fictitious object that had impressed him during his illusion. That is how the figurative word is born before the literal word, when our gaze is held in passionate fascination; and how it is that the first idea it conveys to us is not that of the truth.[13]

The domain of ethnosemiotics is the study of interpretations that are generated by cultural differentiation. When cultures change or collide with one another or when their illogicality is exposed, the shocks and disjunctions lead to creative activities: explanations, excuses, accounts, myths. (We are using creative here in a non-evaluative way—the bringing into being of something new, a new evil as well as good, a new weakness as well as strength.) These interpretations, if accepted at the group level, may themselves eventually become aspects of culture: that is, they may form into a substantial basis for cultural differences that must be interpreted in turn. This is the ongoing synthesis of center and periphery, the engine of perpetual cultural production. Close attention to these matters in concrete cultural contexts leads automatically to a radical transformation of ethnographic method, which has already begun. In the New Ethnography, *interpretation,* which at one time was almost forbidden, is promoted to a central position, and ethnographic *description,* once central, is displaced to the status of the framework for interpretation. Increasingly, one finds that anthropologists of the generation following Lévi-Strauss, Victor Turner, and Clifford Geertz are working the edges between the differentiations of culture, interpreting the interpretations they find there.

From the standpoint of the New Ethnography and ethnosemiotics, it is especially ironic that some anthropologists should continue to cling so tightly to the notion of the "noble savage" and the myth of cultural authenticity as existing elsewhere. The concrete conditions of anthropological fieldwork have always located ethnographers on the edges, fringes, and borders of cultures. They work detached from their own group, never fully accepted into the group they are studying. From a Rousseauian standpoint, ethnographers are automatically situated to know culture in the process of its becoming if they would but remind themselves that they are in the same situation as the "savage": ". . . so he invents another name common to them and to him, such as the name *man,* for example. . . ." Still, some persist in the belief that ethnography is an authentic *re*production of an original culture, not merely a member of a class of cultural productions. The New Ethnography and ethnosemiotics are conscious of themselves as method, a way of framing up culture, and they are aware of the colleagueship of many others in this process. Interpreting culture may be the only social freedom we have ever possessed. Ethnosemiotics understands that culture is not natural in the way that a geological formation is natural; it can never *be* authentic; it dies at precisely the moment it stops questioning its own existence.

An appealing recent example of the New Ethnography is Jean-Paul Dumont's *The Headman and I,* which is a reflection of his field experience among the Panare.[14] When Dumont moved in with the Panare, they called him an *"Americano."* Rather than accepting this as a harmless fiction, Dumont insisted that he was a Frenchman who wanted to study their language, something the Panare did not understand or accept. In trying to explain that he was not from America, Dumont found out that, for the Panare, *Americano* had only trivial geographical connotations and was really their term for missionary, a discovery that only served to increase his frustrations and his desire to enlighten the Panare about his true identity and purpose.

The emotional and methodological intensity of this moment stems from Dumont's insight that his understanding of the Panare and their culture is necessarily a reciprocal function of their understanding of him and his culture. As often happens in these situations, the breakthrough occurred by an accident that Dumont seized upon, motivated, as he put it, "by a practical and spontaneous thought that . . . Lévi-Strauss would call 'savage' '' (1976:13). For several days, the men of the village had been making palm leaf ornaments for a ritual headdress and cape. The finery was made during the day, worn at a night ceremony, and discarded the next morning. On one of these days, watching the men make the ornaments, Dumont thought he saw a peculiar variant in which the Christian cross motif appeared. He asked about it. The Panare, shy at first, eventually admitted that they were, in effect, re-cycling Christian sacred symbolism in a lightly ironic way. What is most interesting about their admission is *their* interpretation of Dumont's reaction to it. For it was then that they realized, as a result of their own skills in ethnosemiotic interpretation, that because Dumont did not take the sign of the cross any more seriously than they did, because he did not become angry or moralistic, he must have been telling the truth all along: he was not an "Americano."

Dumont has aligned ethnographic performance with ethnographic experience, re-centering both on the intersection of cultures. His study is electric with naturally occurring interpretations (his, the Panare's, other's) that arc across cultural differences. There is a great deal of potential in this research design, a great deal more than in conventional ethnography, for the production of knowledge that is valuable in the modern world as it evolves in the direction of a single system. But it should not go unremarked that the goals of traditional ethnography are not necessarily suppressed by this approach. It was only after the Panare became genuinely curious about Paris and French family structure that they began to explain in detail the intricacies of their own to Dumont. In sum, Dumont has provided us with an ethnosemiotic of a system of synchronic differentiations (himself and our culture, the Panare and their culture, the Creoles who live in the region of the Panare) and the ways these differentiations form the meaning of Panare life and the anthropological field experience.

In another of the new ethnographies, Paul Rabinow has explicated a complex series of *diachronic* differentiations. Rabinow's (1975) *Symbolic Domination* is foremost a study of Sidi Lahcen, a Moroccan village in the Atlas Mountains—but one also senses there the quiet presence of Sartre and Ricoeur. Sidi Lahcen claims both its name and divine grace from a minor Muslim saint who lived in the seventeenth century. Rabinow pulls the Moroccans' interpretation of their own situation into the center of the ethnography before developing his analysis. He found that a continuing, literalistic interpretation of religious beliefs, during a history of complex socio-political change (e.g., the nineteenth-century change to a French legal system), was plunging these people ever deeper into raging alienation.[15] According to Rabinow (1975:99), "the symbolic formulations which are the vehicles of meaning changed much less rapidly than did the material conditions. . . . This is a source of both the continuity and profound malaise and disharmony in Moroccan society." It is worthwhile to render this structure as a formula in order to manipulate it theoretically: Alienation (A) is produced when the material conditions (MC) change more rapidly than cultural symbolism (CS).

$$\frac{MC}{CS} \rightarrow A$$

Rabinow does not go as far as one might wish in following his Sartrean impulses back to their Marxist roots; to the negation of alienation in revolution (R). He has, however, opened some interesting theoretical possibilities via the simple inversion of the structure he describes:

$$\frac{CS}{MC} \rightarrow R$$

Or, cultural symbolism that changes more rapidly than material conditions leads to revolution. To have moved beyond ethnography in this way would have carried Rabinow and the people of Sidi Lahcen outside the framework of their Moroccan experience, a move Rabinow, at least, was unwilling to make.[16] Still, there was a close brush here between revolutionary and ethnographic praxis—something that often happens in the new ethnography.

D. MacCannell selected tourists for his research topic because they intentionally violate and transcend cultural unity and isolation.[17] They are time travelers and space travelers *par excellence,* and they like to think of themselves as having a privileged point of view for the interpretation of historical and social phenomena. In other words, he followed the tourists both in the empirical, and in the scholarly, sense of basing his work on their semiotic of cultural differences. He found them to be less disciplined than anthropologists are supposed to be, but more dispersed and better financed. He even found some anthropologists among them. From following them he learned a great deal about the self-images traditional groups construct for tourists (and anthropologists) and the ways tourists interpret these images. Now we are beginning to study some of the ways touristic imagery influences group structure: the ways Amish and Basques have transformed themselves into a traditional-group-for-others, for example, or the ways Eskimos interpret the sculpture they make for sale to tourists.[18]

The new ethnography that we have been citing has departed from the heart of culture in order to attend to historical disruptions and the relations between groups.[19] In other words, it is ethnography that has been re-located and fundamentally re-designed for the modern collective experience, an ethnography of difference. An extensive series of ethnosemiotic studies would stand in sharp contrast to the aggregation of discrete cultural analyses we now have. Such a series would follow the contours of the evolving system of relationships between cultures and reproduce the emerging global cultural synthesis as it is occurring. The work involves comparison, but not mere comparison of the sort that is accomplished by the free play of Western theoretical imagination. Rather, it involves the study of living comparisons—the concrete communication and interpretive links between groups. Some of the implications of this transformation can be grasped by viewing the United States from a post-ethnosemiotic standpoint. Far from being a wasteland, as it appears in the current ethnographic atlas, it would be one of the richest areas for research on the ways the different peoples interact with one another in their arts, folklore, and politics, and the effect of these interpretations on the life of the groups.[20] Some groups, for example, Middle Americans and the Establishment, are pure products of interpretation.

The Roots of Ethnosemiotics in Anthropology

Tendencies toward a general theory of cultural differentiation surface from time to time in exciting and anomalous texts on interstitial phenomena and intercultural relations. Foremost among these are Marcel Mauss's (1967) study of *The Gift* and Robert Redfields's (1941) comparative community studies in Yucatán. Mauss and Redfield went beyond merely aggregative comparison of the sort that can now be routinely performed by manipulating the Human Relations Area Files and began to explicate the general form of the communicative relationship between groups. Lee Drummond has brought this line to its highest degree of refinement in his recent studies of Carib ethnicity. Their comparative ethnographic investigations are technically pre-semiotic in that they are cultural analogues to the situation described by Peirce and Rousseau on philosophical and literary levels.

The greatest barrier to the continued development of ethnosemiotic theory is the idealized anthropological version of its subject matter,

which holds it to be small-scale, unchanging, isolated, primitive societies. Mauss's most quoted remarks on anthropological subject matter and methods make him appear to have fully embraced the prevailing rhetoric of cultural isolation. For example, Merleau-Ponty (1964:115) quoting Mauss approvingly, states: " 'What is true,' Mauss writes, 'is not a prayer or a law but the Melanesian on such and such an island. . . .' "
In the same paragraph where the famous sentence appears, Mauss (1967:78–79) placed greater emphasis on "complex beings," "organized societies and their sub-groups," and collective "ideas and sentiments as interpretations" and "motive forces." Mauss sketched the outlines of a general ethnosemiotic theory in *The Gift,* but he also made it possible for us to ignore it by attending exclusively to his remarks on cultural integrity.

The same could be said for Redfield except that he had an almost perverse tendency to deflect attention away from his own most important contributions. Redfield (1953:12) wrote: "The precivilized society was like the present-day primitive society in those characteristics— isolation, smallness, homogeneity, persistence in the common effort to make a way of living under relatively stable circumstances. . . ." Redfield's great insight, of course, was that the sort of reflective self-consciousness that is so evident a feature of modern civilization cannot have emerged in isolated, culturally homogeneous communities. He analyzes the relationship between folk and urban centers in the same way that structural linguists would eventually come to analyze the relationship of subject and predicate—as the basis for the liberation of the subject from the immediate situation and the use of the imagination to create new cultural worlds.[21] Redfield does not carry his speculations as far as we are suggesting we should carry ours, to the point of asking if culture itself is a form of reflexive self-consciousness (interpretation) which requires differentiation *and* relations between communities and groups.

We have only gone so far as to arrive, once again, at Rousseau's position—that there is only one culture of which the various "cultures" of the world are but partial expressions. This is the view which is more or less explicit in all semiotic anthropologies in structural anthropology, for example.[22] Recall that Lévi-Strauss (1967:16) used no less an occasion than his assuming the new Chair of Anthropology at the Collège de France to advance the claim that anthropology is only a subfield of general semiotics. One would expect a decline of the particularistic view of culture to occur with increasing acceptance of structuralism. Echoing

Redfield on the theme of global synthesis, Lévi-Strauss (1967:24) writes: "Existing societies are the result of great transformations occurring in mankind at certain moments in prehistory and an uninterrupted chain of real events relates these facts to those which we can observe." When we give structural anthropology a close reading, however, rather than discovering the expected decline in the particularistic viewpoint, we find that the tension between particularism and the "family of man" has reached a crisis stage.

Lévi-Strauss himself is determined to advance the notion that primitive societies are absolutely different from modern societies—that they are isolated, undifferentiated, timeless monads; that they function almost purely as objects of anthropological research. He writes: "the social facts which we study are manifested in societies each of which is a *total entity, concrete and cohesive"* (1967:24, his emphasis). "In a word," Lévi-Strauss (1967:47) continues, "we might define these societies as 'cold' in that their internal environment neighbors on the zero of historical temperature." The idea of the Total Social Fact, which is so supple and heuristic in Mauss's expression of it, has here been literalized, concretized, and perhaps killed-off. And, it should be added, quite selfishly on Lévi-Strauss's part, for he hardly had time to refill his pen before he began to violate assumptions of cultural totality as they had never before been violated, not even by Mauss.

Here is one of the most troublesome of the dilemmas facing anthropologists today. Lévi-Strauss claims, we think justly, for the most part, to have devised methods that permit us to transcend the limits of Western science in our understanding of cultural others. In *Mythologiques,* (1970, 1973) guided alternately be hermeneutics and semiotics, his interpretation moves with absolute freedom between the myths without concern for the so-called totality of the groups in which they were found. But, as the critics have reminded us (de Man 1967: 46–47; Derrida 1967a: 414ff.), Lévi-Strauss's viewpoint remains close to that of Western science in that the final interpretation of the myths, though not quite that of an external observer, is still presented as having a life of its own, independent of both scientific subject and ethnographic object. Lévi-Strauss's great contribution is that he faces these problems squarely and attempts to solve them.[23] Now the struggles between inside and outside, center and periphery, the West versus the rest, which have been so long repressed by the academic conscience, are out in the open.

ETHNOSEMIOTICS AND PHENOMENOLOGY

This run of events, which has already begun and is profoundly disturbing the field of anthropology, faces many real obstacles ranging
from unsolved, complex theoretical and methodological problems to
conservative discipline politics. There are also some pseudo-obstacles.
Foremost among these is the opposition of structuralism and semiotics
to phenomenology. Apparently this opposition is the product of some
squabbling that took place among French academics during the early
1960s.[24] Lévi-Strauss (1968:61) may have started it with these famous
lines in *Tristes Tropiques,* read and taken to heart by every anthropologically bound French high school student from 1956 onward:

> I stood out against the new tendencies in metaphysical thinking which
> were then beginning to take shape. Phenomenology I found unaccept-
> able, in so far as it postulated a continuity between experience and
> reality. . . .

This anti-phenomenological position is both understandable and correct when viewing some of the social research of existentialists, ethnomethodologists, and sociologists who follow Alfred Schutz, Harold
Garfinkel, and Peter Berger. Their work often is anthropologically naive
in that it mingles psychology and culture in an un-thought-out (they
would say "taken for granted") fashion. However, if Lévi-Strauss intended his remarks to cover the full potential of phenomenology as it
was originally expressed by Husserl, the tack he and others have taken
eventually rests on forced distinctions. Husserl wrote a semiotic integral
to his phenomenology, just as Charles S. Peirce wrote a phenomenology (he sometimes referred to it as "Phaeneroscopy") integral to his
semiotic. Semiotics and phenomenology in their original and fullest
expressions are the two sides of the question of meaning.

Nowhere does Husserl make the mistake that Lévi-Strauss claims is
endemic to phenomenology, that is, the postulation of a continuity of
meaning. The phenomenological *epoché* is a methodologically imposed break with our familiar acceptance of things as they are, a detachment that is designed to throw the essence of consciousness into
sharp relief. Moreover, according to Husserl (1962:96–100), it is only by
means of this break, suspension, or bracketing of the familiar world that
consciousness becomes accessible to itself. Such an operation cannot
be claimed to have been properly performed unless it can be turned
back onto ethnographic, literary, aesthetic, and other materials: in other

words, considering only the anthropological, unless it throws both consciousness *and* the essential properties of everyday life into sharp relief.

They set out in opposite directions: Lévi-Strauss rigorously gearing his anthropology to the realm of the cultural; Husserl just as rigorously holding to his goal of radical philosphical reflection. But the world of thought is round and extremes meet. Lévi-Strauss's search for the universal characteristics of consciousness carries him into the same unfamiliar territory that Husserl discovered in his search for transcendental intersubjectivity.

As we suggest in the next chapter, the most straightforward way to wrap these matters up and move beyond Husserl and Lévi-Strauss, continuing in an ethnosemiotic direction, is to approach cultural differentiation itself as the first *epochē,* or epoch, in our collective transcendental journey.[25] Cultural texts that treat the same materials from different angles produce, more or less automatically, by their simple juxtaposition, a shock, and at least a momentary awareness of the arbitrariness of all cultural codes. Cultural differentiation corresponds precisely to the phenomenological *epochē* in that it simultaneously detaches us from the world of familiar affairs and throws this world and our thought about it into sharp relief. Note that while this is an acceptable statement from the standpoint of general semiotic theory, it contains an assumption that would be highly problematical to some phenomenologists, those who locate consciousness in the individual psyche. The statement is based on the assumption that culture is a form of consciousness, or is a being that we can live within without consciousness of it, by the simple expedient of letting it be our consciousness for us, until something happens that shocks everything out of alignment.[26]

BEYOND ETHNOGRAPHY

"Beyond" is not here intended to suggest that ethnography is dead —only that it should be possible to build upon it and reconstruct the discipline(s) on a meta-ethnographic basis. Movement beyond ethnography is concomitant with a recentering of research on interpretation and communication links between cultures and the emergence of a semiotic of transcultural materials.[27] The field of anthropology, insofar as it has used the aggregate of ethnographies as its data base, has always been meta-ethnographic "in-itself." But it has had little awareness of its organization "for-itself," that is, of its place in history, until the recent appearance of the theoretical viewpoints discussed in this chapter. The most complete illustration of the results of this theoretical combination and movement is still the *Mythologiques* but there are other meta-ethnographic tendencies on the margins of anthropology.

The Ethnography of Modernity

Students who are attempting to arrive at a basic and holistic understanding of modern societies, who approach a complex structure not as an aggregate of little societies (urban villages, for example), but as a phenomenon *sui generis,* necessarily operate on a meta-ethnographic level. In this regard, we would again call attention to the works of Erving Goffman, which can be used to illustrate more than one point.[28] Goffman has provided us with the best ethnography of modernity we have while rigorously staying on the margins of several disciplines: sociology, anthropology, linguistics, ethnology. His work is a charmed combination of three basic elements: (1) a phenomenology, (2) a semiotic, and (3) unusual savvy about social organization that permits him to dart and weave through class, status, power, ritual, kinship, morality, occupation, etiquette, ethnicity.[29] The semiotics and phenomenology in Goffman's works are at a crude state of development when judged from the standpoint of standards now being established by technicians in these areas. But this only serves to better illustrate the potential that resides in their combination. Goffman's phenomenology, when it is working, can convey to us a sense of ourselves because he has suspended or bracketed everyday experience in his descriptions of it, rendering it accessible to analytical consciousness. These descriptions are interconnected by a practical semiotic of social appearances. The linkages established in this way, while originating on an empirical level, do not reproduce either a geographically bound community or a conceptually bounded class. They express the genetic capacity of social life to reproduce itself through interpretation and to assume different forms.[30]

Comparative Studies of Third-World Communities

Another organized research program, little known and less understood, which is semiotic (although not phenomenological) and meta-ethnographic, is Frank Young's comparative studies of Third-World communities. This work, which apparently received financial support in inverse proportion to its recognition in the field of anthropology, began in Mexico in the 1950s and eventually extended itself to other areas of

Latin America, Asia, Africa, the United States, and to ethnic solidarity and liberation movements.[31] The original study (reported in Young and Young 1960 and elsewhere) is a comparison of twenty-four villages designed to show the relationship between the form of their interactions with one another and their internal structure. The research design is similar in most technical respects to comparative studies using the Human Relations Area Files. The difference is that the Youngs generated their own original ethnographic profiles, selected a system of communities that had formal ties with one another, and focused on the structure of the network as much as on the organization of the component communities. (All these points are illustrated in Young 1964.)

The theoretical component of this work was arrived at inductively outside of the semiotic mainstream but predictably it was formulated in semiotic terms. In a (1966:46) summation of the work to that point, Young wrote: "social change is construed as symbolic transactions and transformations, and the important variables in understanding the dynamics are the information processing capacities of the communities and the communication strategies they use." In his more recent work (Young 1976) he appears to be moving from the conventional sociological notion that "groups produce symbols" to the semiotic and/or phenomenological idea that groups are signs. The innovations here are twofold: (1) symbolic interaction is reconceived as operational between groups and communities, not merely between individuals, and (2) relatively stable and highly predictive measures of group-level communication processes have been constructed. Again, this work is at a relatively crude stage of development, but the ground has been broken for a semiotic of macrostructural change.

These examples diverge greatly from conventional one anthropologist-one group-one book approaches to ethnography. The descriptions of particular groups, situations, and communities are located from the beginning in a wider context of comparison and interpretation. And, as ethnography is made perhaps more important in these comprehensive systems of interpretation, the role of the ethnographer is simultaneously effaced. The ethnographic performance becomes the groundwork for the analysis that follows. In Dean MacCannell's own current research on 650 California towns, the ethnographies are not written by anthropologists but by machines and institutions. Freeways, for example, are a form of writing about California communities. They appear on aerial photographs as a drunken cursive and they describe power relations better than we do.[32] They only require an interpreter who has taken the trouble to learn their language.

A Final Word about the "Political Dimension"

Ethnosemiotics, located as it is between groups, occupies precisely the same ground which is also referred to as the "political arena." Insofar as power is a part of the vocabulary of interpretation at the group level, ethnosemiotic analysis is political analysis. It can be seen immediately, however, that we must be prepared to extend the framework of conventional political science beyond organized politics, beyond class, occupation, and community structure, into the relations between cultural phenomena. And going still further, once we have taken leave of the heart of culture and relocated our studies on the furthest perimeters, we must be prepared to discover revolutionary activity at every turn.

Revolution is used here in the widest possible sense, to incorporate the fights for self-determination that are occurring on a cultural plane. Consider, for example, the opposition we can witness right now between *fiction* and *reality,* which is shaping the modern world in the same way that the opposition between the classes shaped the industrial world. The arts are developing consciousness of themselves in the socio-cultural change process; the film medium in particular is striving to become political ethnography.

Clearly it is time for us to leave this field to occupy higher ground. Whether this move is eventually read as an advance or a retreat will be determined by our skill at interpreting these events, by our ethnosemiotic skills. As we have already suggested, these skills are still most developed and evident in the writings of J. J. Rousseau. Recall some remarks Lévi-Strauss has made:

> Rousseau is our master and our brother, great as has been our ingratitude towards him; and every page of this book *[Tristes Tropiques]* could have been dedicated to him, had the object thus proffered not been unworthy of his great memory. For there is only one way we can escape the contradiction inherent in the notion of the position of the anthropologist, and that is by reformulating, on our own account, the intellectual procedures which allowed Rousseau to move forward from the ruins left by the *Discours sur l'Origine de l'Inégalité* to the ample design of the *Social Contract.* . . . He it is who showed us how, after we have destroyed every existing order, we can still discover the principles which allow us to construct a new order in their stead. [1968:389]

5

The Second Ethnomethodology

The discipline social sciences are already internally fragmented by diverse research programs that are attempting to discover "natural cultural arrangements." The most developed of these counter-disciplinary sub-programs goes by the name of ethnomethodology. We once called ethnomethodology the "New California School of Sociology," but it is not new anymore and not confined to California. Some would argue it is not even sociology. Ethnomethodology appeared on the fringes of mid-twentieth-century American sociology as if set in place by Hegel's own hands; as the antithesis of sociological positivism. Predictably, sociology's response has been aggressive and hostile, to the point of driving some of its most advanced thinkers out of the discipline.[1] In this chapter we open the possibility, on a conceptual and theoretical level, of a rapprochement between ethnomethodology and the semiotic revolution. It seems unlikely that ethnomethodology will find room for advance within sociology, but it has much to offer semiotics and vice versa, we think.

Ethnomethodology was first practiced by a group of dissident sociologists and anthropologists under the influence of Harold Garfinkel. This group included Aaron Cicourel, Harvey Sacks, David Sudnow, and Manny Schegloff. This was a serious and somewhat self-conscious group, touchy about membership and apprenticeship and concerned about the correctness of ideas.

Like many California developments, the first ethnomethodology has involuted or become a tangle of tightly interconnected cul-de-sacs, easy to enter but not easy to get out of. We think it is possible, by steering always in the direction of a semiotics of culture, to find the heart of the first ethnomethodology and move in the direction of a second.

By now almost everyone knows (perhaps some of us have forgotten) that the domain of ethnomethodology is everyday life, that it takes seriously the subjective point of view of the individual, that it is theoretically based on phenomenological philosophy, and that it applies new ethnographic techniques to natural situations in an attempt to discover their "rational" properties: the methods people actually use to accomplish their everyday affairs.[2]

Note that as an offspring of sociology, ethnomethodology's pedigree is in good order. Harold Garfinkel was a graduate student of Talcott Parsons's at Harvard at the time when Parsons held almost the entire field of sociology spellbound. On the phenomenological side, Alfred Schutz, who was Husserl's student, wanted to begin his career in America with an extended re-interpretation of Parsons's *The Structure of Social Action*.[3] In other words, the two main streams of influence on Garfinkel had begun to flow together even before he coined the term ethnomethodology. Nevertheless, its proto-semiotic leanings insured it a very confused reception by the parent discipline. And, of course, as is now well known, the early ethnomethodologists were perverse enough to enjoy their opposition to the discipline. They insisted on the importance of understanding the subjective viewpoint of the actor at a time when everyone else was frantically trying to establish the objective viewpoint of the investigator; they insisted that ethnographic description occupied a methodological ground higher than mere statistical explanation and prediction. These were reasons enough for the repressive mobilization of discipline machinery.

But we think the bedrock basis for the mutual hostility of sociology and the first ethnomethodology is buried deeper still in the bad conscience of the discipline. The most subversive aspect of the first ethnomethodology is its persistent suggestion that an understanding of *culture* is the key to our consciously thought-through research agenda. Goffman studied ritual and drama; Sacks studied language; Schutz, music; Berger, religion; Garfinkel, manners. These are aspects of culture, not the restricted domain discipline sociologists, even some sociologists of art, like to call "social organization." Modern sociology had to distance itself from ethnomethodology as a defensive move to preserve the intellectual status quo: sociology contained no theory or theory fragments that were adequate to the analysis of culture.

Of course, from the vantage point of post-structural semiotics, all the hostile academic posturing within the discipline social sciences during the last ten years appears as silly slapstick. From the standpoint of semiotics, the first ethnomethodologists did not go too far, they fell short in their efforts to unravel the secrets of modern culture. Part of the reason that ethnomethodology has not advanced much beyond its campaign promises is the resistance offered it by sociology, and part is a built-in limitation stemming, we are about to argue, from its intellectual dependence on a version of Husserlian phenomenology.

We do not think the theoretical inhibitions of ethnomethodology are in the general perspective provided by Husserl. Husserl's work remains heuristic to the social sciences. Indeed, it gave intellectual force to an encouraging attack on the discipline social sciences during the 1960s. Rather, it is on the specific ground of Husserl's description of the "natural standpoint" and everyday consciousness that the first ethnomethodology stumbled. But let us back up a bit . . .

Recall that Husserl's starting point was exactly the same as Charles Peirce's, a radical critique of mathematical logic, a critique that led them both (independently) to parallel attempts to establish new ground rules for science. Following Husserl, phenomenology takes as its foundation the factual world, but it refuses to join with science (as we continue to know it) and pre-conceive the things of the world to be either real or ideal. Rather, they are taken as they *are,* that is, as *appearances.* (Phaneron = appearance.) More than this, phenomenology refuses to join with science in its study of the accidental characteristics of things, their weight, volume, length, etc. Phenomenology is the study of *essences,* for example, the essence of thought or the essence of language, etc. Husserl's main discovery, the principle of *intentionality,* assures that phenomenology cannot ultimately break with the world nor can the world break away from philosophical reflection. Intentionality means that consciousness is always consciousness of something— that thought intends its object.[4] Husserl's own investigations demonstrate quite conclusively that there is no *realm* of consciousness, or category of consciousness. If you examine any thought or any perception, it is not possible to discover consciousness on the edges of it, or at the end of it. The thought *is* consciousness—the perception *is* consciousness: all consciousness is consciousness of something. These matters can be clarified for some students by pointing out that Husserl's *consciousness* and *intentionality* correspond to Peirce's (1955:91) "thirdness":

> We are too apt to think that what one *means* and the meaning of a word are quite unrelated meanings of the meaning of the word "meaning." . . . In truth the only difference is that when a person *means* to do anything he is in some state in consequence of which the brute reactions between things will be moulded to conformity to the form to which the man's mind is itself moulded, while the meaning of a word really lies in the way in which it might . . . tend to mould the conduct

of a person into conformity to that which it is itself moulded. Not only will meaning always, more or less, in the long run mould reactions to itself, but it is only in doing so that its own being consists. For this reason I call this element of the phenomenon or object of thought the element of Thirdness.

All advances in the sociology of face-to-face interaction, the ethnography of speaking, the first ethnomethodology have been based on this (Husserl's/Peirce's) insight. In interaction, the individual is condemned to meaningfulness. No matter how much it might be desired, as under conditions where shame and embarrassment (Sacks) are likely outcomes, it is not possible to stop the moulding of meaning to behavior in the presence of others. Even "meaningless" behavior is taken to mean that the person either is insane or is conducting some kind of experiment. (See Goffman 1963, 1967, and his other writings.) And since it is impossible to stop meaning, it is equally impossible to stop the masking and staging that goes with it.

Philosophical phenomenology, which holds itself aloof from sociological phenomenology, takes consciousness itself as its object, or attempts to describe the essence of perception, intuition, ideas, imagination, etc. There has been almost no systematic development of this philosophical field (beyond the usual classroom and textbook discussion) in the United States, but it has undergone continuous and considerable development in Europe. Prominent contributions after Husserl include Heidegger's *Sein und Zeit* (1927), Sartre's *L'imaginaire* (1940) (translated into English under the unfortunate title *The Psychology of the Imagination*), Merleau-Ponty's *Phénoménologie de la Perception* (c. 1945), and Jacques Derrida's *Speech and Phenomena* (1973) and *De la grammatologie* (1967a), which inaugurate the semiotic critique of Husserl. In order to arrive at a description of the essence of perception or the imagination, these students undertake to hold the world in brackets, to reduce it, or freeze it, so that consciousness can return to itself and examine its own features. It is through this examination of itself that consciousness returns to the world and clarifies it. This disciplined act of reflection is the phenomenological method, called the *epochē*, or reduction.

Critique of Husserl's Thesis of the "Natural Standpoint"

It is here on Husserl's positioning of the *epochē* that we might advance by detaching ourselves from phenomenological orthodoxy, and eventually by separating a second ethnomethodology from the first.

Recall that Husserl simultaneously justified his philosophy and staked out the domain of phenomenological sociology by describing a socio-cultural world drained of all thought:

> This world is not here for me as a mere world of facts and affairs, but, with the same immediacy, *as a world of values, a world of goods, a practical world.* Without further effort on my part I find the things before me furnished not only with the qualities that befit their positive nature, but with value-characters such as beautiful or ugly, agreeable or disagreeable, pleasant or unpleasant, and so forth. Things in their immediacy stand there as objects to be used, the "table" with its "books," "the glass to drink from," the "vase," the "piano," and so forth. These values and practicalities, they *too belong to the constitution of the "actually present" objects as such,* irrespective of my turning or not turning to consider them or indeed any other objects. [Husserl 1962:93, his emphasis.]

Elsewhere (91) Husserl describes the world of the natural standpoint as "simply there." And knowledge of this world has "nothing of conceptual thought in it."

There are two ways to approach this powerful image of a mindless world that appears to think. One angle of approach would be to treat it as the origin myth of modern phenomenology: in the beginning the world was exactly the same as it is now, only there was no consciousness. . . . In other words, the "natural standpoint" is a fiction of the presence of pure facts against which all thought originates in opposition. This was Charles S. Peirce's way of describing the "natural standpoint," what he called "Firstness," which he developed into his phenomenology of feeling. Peirce (1955:81–82) wrote:

> By a feeling, I mean an instance of that kind of consciousness which involves no analysis, comparison or any process whatsoever, nor consists in whole or in part of any act by which one stretch of consciousness is distinguished from another, which has its own positive quality which consists in nothing else, and which is of itself all that it is, however it may have been brought about; so that if this feeling is present during a lapse of time, it is wholly and equally present at every moment of that time.

Note that Peirce has written this description in such a way as to render it as unlikely as in Husserl's hands it appears to be likely.

Peirce elaborates his idea of "Firstness" for purposes precisely the opposite of Husserl's in describing the "natural standpoint," namely, to begin a philosophical critique of the "natural standpoint" and to suggest or even to insist upon a radical detachment from the ideas of *presence* and *immediacy.* According to Peirce (1955:91), "Firstness" is the basis of all feeling and he goes on to say:

> The immediate present, could we seize it, would have no character but its Firstness. Not that I mean to say that immediate consciousness *(a pure fiction, by the way)* would be Firstness, but that the *quality* of what we are immediately conscious of, which is no fiction, is Firstness. [our emphasis]

A second approach to Husserl's thesis of the "natural standpoint," the approach Husserl himself appears to have taken, and certainly that of his orthodox followers, is to accept it not as necessary fiction (i.e., myth) but as a provisional but essentially accurate description of everyday social life, and to build upon it. Husserl's remarks on the "natural standpoint" clearly announce themselves as scientific description and programs for a new science, not as fictions: "I am aware of a world. . . . immediately, intuitively, I experience it." Things are *"for me simply there,* in a verbal or figurative sense 'present' . . ." (1962:95). Here is the program statement:

> We do not set ourselves the task of continuing the pure description and raising it to a systematically inclusive and exhaustive characterization of the data, in their full length and breadth, discoverable from the natural standpoint. . . . A task such as this can and must—as scientific —be undertaken, and it is one of extraordinary importance. . . . [1962:95]

The first ethnomethodology is a serious effort to realize and institutionalize Husserl's program. We might question the logic and value of such procedures, not from an external standpoint as has already been done by the field of sociology, but, taking our cues from Peirce, from within.

At least three times scholars of enormous capacity—Sartre, Schutz, and Berger and Luckmann—have tried to complete the pure description of everyday life from the natural standpoint, and have failed. While it is not identified as ethnomethodology, Berger and Luckmann's elegant *Social Construction of Reality* provided illustration: "Among the multiple realities there is one that presents itself as the reality par excellence. This is the reality of everyday life." It seems so true as to be not worth questioning. It appears to have satisfied the phenomenological requirement of getting the essence of the consciousness of everyday reality. But suppose we question it nevertheless, as Peirce suggested we must. What is *immediate presence*? Can there be such a thing and if there is how meaningful is it in-and-of-itself? What is the basis for all these claims being made for immediacy and presence? It is certainly not based on pure description. Even a naive description of presence quickly reduces it either to nothingness or to a fiction of presence, which derives its character from thick semantic layering and syntactic extension into matters often very remote.

Viewed from this vantagepoint (which is also that of post-structural thought), the first ethnomethodology appears as a moment of forgetting or blindness, the kind of moment in the history of a culture that Juri Lotman has described so well. By pretending that consciousness does not exist in the world, but only in philosophy and theory, the first ethnomethodologists were free to create a series of new myths about the origin of the world and to name their myths "scientific discoveries": Berger and Luckmann (1966:19) write:

> The world of everyday life is not only taken for granted as reality by the ordinary members of society in the subjectively meaningful conduct of their lives. It is a world that *originates* in their thoughts and actions, and is maintained as real by these. [Interestingly, their emphasis.]

This is not technically a new myth, but a variant of an old Western idea about the autonomy of the individual, and we should be able to place it under a positive sign (which is clearly Berger and Luckmann's intention) if it were an unambiguous reflection of the spirit of independence. But things are not always what they seem, and the idea of the autonomy of the individual has long since been subverted so that it now breaks up spontaneous solidarities and perpetuates the autonomy of existing organizations and corporate structures, not individuals. In other words, it functions as a myth.

In his critique of Husserl, which is sufficiently trenchant to apply equally to the followers of Husserl, Jacques Derrida suggests that the metaphysics of "presence" within phenomenology is only the latest disguise of the Western transcendental ego. It is interesting to read the following passage from Derrida (1973:6) as a comment on ethnomethodological "descriptions" of the origin of reality in everyday life, or the living present (although the passage was certainly not written as such):

> One ideal form must assure this unity of the infinite and the ideal: this is the *present,* or rather the presence of the *living present.* The ultimate form of ideality, the ideality of ideality. . . . is the *living* present, the self-presence of transcendental life.

Derrida adds ironically:

> Presence has always been and will always, forever, be the form in
> which we can say ... the infinite diversity of contents is produced.

The Displacement of the Epochē and the Second Ethmethodology

Derrida's critique is not motivated by a concern about the false consciousness produced by the myth of the autonomy of the individual. It
is based on a radical philosophical semiotic which holds that it is not
possible to set consciousness in opposition to a world composed of
signs. Consciousness, in the form of meaning, value, is already in the
world. We can return semiotic insights back to phenomenology with the
suggestion that the *epochē* is not philosophical reflection but cultural
processes. [Note that it is possible, though cumbersome, as Peirce was
fond of demonstrating, to keep the analysis flowing in phenomenological rather than semiotic language. We suspect that this strategy has its
limits, but since it also corresponds to the main point of this chapter,
we shall follow it out here.]

Husserl defined the *epochē* as a bracketing of the world, a disconnection and a suspension of judgment, a delicate and unmotivated
holding of the world in consciousness. This bracketing, Husserl suggested, "clamps onto an original, simple thesis and transvalues it in a
peculiar way," opening access to (the transvaluing) consciousness itself. We do not want to question the validity of Husserl's description of
the *epochē,* which we find to be detailed, convincing, and eloquent.
Rather we want to question his desire to monopolize the *epochē* for
philosophy while delegating to the post-disciplinary sciences the task
of describing a mindless world. The question we want to raise against
Husserl is When or Where does the "natural standpoint" leave off and
bracketing begin? Does the break occur only in a philosophic act? Or
does it exist in every object of attention, every cultural form, in every
moment? *Is the suspension first an aspect of the structure of the sign
and only secondarily a description of the contact of consciousness and
the world?* In our first chapter, we suggested that Rousseau and Saussure, prefiguring Lotman and Uspensky's version of the semiotic mechanism, imply that the process of transvaluation may operate
independently of the conscious will. The ongoing sign mechanism of
value creation (comparison and exchange) in the absence of any external criterion was countered in Rousseau's work with a fictional version
of a "self"; Husserl's *epochē* may be a companionate ephemeral
fiction.

In the works of Lotman, Kristeva, and others we find that (while it is not always presented as such) an unmodified version of Husserl's description of the *epoché* reappears as a model for cultural forms that have nothing of the philosophical in them. For example, as a general class, *ritual* is an interpretative form that is designed to produce a disconnection from the world of everyday affairs, to freeze or bracket social meanings or values, to suspend judgment, and to produce consciousness.[5] Social structural differentiation can also be read as a series of detachments or brackets that constantly produce new forms of consciousness. This is explicit in Marx's description of class consciousness, which he bases on the worker/owner differentiation; George Herbert Mead's description of Mind, which he based on the self/other distinction; Robert Redfield's analysis of historical consciousness, which he based on the rural/urban distinction; Goffman's description of self-consciousness, which he based on a front/back differentiation; and Lévi-Strauss's description of the Savage Mind, which he based on a nature/culture distinction (he would call it opposition). Note that a probable byproduct of dislocating the *epoché* along the lines we are suggesting would be a badly needed re-interpretation of all modern social theory.

Our favorite example of a cultural *epoché,* a semiotic transvaluation, is from Rousseau's *Emile.* The passage has been made all the more special for having been selected by Durkheim (1965b:93) for quotation in his study of Rousseau. Rousseau wrote:

> Good social institutions are those which are best able to alter man's nature, to take away his absolute existence . . . and to transfer the self to the community.

A second ethnomethodology, then, would be based on the principle that the *epoché* is not a philosophical act of reflection, but cultural semiosis; that consciousness is not opposed to the world of things, rather it operates through a world of signs; that the second ethnomethodology is semiotics.

Current Uses of the Epoché Within Ethnomethodology

As we have already suggested, the tendencies we have been describing here are being worked through in an un-self-conscious way in phenomenological sociology and ethnomethodology. The changeover to the study of cultural forms is almost complete, even though none of those whose work has been most affected have attempted an explanation of this evident process. Also, ethnomethodologists have developed an alternate, working version of the *epochē*. In fact, it is possible to discern three distinct operational definitions of the *epochē* implicit in the work of ethnomethodologists and phenomenologists.

(1) The *epochē* serves as *method*. Note that in so serving it partakes heavily of the spirit as well as the dicta of the original philosophical definition. Some ethnomethodologists begin their investigations by making a break with our familiar acceptance of everyday affairs so they can throw the essential properties of everyday life into sharp relief. Famous examples of this include the experimental fiddling with everyday expectations undertaken by Garfinkel's students and the widespread lore of the alleged antics of Erving Goffman. This is still a fruitful line, but it would be smarter, we think, to pay more attention to the serious methods for developing new angles on social situations that have been invented in the last ten years, including some of the less colorful techniques of Goffman and Garfinkel. We might look, for example, at the logic and results of Sudnow's (1972) use of the point of view of the still camera for his analysis of the role of the glance in social relations.[6] As a form of anti-sociological method, the *epochē* involves displacement of the everyday attitude in order to arrive at a clarification of the essential properties of everyday life. This was the main progressive interpretation of the *epochē* within the first ethnomethodology, the interpretation that paved the way for the second ethnomethodology.

(2) Cultural semiosis can be approached as a pre-scientific *epochē* . According to this approach, cultural productions serve as consciousness of the world, providing the first organization of its meaning, and providing us with our pre-reflective understanding. This is the position of the post-structuralists, the Tartu school, and others not necessarily identified with ethnomethodology.

(3) Finally, *epochē* can be understood in a psychological way, making of each of us a kind of mini-philosopher, united with our fellow human beings in an intersubjective understanding of the commonalities of our ideas, perceptions, etc. In our opinion, this is the most regressive and weak form of interpretation of the *epochē* found in the first ethnomethodology, a definite obstacle in the path of the development of the second. This superimposition of the philosophical attitude over everyday life separates human individuals from one another and from society, reduces institutional structures to an aggregate of habits, history to the span of attention of a hypothetical individual, and it retreats from conflict, change, and the semiotic revolution.

It should be noted that a psycho-philosophical as opposed to an ethnosemiotic definition of the *epoché* gives not merely different results but opposing results. Perception that is grounded in the psyche is very personal and absolutely individualistic. It is impossible to get so close to another that you perceive exactly what the other perceives. On the other hand, perception that is grounded on a methodological/cultural plane, if it is going to work in the first place, indicates that what it perceives is the true character of the object. The object is more than what is seen; we know it has another side, *even as we see it.* Perception brings us closer to participation in a pre-personal or absolute subjectivity. We have only to turn an object around to discover that it was not the way it seemed from our original point of view—but we knew that already. Our perception was submerged in a non-contingent perceptual knowledge, in culture.

The Concept of Intersubjectivity in the Second Ethnomethodology

In Schutz's writings, intersubjectivity is assumed and behavior is deduced from it. But after Schutz we find a progressive disillusionment with this idea culminating in the second ethnomethodology. Now we know that intersubjectivity is something not "given," rather it is accomplished, worked through, or produced, and it takes the form of both revolutionary and anti-revolutionary signs. The first ethnomethodologists often believed, as Husserl suggested they should, that intersubjectivity is similar to a scientific consensus, an agreement not to deviate from a set of shared ideas and procedures. While this has been the goal of several ethnomethodological investigations, it has not been possible to demonstrate conclusively that intersubjectivity is based on shared ideas and assumptions. Everyday life works and has meaning even under conditions where seemingly critically important assumptions are not shared. There are many aspects of life—courtship is an example—which could not work if the different metaphoric possibilities for interpretation were not maintained in perfect, or near-perfect, balance in behavior.

Garfinkel has demonstrated quite conclusively, it seems to us, that it is a supreme violation, not merely of scientific praxis, but of the norms of everyday life situations, to attempt to impose a precise and literalistic interpretation on the behavior of others. The behavior of the other, in ethnomethodology and in everyday life, is not in- and for-itself looked *at.* Rather, the behavior of the other provides a way of looking at still other behaviors and beliefs. It is looked through. Everyone sees through behavior in both the conventional (i.e., figurative) and non-conventional (i.e., literal) senses of seeing through. Concrete behavior is the basis of our perceptions of future affairs and expectations, previous conditions, and other behaviors in the same situation. When Garfinkel (1964) asked his students to look directly at the behavior of others with whom they were interacting, he found the others would become stupefied and the situation would "explode." Here is Garfinkel's great contribution to the semiotic revolution, where he goes beyond his teachers, Parsons and Schutz, even beyond his own invention, the first ethnomethodology: the subjective point of view of the actor in everyday life (the natural attitude) is in itself a cultural production, a sign that conserves the social order or opposes and changes it.

Compare, for example, a smile with the Pythagorean theorem. The theorem means the same thing to who so may make use of it. A smile may mean any number of things, such as "You are a stupid little man" or "Why don't we go up to my apartment so we can 'talk' "; its meaning(s) depends on the manner in which it is accomplished, who smiles at whom, where it takes place, what precedes and follows it, etc. A gifted actress can manage both meanings with one smile, unambiguously. Its meaning(s) and therefore any possibility for agreement are located not in the mind but in semiosis. Meaning-in-use often appears to arise in a natural, unproblematical way even though its complexities are enormously greater than those surrounding a detail of scientific consensus that requires special training to achieve. It is this *seemingly* unproblematical aspect of ordinary reality that led Husserl to his thesis of the "natural standpoint." But we are suggesting that it might also have led him in the opposite direction, to a consideration of the semiotic mechanism of culture.

Conclusion

It was Harold Garfinkel himself who gave to an essential property of everyday behavior the same name and meaning that Charles Peirce gave to one of his three primary types of signs: index or indexicality. And in his own researches, Garfinkel demonstrated the "indexicality" of behavior, the way it points through to and manipulates subjectivity. In Garfinkel's hands consciousness appears as variations on the theme of social structure. But his material can be re-interpreted from a post-structural standpoint as opening the way to understanding structural energetics by means of an empirically based synthesis of semiosis and subjectivity.

On the empirical level, the second ethnomethodology, without negating the first, has taken leave of the homely terrain of job interviews, plans to go shopping, the dinner table, and crying babies and comforting mothers. The scope of research is expanding to cover ritual, discourse, games, insults, etc. It is the same empirical domain worked by some semioticians who have never identified themselves with ethnomethodology. We are collectively involved in the task of generating cumulative findings on the relationship between specific semiotic systems (drama, ritual, discourse, literature, monuments, design, etc.). Interestingly, the students involved in the development of the first ethnomethodology seem now to be specializing in research on language as they attempt to re-tool.

The empirical successes of the first ethnomethodology have been considerable and should be carried forward. This includes work on jury decision making, suicide prevention, the staging of dying, role conflicts (role "distance" and sex-change operations), the design of airplane cockpits, etc. Of course, we might argue that these apparent successes are spurious, there being little competition from discipline sociology.

From a traditional sociological standpoint, the main weakness of the first ethnomethodology is its retreat from questions about the structure of entire societies. Jack Douglas (1973) has suggested that interaction between individuals is the basis of society, but this formula, extending back to Georg Simmel through Blumer and Mead, still has an anxious, provisional ring to it. Post-Parsonian macrostudies, for example, the work of Bruce Mayhew, Frank Young, or Parsons himself (1977), suggest that Durkheim and Marx were closer to the truth in their claim that the elementary units on this level are not individuals, but communities, social classes, ethnicities, etc. The displacement of the *epoché* to this level, which is occurring in the diverse research activities, and which we have tried to document here and in the next chapter, suggests the imminent appearance of a macro-ethnomethodology. Such a theoretical development would have the potential to extend its scope to the furthest limits of sociology as we know it today and beyond.

Part III

Critical Applications

6

On the Nature of the Literary Sign

On Re-reading Saussure for Literature

What follows is an engagement with the nature of literature from the point of view of a reader—as distinct from that of a speaker or a writer. The peculiar kind of grasping of a vivid image that yet eludes definition as clear and distinct, that is not quite a 'idea', seems to be of the essence in literature. In other words, literature has a "sign-character." Recent interest in developing theories of reading[1] ranging from reception theory to hermeneutics and allegories of reading indicates the importance of uncovering the structure of the act of reading at this moment in our literary history. Our purpose here is not to review these theories but to examine instead the potential a semiotic analysis of reading might have for its structure and process. The contention is that any theory of reading eventually will have a theory of the sign-structure implicit in it. It is the structuralist sign that will occupy the central place in this chapter.

For some versed in semiotic theory, it is Peirce's "pure rhetoric" that would provide an adequate model of the "reading" that is literary.[2] Peirce's definitions have historical affinities with New Criticism, and the notion that literary work can be conceived as the kind of sign that gives birth to other signs (texts engender readings which, as interpretants, are also texts) has enormous appeal for literary formalists. For all his insistence on the concrete presence of the sign for the receiver, however, Peirce often elides the description of the act of reading the sign, of the 'grasping' of its meaning.

Reading is bound up with meaning, and it is meaning that concerns the other semiologist, Ferdinand de Saussure. In thinking over the question of reading, we have noticed several ironies: while Saussure's work has been utilized by students of speech and students of writing (the semiolinguists, Lévi-Strauss, and Derrida) little has been done to explain, analytically, his importance for some of the greatest of modern readers, such as Barthes, Derrida, and Todorov. Moreover, it is Saussure's, not Peirce's, work that has itself given birth to what we can call "readings," texts that are interpretants and that have by now become part of our literary history.[3]

It is our intent to open the discussion of Saussure's essay "On the Nature of the Linguistic Sign" (1959) by drawing out its import for literary study. To be literate is *to read;* even though a reading may be wrong or unconsciously motivated or determined by the manner of presentation of the material. What is read are signs, and if the sign seems somewhat worn-out as a concept, it is nonetheless inextricably linked to the fate of reading.

In re-reading Saussure's linguistic sign as a literary one, we do not hope to go over old debates. We hope instead to re-frame the Saussurian sign for the literary history of ideas. Moreover, this is not an attempt to return to a 'sign' in a mode that pretends to ignore Jacques Derrida's brilliant critique (1967). On the contrary, our aim is to repeat the Derridean movement in which, it must be recalled, Derrida emphasizes his awe and respect for the sign as Saussure so radically conceived it, the sign prior to its metaphysical 'perversion.' Derrida tracked the sign's corruption in the *Course* (its failure to maintain balance between *signifié* and *signifiant*) as a story of the inevitable repression of one aspect by the other. We take a different course: tracking the internal "deconstruction" of the serene sign within Saussure's text, the movement from the apparent totality of the linguistic sign to the moment of its explosion in the associative relation. Derrida writes of the labor of uncovering the metaphysical dimension of the concept of one sign, up to the moment of disclosing its logocentric and ethnocentric limits:

> C'est à ce moment là qu'il faudrait peut-être abandonner ce concept. Mais ce moment est très difficile à déterminer et il n'est jamais pur. Il faut que toutes les ressources euristiques du concept de signe soient epuisées et qu'elles le soient également dans tous les domaines et tous les contextes. [Kristeva et al. 1971:12]

> It is at that moment that it would perhaps be necessary to abandon this concept [the sign]. But that moment is very difficult to determine and it is never pure. It is necessary for all the heuristic resources of the sign to be exhausted and that they be so in all contexts and all domains.

We revert from Saussure's final terminology of signifier/signified to his first approximation for naming the elements of the sign—image and concept. Many doors of the literary and philosophic tradition, in particular the epoch of pre-Romanticism, are open to Saussurian semiotics in this way. Use of image and concept also allows us to integrate criticism with the deconstruction of behavior (chapter 1) and to deal with the peculiar turn given literary criticism by the attention to the signifier. Finally, the current move toward rhetorical figures in literary criticism is seen as a bipolar movement.

SIGNIFIER/SIGNIFIED: IMAGE/CONCEPT

The Saussurian sign, everyone knows, has two components: the signifier and the signified. For Saussure, if for few of his successors, the two are absolutely mutually determinant: neither exists as signifier or signified outside of their mutual determination. The sign composed of signifier and signified is a concrete entity, and although it is not a 'unit' such as a rational science might desire, it is open to study: Saussure writes,

> The signs that make up language are not abstractions but real objects: signs and their relations are what linguistics studies; they are the concrete entities of our science. . . . The linguistic entity exists only through the associating of the signifier with the signified. . . . Whenever only one element is retained, the entity vanishes; instead of a concrete object, we are faced with a mere abstraction. [1966:102]

Like a chemical compound (Saussure's analogy is water), the sign is radically conceived as the total determination *by* a relationship; and it is the sign that makes the signifier and the signified what they are in the situation of their relationship.

What is true of the sign holds, for Saussure, at the level of the linguistic system: there is no language where the two elementary planes of *sound* and *idea* do not relate to each other as *sound-image* and *concept.* Saussure illustrates,

> The linguistic fact can be marked off on both the indefinite plane of jumbled ideas (A) and the equally vague plane of sounds (B). The following diagram gives a rough idea of it:

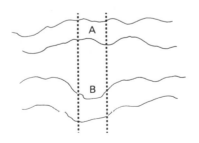

[1966:12]

From both the standpoint of the sign and that of the system of signs the stress is on the idea of mutual determination of elements. Few statements, either scientific or poetic, have so underscored the idea of mutual determination—more than organic—in the production of the third. And not since Wordsworth, perhaps, has the third entity 'produced' proved to be a deceptively simple inversion of parental relations: the third element here (language-child), which seemed to have been engendered by the union of signifer and signified, has itself engendered the union of the father and mother (concept and image; not thought and sound).

What should give us pause in re-reading Saussure for literature is more than its pre-Romantic sophistication in understanding the structure of cultural "production." Rather, it is the fact that this very text has been able to evoke a completely perverse reading of it by semioticians who convey the sense that the two elements of the sign are separable and free to persist as "singles" outside their relationship to each other. Thus we have "modernist"[4] versions of the Saussurian sign among leading semioticians, as in Umberto Eco's formulation:

> *A sign is not a fixed semiotic entity* but rather the meeting ground for two independent elements (coming from two different planes) and meeting on the basis of a coding correlation.
>
> Properly speaking there are no signs, but only *sign-functions* . . . . A sign-function is realized when two *functives* (expression and content) enter into a mutual correlation, thus becoming a different functive and therefore giving rise to a new sign-function. Thus signs are the provisional results of coding rules which establish transitory correlations of elements, each of these elements being entitled to enter, under given coded circumstances into another correlation and thus form a new sign. [1976:49]

One should note that Eco uses Hjelmslev's expression/content division, not Saussure's, and it is this assumption that eventually necessitates notions of *subjectivity* and *form*—again notions that Saussure's formulations can defer. Moreover, despite the attractiveness of the mobility assigned to the sign-functive over the seemingly static identy of the Saussurian sign,[5] Eco's version only brings out one facet of the sign's existence, or its actual functioning: its arbitrariness. For, although Saussure notes the necessary *arbitrariness* of the linguistic sign (as would anyone who had ever heard a language other than one's own), he notes that the sign has an equally important existence that is *traditional:*

> At every moment solidarity with the past checks freedom of choice. We say man and dog. This does not prevent the existence in the total phenomenon of a bond between the two antithetical forces—arbitrary convention by virtue of which choice is free and time which causes choice to be fixed. Because the sign is arbitrary, it follows no law other than that of tradition, and because it is based on tradition, it is arbitrary. [1966:74]

The transitoriness that is so striking and salient a feature of Eco's ahistorical and scientistic attitude* is in direct contrast to the Saussurian vision. The sign is arbitrarily instituted; to be sure, it is not motivated either by God or by nature, yet once instituted, any change in the sign is never less than catastrophic:

> Regardless of what the forces of change are, . . . they always result in *a shift in the relationship between signified and signifer;* . . . It Is useless to separate the two parts of the phenomenon; it is sufficient to state with respect to the whole that the bond between the idea and the sign was loosened. [1966:75]

Theoretically language is sheer arbitrariness and the locus of a potentially free-wheeling "associating of any idea whatsoever with any sequence of sounds" (1966:76); it is not so in fact, in practice. We are not daily reminded that the absolute freedom to have been or to become anything at all is the chief constituent of language. Eco's abstract portrayal is exciting but eventually more heavy-handed than Saussure's: the sociological sophistication of Saussure's supple handling of the traditional, social-institution aspect of language has been noticed by such critics as Jonathan Culler, who compares Saussure to Durkheim (1976:71), and it is much less deterministic than Eco's coding "rules," whose preexistence ironically undermines the apparent freedom of the detachable *functives.* Clearly Saussure is heir to the post-Rousseauian, post-Kantian revision of the individual identity *versus* group identity split —its reformulation as a tension between *person* and *community* in which the definition of each depends on its relationship to the other.[7] (In this version language allows no subjective 'freedom to mean'—its *meaning* is in the response to it; the identity of the self is in the relation to the other, etc.)

*This is in no way meant to imply that Professor Eco does not attend to history and its literary monuments—his work has been indispensable for heightening awareness of the semiotic dimension in many literary works, such as Stendhal's *Chartreuse.* His thesis emphasizes the arbitrary over the traditional character of the sign, and his *signifier* is the detachable *concept*—like that of science—not the *material image* that is detachable in 'wild thought'.[6]

While it is possible to situate Saussure and his linguistic sign and sign-system within the movements of post-rational thought, as we have tried to do in the previous chapter, that is not our purpose here. The real question, the literary pertinence of the sign, can and should take as its point of departure the manner in which literary theorists have utilized it: if a pattern of resistance emerges, that in itself is important for uncovering the uses, misuses, and abuses of the sign for literary reading.

What then are the elements in the Saussurian text that have inspired theories of the sign (Eco is not alone) that are quite resistive to its spirit and direction? Why has there been no major and/or overt effort to analyze and utilize the *sign* as conceived by Saussure without first decomposing it into signifier *versus* signified—and then concentrating all one's attention on one or the other in the absence of its mate? For although one might argue, as do Carontini and Peraya (1975), that one is either for or against the "ideologism of the sign," it is much more correct to say that it is rather a choosing of either the signifier or the signified that divides recent theoreticians: Deleuze favors the signified, Barthes the signifier, etc. As with Eco, the "sign considered in its totality," to borrow a chapter heading from Saussure, is something of an embarrassment to literary semioticians.

Derrida (1967) has dissected the phonological bias, the verbal-/logical/mythic identity complex in Saussure; and he has noted the repression of the graphic signifier by the phonic one in semiology. But there is more than this repression of the signifier by another signifier, more even than the repression of the signifier by the signified—the sign is the locus of repression in general. What is repressed by the sign may not only be the material signifier—phonic or graphic—its becoming transparent to meaning; the signified, or rather signifieds, may also be repressed, not because the signified has been rendered transparent, but because it is apparent: the appearance as *the* signified represses alternative differential *meanings* that are latent in the sign.

What seems important in retaining the *sign,* as opposed to dividing it, is that it may be a potential model of the text and of literary relations —as bearing both the quality of the puzzling enigma and the sure sign. The association of a signifier with a signified is the exemplary literary act, in terms both of reading and writing, and the avoidance of the sign may well be one source of methodological difficulties in literary analysis.

In reviewing the Saussurian sign for literature we return first to the chapter in the *Course* (I,i) on "The Nature of the Linguistic Sign." This essay is renowned for two things, its differentiating language from no-menclature and its model of the sign. "The linguistic sign unites, not a thing and a name, but a concept and a sound-image" (1966:66). Few readers have remarked (see D. MacCannell 1976 and chapter 3 of this book) on Saussure's intitial formulation of the signifier as an *image.* Saussure is actually quite adamant on this point: "The latter [the sound-image] is not the material sound, a purely physical thing, but the psycho-logical imprint of the sound, the impression that it makes on our senses," and he concedes that he will call the signifier "sounds and syllables . . . provided that we remember that these names refer to the sound-image" (1966:66). This mental impression, or writing, is usually seen as a part of Saussure's 'formalism'—yet it is so bound to its 'content' that it would hardly warrant the term 'form'. And the definition of the sign Saussure makes on its basis is important enough that he presents the first of a series of diagrams of the sign thusly: fig. 2 (66)

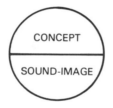

And then the second: fig. 3 (67)

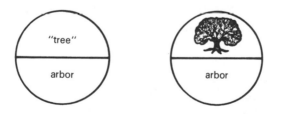

The supreme irony—or a joke? The initial formulation of the *linguistic* sign is as a *picture,* the so-called phonic substance is a graphic image, and the entire sign, often assumed identical to the word or verbal unit, is an icon or hypotyposis, an existential graph. It is only on the third try that this graphic entity incorporates the notion of representation—the

natural object, the tree, is there—yet it is hardly clear what is representing what. The tree, one notes, is the concept and not an image in the relationship; yet the concept itself is markedly only an image:
(It is possible that this third figure is apocryphal; nonetheless its use would not have been inconsistent with Saussure's terminology.)

We find from the outset two striking things about the 'nature of the linguistic sign': (1) as "image" the signifier can substitute sight for sound or sound for sight, depending on the temporal or spatial mode (1966:70), and (2) it is well nigh impossible to distinguish "concept" from "image." The concept, as in the version of the classical *figura,* partakes of the same mode of being as the image. In breaking new linguistic ground Saussure has in effect undone both classical rationalist versions of how language works (language is the picture of thought) and Enlightenment versions (thought is the product of the linking or placement side by side of images.)[8] He has placed two images together, but with the result that each acquires a new existence—*as* signifier and *as* signified—from the relationship. The loss of identity as a separate element in each case results from the relationship.

What follows is an effort to relate the Saussurian 'linguistic' sign to the 'literary' one; debates concerning the verbal and/or iconic character of literature will, we hope, benefit from casting the discussion in this way; so also will the less semiotechnical and philosophic movements in the contemporary rebirth of literature-as-rhetoric.

Applying Saussure's semiology to literature has led in two distinct directions and may require yet a third. Attention to the signifier has dominated much of the methodologically self-conscious Continental literary semiotics; both the verbal narrative, the 'linear' signifier unfolding in time and the graphic, spatial image have been exhaustively examined by semiologically oriented critics. Even those concerned with figures can be distinguished on the basis of their implicit conception of the *figure* as aligned more with the image or with the concept side of the kind of sign Saussure was attempting to uncover. Since it is the *figure* that appears throughout our literary history as intimately bound up with the 'nature of the literary sign,' it seems essential at this point to look at what has happened to the sign-as-figure as a result of the division of signifier from signified in recent theoretical developments.

Figures of Speech

If we split the image-concept bond we lose whatever it was Saussure was trying to convey by the *sign,* something like a "meaning to be read." This loss of the sign, with its vague innuendo of a meaning that is always somehow ungraspable, or dissolves into being a mere image, has seemed to many to be a gain. By using the terms *concept* and *signified,* Saussure suggested the sense of seizing or grasping, of 'getting' the meaning—only to withdraw this suggestion with the revelation that the concept is fundamentally imagistic in nature.*The Sartrean bad faith of such a gesture does not apply if we leave off the problem of the concept and restrict our semioanalysis to signifiers, not to signs. And for this Saussure provided the exemplary methodology: analysis of the signifier for him proceeds along clear-cut lines.

The signifier is distinguished by its syntagmatic (sequential opposition) character. Both temporally constituted speech and the graphic spatial instance of writing are for Saussure in the realm of the signifier: even though it is Saussure's subordination of the latter to the former that has occasioned some controversy, it is important to recall that Saussure at no point ignores either form of the signifier (or image):

> [The auditory signifier] represents a span, and the span is measurable in a single dimension; it is a line. . . . [Auditory signifiers] are presented only in succession; they form a chain. This feature becomes readily apparent when they are represented in writing and the spatial line of graphic marks is substituted for succession in time. [1966:70]

Saussure's first imperative in discussing the signifier is to deny it the capacity to be perceived in "simultaneous groupings in several dimensions," as can "visual signifiers"—auditory signifiers can only be sequential. The bias in favor of the auditory signifier at this point appears to restrict analysis to the narrative dimension, to the flow of discourse.

It was the genius of structuralism to have brought out the *paradigm* as a way of accommodating "simultaneity in several dimensions" even for the analysis of signifiers—signifiers that owe their existence to the syntagmatic or chained (sequential) oppositions. For Lévi-Strauss, for Barthes, paradigms are groupings of opposites in sets which can be superimposed to show that they are so many variations on a single theme (Lévi-Strauss 1970:339–41); Barthes discusses paradigms similarly in what may be his most structural study, *Système de la mode* (1967).

The paradigmatic outgrowth of the signifier (exclusive of the signified; destructive of the sign) has been used for literary criticism. On the one

---

*Of course this is the problem: 'image' in nature, in a sign-relationship it is denatured and acquires a new life. It is this bizarre existence that creates methodological difficulties.

hand, it appeals directly to the sense that literature exists at many different levels, much like Lévi-Strauss's description of the structure of a myth:

> The layered structure of myth ... allows us to look upon myth as a matrix of meanings which are arranged in lines or columns, but in which each level always refers to some other level, whichever way the myth is read. [1970:340]

The idea of superposition, of overlapping levels of the literary figure seems naturally to fit the paradigmatic structure; Jakobson, for example, describes "poetic language" in this way: "Poetic language draws attention to itself by forcing us to consider the paradigmatic aspect of language. This is precisely what we do when we are aware of the presence of a figure" (cited in Scholes 1974:161). Literary critics may take differing positions as to whether what is layered are, as in Lévi-Strauss, "meanings" in the guise of a palimpsest (semi-hidden meanings à la Genette). Or they may, objecting to the hiddenness of meaning, purify the paradigm of the relation to meaning and retain a structure of superposition and figuration (Todorov 1971:246–47 and Shapiro and Shapiro 1976:1–6).

As the structural figure (metaphor) erected from the material of signifiers of syntagmatic origin, the paradigm performs an extremely important function for structuralist literary criticism. Paradigms are relations between signifiers that can replace each other, alternative pairs that seem distinct; by retaining the clarity and distinctness of these oppositions on a metonymic base—in which value is created by the relations to preceding and succeeding terms—structuralism is in a sense, *enabled* in relation to literature. The figurative aspect of literary language can be shown to be based in the syntagmatic axis of language —as the paradigm's "distinctness" is a kind of provisional resting place in the flow, the syntagmatic unfolding of signifiers. The paradigm is a kind of illusory or transitory revelation of central 'theme' or set of contrasts—the Greek etymology of the term is 'to show side by side'—and it is the syntagmatic axis of language that can reintegrate the paradigm into the discursive chain. Literature can be shown to be, finally, discourse, and literary methodology can be enriched with the work of the linguists who study speech acts.

Figures of Thought

The question of meaning—of the signified—is deftly sidestepped by the structuralist critic's affection for the signifier, an attachment perhaps akin to the Romantic respect for the *image* skillfully analyzed by Paul de Man (1960). The place of meaning in cultural productions is difficult to ascertain: Saussure designated it in the sign as the "signified" while undermining any suggestion that it have any existence by itself. "Meaning," the meaning perpetrated by signs, often appears as anything but a neutral term, politically and morally; and in a critic like Barthes, for example, one senses resistance to imposed meanings throughout his entire *oeuvre,* resorting to the signifier as a primary defense. For others, like Todorov and Lévi-Strauss in the quote on the "levels" in myth cited above, meaning is a purely relational term. For still others meaning is inherent in form. Does restriction to the signifier effectively dispel the illusion of the immanence of meaning in the sign, at least for literary critics? Here it seems to us to be the capital question for literature. We wish to trace now several alternative critical patterns in those who limit analysis to the signifier, and we will then turn to those who deal more directly with the problem of the signified, particularly hermeneuticists and post-structural theorists, in the analysis of the other mode of rhetoric, the trope, or figure of thought.

The Formalist Tendency in the Attention to the Signifier

Even the most neutral-seeming signifiers acquire meanings for us: one need not assign a transcendental signified to them, nor go to the sophistication of a Freud to support this statement. One need only look close to home and to the subject at hand, literary theory, to find "meaning" intertwined with signifiers. William Wimsatt and Monroe Beardsley are perhaps justly famous for their attack on "intentionality" (for discussion, see de Man 1971), yet theirs is an attack that in no way precludes "meaning":[9]

> A poem can only *be* through its *meaning,* since its medium is words —yet it *is,* simply *is* in the sense that we have no excuse for enquiring what part is intended or meant. Poetry is a feat of style by which a complex of meaning is handled all at once. [1960:199]

The assumption that poetic language "contains" meaning despite the intentions of the author is clearly in contrast to the structural sense of literature as *parole,* the subjective speech act. Yet there where the structuralist would see only signifiers from which implications of "meaning" are healthily absent—in rhythms, meter, sound-patterns—Wimsatt locates meaning: "Sentence patterns recur, like declensions and conjugations; but they are still expressive forms," writes Wimsatt (Wellek and Warren 1942:179), and his approving fellow formalists remark, "Rhyme

has meaning. . . . Several aspects of this semantic function of rhyme
can be distinguished" (Wellek and Warren 1942:160).

One can imagine Todorovian horror at some of these formalist propositions, but nevertheless they indicate the profundity of Saussure's
insight: there where a signifier is so will meaning (the signified) be.

The structuralist alternative to the formalist feeling that meaning inheres in isolated units is clear and simple: "meaning" is a feature of
literature, to be sure, but must be viewed, according to structuralist
poetics and semiotic theory, as a relation between levels. As in Lévi-
Strauss's description of mythic meaning cited above and Emile Benveniste's similar notion of linguistic levels, Tzvetan Todorov attacks
formalist versions of meaning for literature.

> What is meaning? According to Benveniste, it is the capacity of a
> linguistic unit to integrate a higher level unit. A word's meaning is
> delimited by the combinations in which it can fulfill its linguistic func-
> tion. A word's meaning is the sum of its possible relations with other
> words. [1977:24]

The syntagmatic/paradigmatic solution is appealing: yet it works only
on several conditions. Chief among these is the structuralist capacity
to sidestep certain obscurities in Saussure's text which develop in the
analysis of the sign as a totality, as distinct from the analysis of signifiers. For example, Saussure repeatedly indicates that the "linguistic
unit" is not a clearly identifiable isolate (1966:105–7), particularly from
the point of view of synchronic linguistics, or the analysis of *la langue.*
(On this point Benveniste is in disagreement, since he claims that the
smallest units of language are 'meaningful signs' [1969:11–12].) Somewhat ironically, the structuralist response to the formalist assumption
that meaning inheres in isolated units eventually will appear as parallel.
Recall that Wimsatt writes that "Poetry is a feat of style by which a
complex of meaning is handled all at once" (1960:199); now hear
Todorov:

> Whereas in speech [as distinct from *literary discourse*] the integration
> of units does not exceed the level of the sentence, in literature, the
> sentences are once again integrated into utterances, and the utter-
> ances, in their turn, are integrated into units of larger dimensions until
> we reach the work as a whole. [1977:24]

Meaning is a relation among signifiers, signifiers lifted from the syntagmatic combinations, and arranged paradigmatically to produce the figure: the overlaying of different, but transparent levels, traversible by an

integrating vision. The meaning will not have a 'locus' either in itself nor in the perceiving mind: it will be a set of structured relationships based on paradigmatic contrasts and syntagmatic combinations. Yet the 'product'—'the work as a whole'—which finally appears in the process bears at least a temporal affinity with Wimsatt's own version of textual presence: 'all at once'.

It is in the poetics of structural literary theory that the 'modernism', or the sense of radical arbitrariness of the sign, in Saussure is lost for literature. Just as Eco's overemphasis on the mobile ever-changing quality of the sign devalues tradition, so too the over-identification of literature with Discourse finally has a traditionalizing and conservatory effect that belies the modern. Foucault writes that discourse is what it is because it is *rule-governed* (1971:38), restricted by convention, or in Saussure's terms, 'tradition'. By deriving its models entirely from the analysis of the signifier, and in particular the auditory signifier, structural literary theory seems to go on to become Neo-Classical, arguing for 'literariness' by opposing literary discourse to ordinary discourse. Before Todorov wrote to distinguish literature from "everyday speech" (1977:24), Wordsworth was championing the reverse—literature's counter-adoption of the "very language of men" (1961 [1802]:8). For Wordsworth it is poetic diction that is abusive and capricious: "The reader is utterly at the mercy of the poet respecting what imagery or diction he may choose to connect with the passion" (21); and the abuse results from the arbitrary bond between an *image* ("imagery and diction") and a *concept* ("passion": for Wordsworth, our *thoughts* are "the representatives of all our past feelings" [6]). The poet abuses everyday speech when in fact he should use it. The drive for "rule-governed creativity," latent in Todorov, manifest in critics like Jonathan Culler, arises at least in part from using the model of speech, the analysis of the signifier (paradigm and syntagm), and the deferral of the question of meaning to the question of levels. The model of discourse generally entails the distinction between 'ordinary' or 'everyday' speech and 'literary discourse', to be sure, but the former bears more than its share of the burden of the definition of literature in structuralism.

On the one hand, that is, "everyday speech" is positioned by the unconsciously assimilated set of rules that language is; on the other, it is the source of change and creativity. Culler writes, "Change originates in linguistic performance, in *parole,* not in *la langue,* and what is modified are individual elements of the system of usage" (1976:41). Neo-Saussurian semiologists see language, *la langue,* as did Hjelmslev, as an abstract set of norms and forms fulfilled or realized in the *parole* or speech act. The tendency is then to identify poetic or literary language with the *parole,* inasmuch as for Saussure, as well as for the later Chomsky, it is performance that is the realm of creativity and change: a "rule-governed creativity" to be sure (Culler 1976:41, 84). Poetics, or literary structure, then would be logically akin to Saussure's *langue*— the abstract norm scheme.

Logic fails in cultural institutions—they are bizarre and not rational— and it seems inevitable that the clear-cut parallels drawn above could not hold for so complex a cultural production as literature. From the point of view of literature, it is often in the realm of "everyday speech" that norms, forms, and rules are not latent, but patent. Decorum, etiquette, and *politesse* show in everyday talk; the 'creative' side of *parole* is, even for Saussure, limited to pure change. It is entirely possible that the identification of literature with speech and poetics with *langue* needs to be inverted. This seems true at least for some literary epochs, as the citation from Wordsworth, among others, would indicate. At any rate, for at least some literary epochs, the plane on which image and concept are bonded is associated with the "arbitrariness" and freedom of will that is linked to literature. Change, here, is not in the signifier, but in the signified, or to be more exact, in the relationship of signifier to signified. In the concept, turned, twisted, or deviated, the arbitrary shows: such is the version of literature as trope, or figure of thought.

STRUCTURALISM AND HERMENEUTICS

The important point to retain from our analysis of structural reading here is that, with the device of the figure-as-paradigm the structuralist reader's aim is total clarity, or a kind of *totum simul.* Radicalizing Saussure's presentation of the concept as merely another image makes of meaning, as it can be clearly mapped at different levels, a transitory illusion produced by the arrangement among (syntagm) and between (paradigm) images (signifiers). One might call the structural reading explicative rather than understanding, to revert to Diltheyian terms. Reading is the revelation of a purely relational "meaning"—it is not interpretation. Born at the moment when relationships are laid out, the figure-paradigm is quite other than the palimpsest model for literary texts: in the former nothing is hidden; in the latter meanings are hidden. It might be said that the joy of structuralism is the fact that meaning is so completely sustained by the perceptible relations between signifiers and can expand, like the concrete universal, from the simple signifier to the totality.

What is absent from the discursive view of literature is nevertheless the other version of the figure, pointed to above: the trope. Tropes are twists or turns, deviations in meaning, figures of thought; and for some it is in the realm of the *signified* that one should look for the model of literature. The trope is, in a sense, the figure whose meaning is incapable of being grasped only at the level of the signifier, as in the structuralist vision. But it is also that figure whose trajectory through levels cannot be traced in a clear, open, and direct manner. The palimpsest to which Todorov objects as a description of reading—the layered set of significations or hidden meanings—is nevertheless appropriate as a description of reading in relation to understanding. The trope is not contemporary to, nor coextensive with, nor even coeval with the signifier. Like Rousseau's "figure" in the *Essay on the Origin of Language,* in which the "proper meaning" is found later, the trope exists by virtue of the bar—temporal essentially—dividing signifier from signified. Hermeneuticists may deal with the trope as a deviation from an original meaning; post-structuralists like Derrida may deal with it as a mixture of deferred and repressed meanings (plural). In the former, the hermeneutic, reading the trope is an act of faith in the potential for understanding (retrieving or conceiving) meaning that is not immediately present; in the latter, reading is the threat of misunderstanding the meaning. What was once a tentative pact linking structuralism and hermeneutics (Barthes interfolds a hermeneutic code as one among several required for understanding) threatens to break down with the purely discursive model of literature in the younger structuralist critics. And although it is the differences between "hermeneutics" and "deconstruction" that are today being highlighted, our semioanalysis here has perhaps allowed us to divide both from structuralism on the basis of the attention to the signifier and to the process of reading.

Non-structural reading is not clear and distinct, nor even 'innocent'; signs, unlike paradigms, do not only have sides that show. Signs, that is, are not *ad hoc,* pristine, and happenstantial: they carry, by Saussure's still unexcelled description the germ (in the pernicious as well as the reproductive sense) of meaning in their hearts. They have past histories—the elegiac past and/or the accretion and repression of past (often pathological) associations; and they have futures—the hermeneutic expectation of understanding and/or the deferred never-to-be-clear-and-present *later* Derridean signified.

In point of fact Derrida remains more respectful of the Saussurian *signifié* than have some hermeneuticists. We refer not to the very important debate between Ricoeur and Derrida over the relationship of metaphor and metaphysical truth, which we mention in the notes. We are thinking of this line from Gadamer confronting meaning: "Understanding means primarily to understand the *content* of what is said, and only secondarily to isolate another's *meaning* as such" (1975:262; our emphasis). Here the hermeneut has divorced *content* from meaning; how different is this from Wimsatt's locating meaning in *form?* Few writers indeed have sustained as Derrida has Saussurian insights into the absolute bonding through difference of signifier and signified and the catastrophic import of separating them.

In many areas of existence the syntactical difference between signifiers is precisely the same as the difference between the signifier and the signified: a mere difference (see Merleau-Ponty 1963:121–22 and Dean MacCannell 1976). In some situations it is the relation or relay of meaning from signifier to signifier (as in structuralism) that captures our attention as analysts: we can "map" social intercourse, "suspend" it for inspection. In the case of literature, however, it seems that the focus is, or ought to be, on the differential relation of signifier to signified. Saussure's icon of the sign, itself an ironic conflation of verbal and pictorial, shows the impossibility of defining either image or concept, signifier or signified, external to their relation in the sign. That is, it is not possible outside of their relation to each other in the sign, to define what a signifier or a signified *is.* By itself, the Saussurian signified or concept is just an image, an image like 🌳 , which can be said neither to contain nor to be a meaning. In the same way the image-signifier "arbor" could always be taken as a meaning and not just a graphic image. Saussure's differential bar between the images is what must be emphasized, for this sign is, unlike the paradigm, the locus of an almost pure difference without systematic opposition based on substitution or replaceability of one part for the other. For while it is true that *arbor* can, in any of the graphs presented here, be taken as either signifier or signified, in any one of the specifically designated relationships this is not the case. Whenever an image relates to another through differentiation, it loses its 'nature' as an image and becomes a signifier or a signified in regard to the other. There where a signifier is so shall a 'signified' be. A mere image, that is, can appear to convey and also to be a meaning.

One can operate on the sign and demystify it as a sheer conjunction —happenstantial as it were—of two distinct images, or signifiers, in which 'meaning' is only always an irrelevant illusion. Yet what seems to us to be important *about* the sign and *for* literature is that it is precisely the meaning which is unavoidable: not the meaning, or the only meaning, but a 'meaning' that arises out of the differential relation and that always remains an enigma. The elementary analysis of the linguistic sign brings out the mechanism of meaning-production, yet without thereby doing away with the meaning.

Literary study based in the linguistic source of meaning-production with the alogical possiblity of meaning prior to referentiality would thus be *tropic:* the study of vicissitudes, turns, of a necessary écart, or deviation, from a literal or specific referent in the sign relation. It is no accident, perhaps, that although they conflict with each other dramatically, post-structuralism and hermeneutics often agree to disagree about the same texts,[10] while structural readings tend to be more serene. For whether they deal with the trope as the deviation from an original referent that has somehow lost its rapport with the present text, or whether the trope is seen as a mixture of deferred and repressed referents in the never-to-be understood character of the Derridean sign, it is at least the sign-character of the text that is at stake both for the hermeneuticist and the post-structuralist. The former may still have faith in the possibility of understanding meaning, the latter may assume that reading is possible only on condition of misunderstanding the meaning —but it is still meaning that is the problem, not reference or opposition.

Such is not the case for structural reading, which is clear and distinct because meaning is based in *systematic* opposition. Meaning is that which is *ad hoc* and relational, and by definition it cannot exceed what is given in the discursive version of texts. The alternative or post-structural reading is that meaning spills over into a textuality in which oppositions are derivative and not conditional: meaning, a product of the sign, of the difference that makes a sign, is never yet systematizable as being opposed to and substitutable for the signifier. This is because it is not only an *arbitrary* opposition to the signifier that makes it a signified: it is because meaning also has to bear the burden of *tradition* —to revert to Saussure's terms once again. Sign meanings have "histories," although these histories are not necessarily empirical nor yet the diachronic story of transformation and change.

This brings us to the final and necessarlly speculative section of our chapter. Saussure raised the possibility of introducing a temporal dimension into the analysis of the synchronic language state, the state semiologists have up to now seen clearly as the realm allied linguistically with grammar and literarily with poetics. It is our feeling that even within the synchronic analysis of *langue* Saussure was able to describe one of the two constitutive relations of language—the *association* and the *syntagm*—in such a way as to make the former relevant to the type of 'history' that pertains to literature.

Rewriting Saussure: Associative and Syntagmatic Relationships in Language

Saussure did not tarry overlong with the unitary, isolated sign. He moved quickly into the analysis of the structured relationship of signifiers to each other, and eventually to concepts of the overall creation of linguistic values out of the system of differences. As distinct from signification or meaning, value ("significance"?), the relative salience of one sign over another ("hierarchy"? or "prestige"?), is a possibility afforded by a mechanism in language. It is here that we may look for a model of the *figure* or the trope that seems essential to literary work, yet differs from the figure derived from the syntagmatic and paradigmatic opposition. Saussure discovers, at the level of *la langue,* a type of relation that supplements the oppositional-structural one that holds for signifiers. This supplementary relationship is called "associative." The association (1966:125–27) is a kind of knot of differential values *and* meanings that make it pivotal in linguistic (and potentially literary) creation or production.

As in all his other discussions, Saussure has recourse to an icon or diagram. He distinguishes the *syntagmatic relation* by means of several features: it is present, formed by a series of oppositions, and it occurs *in discourse.* His image for this is that of the relationship, oppositional but supportive, between a column and an architrave. On the other hand, *associative relations* are *"in absentia,"* and their terms are united only in a "potential mnemonic series" (123). They do not require a speaking presence, and they are not solidly structural as are syntagmatic relations. They have only the imaginary being of memories: as when a "Doric column . . . suggests a mental comparison of this style with others (Ionic, Corinthian, etc.)" (124). Based on a kind of material, but not simply historical, "memory," the associative relationship can be schematized spatially. Contrasting it with the paradigm figure based on syntagmatic relations (the paradigm being clear groupings of 'theme parts'—e.g., noun stem, suffix, etc.—in a defined and finite series), Saussure diagrams the associative relationship: [126]

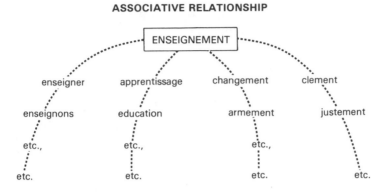

ASSOCIATIVE RELATIONSHIP

A constellation: a "point of convergence of an indefinite number of co-ordinated terms . . . [in] indeterminate order and indefinite number" (126). A bundle of differences prior to or at least coequal with those based in opposition. There is no simple pattern here, no structural way in which members of any one of the strands or series could be transformed into and/or substituted for members of another series. Yet this is, for Saussure, *one of the two constitutive relationships in language.* And Saussure underscores the distinction he is making between this type of relation and the paradigm—a point no structuralist to our knowledge has developed (Culler 1976:48–49; Barthes 1967, prior to his *Pleasure of the Text* [1975], sees "associations" as impossible in the *Système de la mode*). 1. As distinct from the paradigm, which is the arbitrary arrangement of *signifiers* in oppositional and coequal pairs in a defined structural series (there is no reason, Saussure writes, [1966:127] why the "nominative case" should be "the first one in the declension series"), the associative relation is based on both *signifiers* and *signifieds.* We have *enseignement* linked to *éducation* (conceptual); to *armement* (auditory and graphic signifier-*ment*); to *enseigner, enseignons* (a structural verb paradigm); and to *clément, justement* (both on the basis of the signifier-*ment,* but also vaguely in terms of values, the values of education.)

None of the above associations is awarded priority in terms of truth or correctness, none dominates—at least not in the tableau given. The sign *enseignement* is here 'liberated' in a sense, it is no closer to being restricted or limited in its possible relations either by its signifier or its signified. There is as well a sense that in the strands or links of association any one of them may, because it is not structurally and simply opposed to any of the other strands, equally become a ligation, or a *liaison dangereuse.* It can acquire dominance in the definitional chain and in effect repress the claims to relationship of the other strands or filiations. 2. The central sign here, *enseignement,* appears clear and distinct, but there is a sense of diminishment as we move to the periphery. We are taken with the double "etc., etc." at the end of each associational string: implying and denying the infiniteness of the line.* This diminishing in power or light is indeed what first reminded us of Lacan's "points de capiton"—the privileged signifiers that achieve (transitory) prestige over other signifiers. Only in this instance it is a *sign* that appears central, and then it is only through the impossibility of assigning structural dominance or prestige to any one over the other of its associative links. More relevant perhaps than the Lacanian is the Freudian notion of the "condensation point," which suggests both a tying up and an unravelling of strands. And more than a simple indeterminacy being constitutive or a source of figurative power here, we have, in a sense, overdeterminacy, or a kind of instability in which all is still possible, nothing is decided. Saussure's diagram, in both the simultaneous clarity of the conceptual image and the indistinctness ("etc., etc.") which reminds us of its sign-character, reminds us of its capacity to allude to something besides itself.

The suggestion here, then, is that there is a surplus of both signifiers and signifieds; it seems to us that this kind of supplementarity is parallel to the relationship between image and concept in Saussure's first and deceptively simple diagram of the sign. Concepts are surpluses over images, and they do not differ in nature from images; but they differ *in the sign relation.* In the associative relation in language, we have the double and reverse: Concepts and images are surpluses over signs, and they differ in nature from the sign, but in the associative relation they are equivalent or the same. The multiple associative relation is also a "sign" of the type that one reads in "literature." Not yet oppositional, not yet simply conflictual, its scene is that of a bounded multiplicity. And it is a scene in which 'meaning' has the suspended character of a wish, or a 'meaning to'.

The singular sign, the one::one relation of image to concept in the Saussurian sign, has proved to be an enormously transparent obstacle

---

*One thinks again of Stendhal's famous ellipses. . . .

to literary semioticians; in overattending to the simple linguistic sign and the paradigm/syntagm needed to analyze it, we have failed to explore the system of *langue* as a potentially more fruitful ground for uncovering literary sign systems.[11] *Langue*, we believe, is not only a set of abstract norms that structure *parole;* it is in *langue* (which also means *tongue*) that the axes turn that twist language structures into new shapes.

It should by now be clear that Saussure's text has in effect deconstructed itself. Having produced *language* through the operation of the syntagmatic relation—so tellingly visualized as a *Greek* column (of a sacred, social institution, of a temple, perhaps)—Saussure proceeds to give us the catastrophe by which the solidity of structure undoes itself. The mannerist conjunction of differing styles (Doric, Ionic, etc.) is not simply an innocent or neutral association of ideas, a mental comparison; it is a profanation, a violence done to the classical, structured moment. The icon of the "association" is not only that of a flowering but of an explosion as well, an original repetition of the movement from classic to romantic. . . .

In the (twisted) movement between the two axes of Saussure's fictive 'language-state' we can trace not a firm structure, but a deconstructing process, that of making the linguistic into the literary, the fixed paradigmatic figure (metaphor) into the open trope. The story of this movement always generates 'history' (a fictive history), condemned ever to restage the same scene: the passage not from culture to nature (as in the *sign*), but from "culture" (the stable temple column) back to "nature" (the neonature of pure difference prior to systematic oppositions). This passage—variously from social structural institution to free association, from the traditional to the arbitrary, from poetics to literature, from rhetoric to tropology—is the mode of being of modern culture.

Conclusion

Guided by our interest in reading we have here attempted a review of Saussure's sign(s). Only when one has signs (signifiers with signifieds) does one have reading; only when one has the potential for relationships based on absence or lack (as in association) does one have literature. As Saussure once wrote, literature's fundamental identity problem lies in the fact that it "continually draws from [prior signs] new meanings" (in Culler 1976:105). And whenever one has the potential to read one has the potential to be uncertain. In the absence of 'total' signs one can have criticism, one can have poetics, one can have forms and structures, but one cannot read in the specific sense of relating an image to a concept. And reading always seems to be both below structure and beyond subjective certainty. As an icon of 'reading' the 'associative relation' seems to us to begin to capture the literary relation, the suspense of not quite knowing, of not yet deciding the hierarchical value and meaning of a sign and its subsystem—its text. In a manner typical of literary obliquity we have most likely worked our way back to Peirce: with Saussure's sign now seen *as* a reading, we can see the parallel with Peirce's "interpretant."

The great structuralist labor of working out the relevance of the *parole* for literature—the analysis of the signifier, the image, and the syntagm/paradigm—must never be underestimated. In bringing up the association we may dissipate somewhat the elegant and classic clarity of the purely structural approach, but we may regain language from grammar. Literature surely proffers both figures of speech and figures of thought; and if we can aspire to even half the analytic potential the work on *parole* has given us by our now having recourse to Saussure's description of *langue* for literature, we will be fortunate indeed.

7

On the Discriminations of Signs

Phenomenology, structuralism, existentialism, and semiotics constitute the most important intellectual development of the past century. Develop*ment,* not plural. The theory of culture that this book sets forth is based on the assumption that these major intellectual works of the twentieth century are interrelated. In this chapter, we argue that even though they have opposed each other they are linked empirically, historically, and conceptually. And we shall try to describe the exact nature of these links.

Phenomenology, structuralism, existentialism, hermeneutics, and semiotics all stand on the same side of a major cleavage, on the side of a post-rational world whose ground differs ultimately from that divided long ago by Reason into subjects and objects, minds and bodies, theory and practice, thought and action, being and doing. By *post-rational* we do not mean *irrational.* Reason and unreason constitute the foundational mythic opposition that establishes the authority of Western sciences and philosophy and their claim to be the only legitimate forms of subjectivity. Any form of consciousness not equated with Reason is seen as 'mere subjectivity' and is 'unreasonable' if not found in these forms; as such it is not to be entrusted with the development of culture. The *post-rational* perspective differs from the rational by being that position that cannot honor absolutely the fundamental claims Reason makes as to the necessity of its divisions; it knows them to be arbitrary. (Cartesian scientific method begins by dividing, then subjecting the parts to order.)[1]

Specialists in the fields and subfields of phenomenology, existentialism et al. will object to becoming once more bedfellows of those from whom they have struggled to divorce themselves; and rightly so, as each internal differentiation of the post-rational stance has produced its own peculiar effects. Nonetheless, those close to the developments in these specialties have tended of late to lose sight of their solidarity in the face of rationalism. They have also been somewhat remiss in not characterizing for a wide audience their overall importance, especially at a time when the vast majority of humanists and scholars are in need both of guidelines and of defense for their very existence. They may soon find themselves without a constituency, as the rational sciences take over cultural theory and absorb the learning time of students in the engineering and technical arts. Sociobiology's Edward Wilson is a spokesman here.[2] For Wilson human nature is an absolute, the genes irrational "forces" (like the Furies) against which man defines himself as human only by repressing or quelling them with Reason, whose greatest form is science. Post-rational thought really ought no longer to view itself or be viewed as a single minority and fringe element; it should take its place at the center of humanist thought, with all its diversified directions open for inspection and evaluation.

It is with this general programme in mind that we have suggested that semiotics assume leadership in the movement. Semiotics does not require either a philosophical attitude or philosophical preparation; it does not involve the student, as both phenomenology and existentialism do, in the temptations of terminology and of reflection; neither does it suck one up into the spiralling of the hermeneutic circle of understanding, nor does it humble one with the forestructuring of one's experience as do Heideggerian hermeneutics and structural/existentialism. Not at first, anyway. It is semiotics' contribution to post-rational thought that it offers a method that begins on the other side of the debate with rationalism; it does not involve itself first with the rational adversary, then with its subject matter. Instead it operationally defers questions of origin and aim, the whys and wherefores, and concerns itself with the hows. (This is not to imply that semiotics ultimately ignores questions of the context of knowledge. What we suggest rather is that up to now, at least, the semiotic is *the* unexamined context of our knowledge.) It plunges into the midst of the bizarre entity culture is. Phenomology and existentialism can offer justifications for such a position—'sources' are never single, and the goal is always death—but it is semio*analysis* that is the center of semiotics, not its speculative branches. And it seems clear that, as in traditional humanistic education, this kind of experience is the best teacher. Phenomenology and hermeneutic interpretation require long practice in order to appreciate their insights, and they will remain the esoteric-sounding underground of our intellectual life if they do not support semiotic praxis as the prelude to their study.

The aim of this chapter is to set the stage for examining the significance of the recent developments of semiotics from a wider historical perspective and to offer a point of view on this history. It will necessarily be more broad than deep, perhaps too "Continental" for the tastes of some. But the risk of appearing unprofound and un-American must be weighed against the risk of ignoring what is at stake: the present fate and future of the humanities.

Phenomenology and Cartesianism

Husserl and Peirce are the modern philosophers of post-rationalism. Husserl developed phenomenology—and also wrote a semiotic. Peirce developed semiotics—and also wrote a phenomenology (phaeneroscopy). In inverse proportion each made a link between semiotics and phenomenology at the outset, and they did so in the context of their adversary position vis-à-vis Descartes.

For Descartes, signs were either natural (ultimately God-given) or conventional (man-made; like mathematical symbols).[3] Husserl criticized the natural standpoint; Peirce the conventional (he made a critique of the framework of assumptions of a science). Though the type of sign each philosopher had in mind differed from the other's, they were in basic agreement as to the falseness of the natural/conventional split. Their signs—Husserl's *Zeichen (Ausdruck* and *Anzeichen)* and Peirce's triad—concur in the central concern with *meaning*: and meaning *for an interpreter.* Like their Romantic precursor, Kant, they are interested in the Understanding as the important supplement to Reason. Husserl named this understanding Consciousness; Peirce, the Interpretant. In neither is understanding located exclusively in an individual person or subjective process; it is a post-rational structure. (We may here remind the reader that Locke, too, wrote a semiotic in tandem with his Cartesian critique.)

Husserl's stunning *Cartesian Meditations* set up the criticism. Assumptions about the simple origin of understanding—the thinking subject—had to be reviewed. Thinking, thought, is replaced by Husserl with consciousness, and a consciousness that it is impossible to divorce from its contents: it intends them. And the subject, in all its apparent unity and simplicity, is at least double: transcendental and empirical, imbued with otherness in its essence. Consciousness is a composition or synthesis that can be temporally or spatially arrayed and analyzed; the subject can be viewed at different levels of existence. This double analysis of consciousness as synthetic and of phenomena as consciousness is the phenomenological method, a method opposed to

Descartes's, and it avoids subject/object, mind/body, inner/outer and self/other, origin/aim divisions. It is a radical critique of the scientific attitude.

So far so good, but the scientific method was not about to capitulate at once to the phenomenological one. Still a fresh start, a renewal of the Kantian style of criticism had been made.

But phenomenology has had the peculiar fate, in the European history of ideas, of having each of the advances made in it appear as a radical reevaluation of it. The same has not been the case for Peirce, who hardly had time to name a new aspect of his theory, before it was used by his friends like Will James and became in altered form[4] the uncriticized basis for much research. The Peirce revival has so far taken the form of an archival admiration,[5] not a philosophical rereading. Peirce with irrepressible self-irony and an evident distaste for discipleship managed the one-man show of self-criticism; Husserl seemed fated to suffer Oedipalization. Phenomenology barely had been named as such when it underwent the existential revolt led by Heidegger and then Sartre and Merleau-Ponty, and that was only the beginning. Existentialism attacked phenomenology; structuralism attacked existentialism; semiotics attacked structuralism ... The seemingly endless conflicts masked the general post-rational alliance of these "adversaries."

The growth of insight into structure is not a simple process, and even the "Oedipal" history we have sketched here is a fiction. Husserl's work did not flower into immediate fruit—there was Hitler, the war, the friends become enemies, the religious questions yet to be resolved, and overall the continuing expansion of rational science and its technologies. Let us now trace the drama by which semiotics reclaimed for itself a cardinal position in post-rational thought, rediscovering its dual philosophical source in both Husserl and Peirce, but also developing its own complex style independent of philosophical debates. Even more than its genealogy it is its critical varieties that constitute the "history" of semiotics.

The Drama of Semiotics: Existentialism, Structuralism, and the Hermeneutic Method

The existentialism of Martin Heidegger and that of Husserl's students who also followed Heidegger continued phenomenology in the same directions, essentially the same two directions proposed by the master: consciousness and phenomena studied together. The fundamental effort was to advance the phenomenological method into a non-philosophical setting; to show how consciousness and phenomena are twin manifestations not of the same essence, but the same existence. The undoing of rationalistic oppositions continued: Merleau-Ponty sought to work over the mind/body split; Sartre the self/other dichotomy; Heidegger the past/present opposition. Two processes were involved: unifying consciousness and its contents in concrete form and advancing the assumption that all of experience is potentially meaningful: but only to the Understanding—'meanings' do not exist without Interpretation.

It was Martin Heidegger's *Sein und Zeit* (1927) that led the advance of phenomenology into the arena of everyday life. Although Heidegger criticized Descartes's *ontology*, he cut short the debate with scientific rationalism over the subject. His work began firmly within the neo-Kantian post-rational philosophy, as a critique of Wilhelm Dilthey's hermeneutic method of interpretation. The disagreement has its roots in eighteenth-century European notions of "pity" (identification with the other; sympathy) and "self-love"[6] as epitomized by the difference, say, between Rousseau and Adam Smith. The Romantic conclusion that the *imagination* is the locus of the capacity to sympathize (cf. Kant, Hazlitt, et al.) eventually entailed the revival of the hermeneutic method for Understanding the Other. (Hermeneutics is the science of textual interpretation; some place its origins in Hesiod; some in the work of Philo the Jew of Alexandria and his reconciliation via allegorical methods of the Old and New Testaments. Some modern anthropologists such as Clifford Geertz also use the method.) Heidegger begins his *chef d'oeuvre* with an attack on the way the neo-Kantians applied hermeneutics, attempting to reconstruct a lost totality, lost because 'past'. Heidegger questioned the assumption of the definitive split between past and present, and also desacralized the 'texts' to which hermeneutic methods could be applied. Heidegger's is perhaps the first post-medieval though non-religious return to the notion that experience itself could be *significant,* i.e., interpretable as meaningful to someone. Heidegger's improvement upon the hermeneutic method involved the introduction of non-chronological time into the process of understanding, with knowledge always being prefigured, or having the structure of fore-knowledge. Knowing was like a circle, a return, at a higher level, to something already in some way 'known'. Imagination, the figurative and prefigurative, language in its most poetical form, bear in this system great powers of insight; they are closest to the structured circle of Understanding that constitutes our most profound existence.

Everyday life's "talk," paintings, jazz, lyric poems, clothing styles, behaviors, politics, can now be viewed as *texts,* open to hermeneutic understanding and not subject to heavily moral distinctions between sacred and profane, authentic and inauthentic. Representations themselves no longer bear the burden of being 'mere' representations, but are instead conceived of as the very "stuff" of our existence. Indeed literary criticism was one of the first great beneficiaries of this existentialism,[7] for it lent the linguistic arts greater prestige, perhaps, than they had ever before enjoyed. Their representativity was no longer simply an unreal image, a superfluity; it participated in the very structure of all existence.

Social scientists did not long ignore the potential Heidegger's existentialism held as an alternative to the rationalist/behaviorist theories of behavior. But since existentialism remained at first primarily in the hands of philosophic and religio-ethical thinkers—Sartre, Merleau-Ponty, Maritain, Jaspers, et al.—empirical social investigators found frustration. True, Sartre was enamored with the political engagement and applicability of the analysis of consciousness to experience, and Merleau-Ponty wrote on the structure of behavior. But one had to admit that they seemed to do so mainly for the sake of the mode of consciousness they analyzed—Sartre took the imagination, Merleau-Ponty the perception—rather than for the sake of the intentional objects or contents of the consciousness. (It remained for Emmanuel Lévinas and his student Jacques Derrida[8] to work out the modality of memory—but that is another story and its irony is made clear below.) And as philosophers, Sartre and Merleau-Ponty could remain methodologically open, but the empirical researcher often needed something more *ad hoc,* concrete, and operational than a reflective method or a hermeneutics. For even though Heidegger worked out the justification for envisioning all of life as a text or network of associations, the anthropologist or psychoanalyst needed to demonstrate the particular textuality of their subject/matter before hermeneutic methods could be applied: a cumbersome process, perhaps even inappropriate for studying unlettered peoples or peoples with different versions of being and time.[9]

It is in this context that one should view the work of Jacques Lacan, Claude Lévi-Strauss, and Emile Benveniste: psychoanalyst, anthropologist, and linguist. They seemed at first startlingly different in approach from their contemporaries Sartre and Merleau-Ponty, although all were friends and associates, and all were loyal to existential tenets. The great division between the "existentialism" and the "structuralism" of these researchers is that the social scientists literally honored their subject/matter as bearing the burden of intentional consciousness, subordinating interpretation to it, rather than vice versa. Following Heidegger, structuralists made the strange familiar and the familiar strange. They uncovered the byways of what Heidegger called *Dasein*—the unthought yet continual structuring of the world by the prefigurative consciousness, best exemplified by *language,* but also evident in class consciousness and class conflict, etc.

But structuralism foresook the *hermeneutic* method that was so much a part of the Heideggerian programme. And it took Husserl's "transcendental" ego not as a classical autonomous self but *as* this expanding structuring and forestructuring, à la Kant. In seeing this structuring as being "like a language" the structuralists adopted a method of language analysis more applicable than hermeneutics to mundane, 'profane' matters, more systematic and researchable: Saussure's *semiotics.*

A radical move, and important both for the future and the past—for in reaching back behind Kant to Rousseau and to his later Swiss compatriot, structuralists opted for a method that faced head on the process of meaning-making *(semiosis)* without their having the security of a speculative position from which to view the process and without being able to deal with already "worked up" textualized materials. Both Rousseau and Saussure accepted the sheer arbitrariness and traditionalism of all our social institutions, of which speech appears to be the prime example. But even speech is only a special case of semiosis, the production of meanings (or Heidegger's play of representations), the archetypal set of meanings that we always feel need to be *understood.* Semiosis produces meaningful entities entirely in the absence of any "reasonable basis" for their existence.

Lévi-Strauss, Lacan, and Benveniste were quick to seize upon the sign and its meaning-producing mechanism as the most effective means of organizing and analyzing the structure of *Dasein.* Moreover, the *Dasein* to be scrutinized is the unconscious manifestation of the general consciousness: it is, that is, not self-conscious, not worked up as an art or science; yet even though it seems 'natural', it is no less structured as a set of signs or network of representations than any art or science may be. In turning up evidence for this un/conscious structure at every juncture structuralism implicitly resuscitated the transcendental self—that which is originary in "giving the world"—even though one first perceived structuralism as a shock because it had no center, no "subjects."[10] As in the early Heidegger, questions of authenticity and profundity could be put aside and the elaboration of crystallized (traditional) institutions derived from purely arbitrary beginnings could be undertaken. For Lévi-Strauss, simple oppositions analogous to the arbitrary phonemic ones of language generated other sets of oppositions, which "read" or interpreted each other without the fiction of an authoritative mind creating the link between them: oppositions (the *syntagmatic* relationship in Saussure's terminology) seemed always to generate a mediating term or opposition to the opposition: thus the division raw/cooked, which encoded the nature/culture division, produced a new sign, the "rotten," which embodied the fundamental characteristics of each side—the *natural* yet *processed* food. Lest there be any mistake that this is an abstract formalism, Lévi-Strauss insists that these patterns must have a concrete content for them to be structures. Structures are not forms, but the interplay between formal oppositions *and* material oppositions.

For Lacan, too, the initial syntagmatic relationship—the opposition—generates a structure, the psyche. The ego is to the id as the self is to the other, and langage is the other within the self, etc. Benveniste's linguistics proceeds also by means of primary binary oppositions that generate a third term: the person "I" opposes itself to "you" and together they oppose the "they" or "he," the third person.

Structuralism was not of course welcomed at first by existentialism, nor did structuralism always agree with existential theses; but the link is there, they are in the same general enterprise. Lévi-Strauss dialogues with Sartre at the end of *The Savage Mind,* but he dedicates the book to Merleau-Ponty. Both existentialism and structuralism had opted to venture into the post-rational world.

Post-structuralism: The Semiotic Critique of Semiotics

Structuralism re-emphasized the dual levels of consciousness that existential theory had found too idealistic and problematic for the politics of experience. In their attention to the un/thought or un/conscious* (the 'foreknowledge' of Heidegger's circle of understanding) as a concrete set of structures—empirical, analyzable, determinable—structur-

*We use the term "un/conscious" to denote the existential/phenomenological version of the unconscious as a mode of consciousness. "Unconscious" will designate the Freudian concept proper.

alists redressed a certain imbalance and out-existentialled the existentialists by researching these structures and not leaving them to speculation. Mythic foundations, psychical history, natural language itself, were the "un/conscious": and they were accessible because they were essentially the other modality of consciousness, its alter ego.

And though the risk of reintroducing idealism into the post-rational project was grave, it was clear that the structuralists had something there. Linguistic structure, the everyday forms of speech do "found" our ways of being in the world, our subjective sense of our own present and presence as Benveniste demonstrated.[11] "Myths were good to think with," constituting the substance of our understanding in an unreflected way, as Lévi-Strauss showed for Amerindians and Barthes, ironically, for the French bourgeoisie.[12] Our primary experiences prefigure our secondary ones, shaping our persons, just as they had been prefigured by symbolic structures, as Lacan showed. And the methods are not difficult. Restricting semiotics to the level of the signifier—the speech event, the acoustic image, the material signifier—seems a fair guarantee in effect against idealizing or ideologizing the sign's 'meaning' apart from its lived context. Meaning could not be idealized if it were only the 'meaning-effect' of the relationship between mere signifiers.

The structural methods, too, are marvelous devices and they *work,* they give us impressive insight into the ways experience is organized. For example, after our students had studied *The Savage Mind,* we assigned landscaping as a topic for analysis. The students were quick to 'read' landscaping not as nature vs. culture, but as nature *and* culture vs. agriculture (aesthetic vs. utilitarian). The great power of these methods may lie in their being *semiotic,* that is, they link *meaning* to a concrete experiential, not an abstract, sign.

Yet the tendency toward idealism is there, at both the operational level and the thematic level: operationally the insensitive investigator will tend toward automatism (but then so do signs, in their cultural development). The tendency is perhaps more disturbing, however, when it seems the necessary result of the *spirit* of the structuralist enterprise, or further yet, of the post-rational one: the overcoming of divisions. For it is one thing to point out the arbitrariness and traditionalism of oppositions; it is still another to devote oneself to the overcoming of these oppositions at the expense of developing others.

It had to happen. Restricting analysis to the syntagmatic (and, by extension, paradigmatic) relationship (oppositional)[13] one seems always to generate a third or mediating term and then further oppositions and more new signs, until a saturation point is reached in which there is to be no more room for differences. Look at the case thematically, from the ethnic and personal myths studied by Lévi-Strauss and Lacan. Lévi-Strauss's work in the context of the European history of ideas is radical indeed, for in a deep sense it overcomes the great division made since the Romantics (Mme. de Staël, Chateaubriand, Matthew Arnold) between the Judaeo-Christian and the Greek foundations of our culture. (Stendhal, Nietzsche, and Freud each tried to overcome these distinctions too.) Faced with a subject matter (Amerindians) clearly foreign to these twin sources, Lévi-Strauss resorts to both the Oedipus and the Holy Grail myths for models.[14] How radical a move this is, and how much it is a practical sublation of the Romantic division between naive and complex cultures, becomes apparent when Lévi-Strauss's work is set beside analyses of Western culture that are written "from within," most of which, including even contemporary work like Auerbach's *Mimesis,* are based on this initial and all-pervading division between Hebraism and Hellenism. It might also be said that Lacan operates this reconciliation, integrating the Greek with the Christian myths into the constitution of the self: the symbolic plus imaginary produces the real. "Jewgreek is Greekjew"—Derrida cites Joyce, and senses that with the structuralists closure is at hand.

Only to slip away. For no sooner had the apparent saturation point been reached than the next rewriting of the phenomenology began.

Jacques Derrida honored the importance of the semiotization that structuralism brought to existential analysis. So much so that he undertook to reestablish it on different grounds. His own radical revision takes him back to Husserl (to a different Husserl from the one we saw through existential eyes) and to the sign. He reformulates first the genealogy, then the methodology: like Sartre and Merleau-Ponty, Derrida continues the "faculty" analysis of consciousness by studying the *memory;* like Nietzsche and Heidegger, he finds forgetting a crucial aspect of memory;[15] and like his phenomenological predecessors, he finds the sign to be of the essence. But instead of going to Heidegger for his version of the un/conscious—he goes to Freud—to an unconscious that is *not* a modality of the consciousness as is Heidegger's unthought. And rather than going to Saussure for a model of the sign, he goes to Peirce:

> In his project of semiotics, Peirce seems to have been more attentive than Saussure to the irreducibility of this becoming unmotivated [of the sign]. In his terminology, one must speak of a becoming-unmotivated

of the *symbol,* the notion of the symbol playing here a role analogous
to that of the sign which Saussure opposes precisely to the symbol.
[1976:48–50]

(Derrida's warrant for this move in Husserl's phenomenology is discussed below.) And on the question of meaning he does not join the
existential revolt against the signified in the name of the signifier so
much as he differentiates and pluralizes meanings: the "sign" is a
bounded multiplicity, like Nietzsche's, having the relationship between
signifier and signified determined by the history of the repression of one
meaning by another.

Derrida's double substitution of Freud for Heidegger and Peirce for
Saussure separates post-structuralism from structuralism, and has far-
reaching implications. Not only does the type of analysis differ, but its
overall emphasis on recovering difference rather than overcoming oppositions implies a much more active total structure than that finally
envisaged by Lévi-Strauss: Derrida undertakes his reading of Lévi-
Strauss's *Tristes Tropiques* in *Of Grammatology,* part II, "Nature, Culture, Writing." He does so again in a later essay (1970:255–59). Derrida
does not draw attention to the different "signs" used by himself and
Lévi-Strauss, but one should note that Derrida uses "sign" at every
point where Lévi-Strauss uses "signifier" to characterize the notion of
"freeplay." (Freeplay is "a field of infinite substitutions within the closure of a finite ensemble," a finite ensemble being, for Lévi-Strauss,
one of the chief aspects of a *mythic* as opposed to a *scientific* system
[1966:16–19].) Within this system, magic's all-embracing determinism
operates by means of a "superabundance of signifiers" (tantamount to
primitive "mana": like the zero phoneme in phonetics, and the phallus
in Lacan's theory, these are signifiers that lack a signified. See Lévi-
Strauss, 1950). Derrida uses the term "sign" rather than "signifier" to
describe this supplementary structure (1970:260). With wonderful irony
Derrida masterfully links even the notion of a mythic closed totality to
the totality of Western metaphysics. A further irony is that an 'enclosure'
is one of two founding signs—the female (vaginal) sign—as distinguished from the conceptual, scientific, male, detachable part-object
(phallic) one.

Structuralists have not often responded directly to this new development in post-rationalism, but one has heard oblique objections. For
example, Benveniste makes it a point in the essay that founds the
International journal *Semiotica* to decry the *world* implicit in a Peircian
semiotic:

L'homme entier est un signe; sa pensée est un signe, son émotion est un signe. Mais finalement ces signes, étant tous signes les uns des autres, de quoi pourront-ils être signe qui *ne soit pas signe?* [1969a:2].

The entire man is a sign; his thought is a sign, his emotion is a sign. But finally these signs, being all signs one of the other, of what can they be signs that *is not itself a sign?*

Benveniste opts instead for a linguistic Saussure—for a version of the Saussurian sign in which the phonological, acoustical signifier is the unit of analysis, predominating over and determining the signified. But the drama of the transition from structuralism to post-structuralism is the drama of the return of the sign—the signifier *and* the signifieds *and* the interpreter—such as Peirce and (as we shall argue) Saussure himself intended it. (The reader might recall our discussion of the difficulties involved in a semiology that subordinates itself to linguistics in the first chapter.)

For ultimately it is the sign itself (its history of pervading the world with meanings) that requires the development of semiotics—even if only to preserve our capacity of signing off from time to time.

SEMIOSIS AND THE DISCRIMINATIONS OF SIGNS

At the same time that there has been a global expansion of semiotic theory and practice there has been an inflation of the sign as well in all aspects of culture. Even before Nietzsche mobilized his "army of metaphors and metonymies" for a vision of semiosis uncontrolled and unwilled by a subject, other indications that the birth of signs was proceeding at an alarming pace appeared. Romantic literature offered both the chief offense and the chief counterattack: one need only review the luxuriating in metaphoric powers exhibited and expressed as such by Chateaubriand, for example, in *Atala* and the immediate critique of this style by Stendhal (in *Racine et Shakespeare*); Poe's ironization of Coleridgian language is another example. It is as if a mechanism had been discovered for producing texts—one could associate any concept with any image and create a sign, a meaning-effect. Tear-jerking, thrills and chills, suspicion, the supernatural could all be automated, so to speak, or at least engineered by setting the sign-mechanism in motion, not merely in drama proper but, as Goffman has taught us, in the drama of everyday social life. And the *deus ex machina* could always be exposed, via Romantic irony, for yet another dimension. The popularity of the detective novel, of stories about confidence men, of ambiguous states of mind and soul, Poe's tales of terror and his treatise on the mechanics of poetry, are exemplary evidence of a growing mastery of the sign-mechanism. And these are only the good examples: the sign-mechanism could make any signifier mean any signified and let the critics be damned. Modern literature has attempted to break the hold over art of total representation by signs (Mallarmé against Wagner) by a restriction to the signifier and an attack on the signified. "Meaning" as anything above or beyond signifiers could simply be disavowed: and literature need only "mean" itself. Joycean laughter rings, as he assembles and reassembles signifiers to demystify the automatism of the signifier/signified relationship.

In science and in philosophy signs have competed with nature as both mother and legislator: "Symbols grow," wrote Peirce, *"Omne symbolum de symbolo"* (1955:114–15), and they legislate the birth and type of other symbols. Barthes (1972:141–42) writes pithily of the transformation of culture from anti-nature to pseudo-nature that the Peircean dictum implies:

> The first bourgeois philosophers pervaded the world with significations, subjected all things to an idea of the rational, and decreed that they were meant for man: bourgeois ideology is of the scientistic or intuitive kind, it records facts or perceives values, but refuses explanations; the order of the world can be seen as sufficient or ineffable; it is never seen as signification.

Science no longer takes 'nature' as its opponent to be dominated, but creates an ideologized neo-nature, a nature constructed of signs.[16]

Economically and politically too the sign mechanism appears to prevail. Marx's commodity—the equivalences of values that are not only unequal but incommensurable—is technically a *sign.*[17]

> It is only by being exchanged that the products of labour acquire, as values, one uniform status. . . . The equalization of the most different kinds of labour can only be the result of an abstraction from their inequalities. . . . these quantities vary continually, independently of the will, foresight, and action of the producers. [1965:73–75]

Nietzsche once called this metaphor the process of equating unlikes, and it is the representative sign-character of the commodity that so amazes Marx as he opens his *Capital* with the picture of the wealth of capitalist nations displaying itself as an "immense accumulation of commodities." Marx is indignant that, as with Peirce's symbol, these representations could have a "life" of their own and enter into social relations with each other. (1965:71–83)

Today semioticians are beginning to observe the "oversaturation of semiosis in mid-twentieth-century culture" (Lotman 1977:338), as they review the plethora of primary, secondary, and even tertiary modelling systems. Entropy threatens as systematization reaches this point—the endpoint of structuralism sensed by Derrida. Where it bursts the bounds of fictitious hierarchizations and levels we need to deal with semiosis *per se,* meanings produced at the distributional, disseminational, and uncontrollable level.

> Man would rather have a void for his purpose than be void of purpose.
> [Nietzsche, *The Genealogy of Morals* (299)]

Semiosis and the Sign: Varieties

In this book we have tried to correct for the tendency to blur the differences between structural and post-structural thought. And, at the same time, we want to correct for an associated error of an opposite kind: the tendency to overstress the *differences* between the Peircian and Saussurian models of the sign. They overlap as much as they diverge. The essential definition of their basic unit is that it is not a 'unit' but at least double or triple in its structure—*the sign is always a "sign of."*[18] Saussure's sign is a relationship between a signifier and a signified. A derivative example would be New Critical versions of metaphor wherein the vehicle would be the signifier and the tenor signified. Peirce's formulations seem slightly more modern in that they include a third part to the sign: the act of interpretation or reading, which is built right into the structure of the sign. The Peircian model of the sign can be diagrammed as follows:

[signifier/interpretant/signified]

sign

Interestingly, this model was the ostensible one appended by B. Malinowski to Ogden and Richard's (1946[1922]:324) *The Meaning of Meaning,* but their working definition of metaphor was closer to the Saussurian, rather than the Peircian, sign.[19] (A very good comparison, relevant both for literary and anthropological theory, to be made is that between the model of the sign used in the Ogden and Richards texts and that used by Lévi-Strauss.)

It is the Saussurian sign that has operated in the course of the development of continental European semiotics to unleash simultaneously a wealth of studies of signs and sign-systems and a certain hostility to the sign—the same sort of hostility evident in respect to metaphors that imply the equivalence of one item for another. Thus it is that we find an astonishing depth to the types of semiological linguistic analyses inspired by Saussurian formulations.[20] Yet these semiological studies, systematic though they have been, have been biased toward the material signifier, the sound-image, and the speech act, of *"parole,"* aspect of language itself.[21]

This bias is partly due to the *existential* appeal of the speech act. In his definitions, Saussure names all the elements that will strike a particularly responsive chord in existentialists and structuralists:

> The signifier, being auditory, is unfolded solely in time, from which it gets the following characteristics: (a) it represents a span, and (b) the span is measurable in a single dimension; it is a line. . . . Auditory signifiers have at their command only the dimension of time. Their elements are presented in succession; they form a chain. [1966:70]

The signifier in effect is paradigmatic of existence, while the signified is basically 'metaphysical' or unavailable for direct inspection. Thus the phonological semiologists concentrated their attention on signifiers and made structural gains by discovering relationships of binary oppositions and their mediations (e.g., Jakobson's phonemic triangles) as forms that required actual "concrete" existents to fill them and make meaningful structures.

A more dramatic radicalization of this existential reading of Saussure developed by way of Saussure's "French connection"—in the work of Jacques Lacan and Roland Barthes.* Here the primacy of the signifier is announced with fanfare; the instance of the "event" or speech act gains a centrality that is framed ethically and politically. The unity of the sign as designated by Saussure, the absolute mutual determination of the sound-image and the concept is for these French writers tan-

---

*It is of the utmost importance to note here the absolutely fundamental contribution made by the late Roland Barthes to literature, semiotics, and more important, to our society itself. His fluidity and capacity to develop and change his perspective makes him less than a "theorist" but all the more exemplary. Our remarks about his giving "prestige" to speech here, an attribute of his earlier works, in no way imply that such is his "philosophical" position. In point of fact Barthes reversed this stand upon taking the chair in Literary Semiology at the Collège de France in 1977. Barthes modified his methods, but never lost sight of his goal, to understand the specificity of the relationship of literary, figurative thinking to other modern structures. His essay "Myth Today" (1972) is probably the single most important theoretical essay on literary and sociological semiotic methods in existence.

tamount to metaphor, and a metaphor of a particularly pernicious sort. For Lacan the sign-as-metaphor is the capital symptom; for Barthes the sign-as-metaphor is a pseudo-unification of opposites, the epitome of false consciousness. The sign is hysterical for Lacan; bourgeois for Barthes. According to their formulations, the sign must be "corrected": analyzed, the false associations or links dissolved, decomposed, decoded.

There has actually been a considerable unreflected agreement as to the means for decomposing the Saussurian sign/metaphor into analyzable and controllable parts: it is clear that what is lacking is the "subject" of the speech act, the purveyor of the sign, the addresser and the addressee, who are implicated in it. Jakobson makes this move, without the French fanfare, in his essay "Closing Statements" in which he suggests the receiver/sender/context and code are all necessary for semioanalysis.[22] It is equally so for Lacan and Barthes. Lacan insists we ask "Who is speaking and to whom?" as Freud did in his analysis of the phrase "A child is being beaten." And Barthes never seems to tire of dissecting the anonymous voice—like Heidegger's *"on dit"*—that addresses us, assaults us at every turn in our daily lives. Barthes achieves some of his finest effects by his uncovering the "representation" that parades as a mere "presentation"—the famous picture of the colonized Negro conscript saluting the tricolor—and then discovering *who* has perpetrated this representation (1972:121–26). For Barthes the source, the addresser, is the bourgeoisie itself, and so is the addressee: the aim is its own mythification.

The need for supplementing Saussure's sign with a subject, conscious or unconscious, neutral or innocent, motivated or unmotivated, derives from the attention to the signifier. As distinct from Peirce's formulation of the sign noted above, it is the absence of the term (interpretant) corresponding to a subject that liberated semiology from subjectivity and left semiology open to freeplay. In the absence of an identifiable subject, the potential for uncontrolled semiosis (pathological associations, the deployment of unconscious representations) is enormous, and the linguists, psychoanalysts, and critics we have been discussing here supply a subject to Saussure's sign. This subject takes the form of an analytical intellect, the individual as interpreter or theory itself.

Thus we have, for example, Barthes's development of the structural study of narrative in which literature is removed to the arena of discourse *(parole)* and a programme for its analysis is laid out (1975:237–

71). Carrying a semiology that is centered on the *signifier* out to its fullest limits, Barthes shows how one can master the meaning of semiotic systems on the model of linguistics by a movement between levels of analysis. It is the intellect that takes what is at each distributional level of semiosis a meaningless signifier and integrates it into a higher system level. In this construction, linguistics yields its grammar to the wider rules of Discourse. These rules are, of course, *rhetoric.* [23] Doing the poetics of prose-as-speech-act is indeed one of the only options open to literary analysis within the limits of the signifier and speech event. Derrida recognizes this, when at the end of his lengthy critique of phonological semiolinguistics he praises Barthes for resubordinating semiology to language, a move he terms "fecund and indispensable" (1976:52). Practioners such as Greimas, Todorov, and Benveniste are evidence of the fecundity Derrida cites, as are the critics around the journal *Poétique,* such as Gérard Genette, Paul de Man, and Philippe Lejeune.

Even though his own grammatology aims at meaning which is at the distributional level, Derrida does not object to Barthes's remaining within the limits of Discourse because Barthes's efforts have been in many ways salutary for a discipline (criticism) that, like psychology, is always in danger of unconsciously censoring or restricting semiosis and preparing rigid codes of "meanings" ("The poem means this," "the tower means that," etc.). It is then "meanings" that must be attacked (in the name of the signifier alone) by resorting to the hypothetical possibility of a literature that refuses to signify (or a psyche, in the case of Lacan). The notion that literature refers to "nothing,"[24] so popular with the group around Barthes, is basically a rhetorical definition of literature, in which only a controlled intellect, capable of an essentially allegoric process of reading signs, can produce meaning through its powers of integration. We always have the exciting prospect of discovering at least two *levels* of significance in the Barthesian type of analysis: Todorov can reveal the "grammar" of the *Decameron;* Greimas can produce a meaning-effect by using the syntactical subject/object relationship as a way of naming divisions in novels; Benveniste can talk about grammatical *persons* and *tenses* so as to make one feel that a revelation about the subject and temporality is at hand. Barthes and his group have achieved a way back to literature from linguistics, not only to save an outmoded institution, but because literature is the best ally one can recruit to attack the bourgeois and synthetic unity of the sign, to retrieve semiotic (communicative) language from mythic metalanguage. Literature, that is, has always been enemy to the hypostatized entity of "language," especially in the form of grammar. It is no accident that one of the signs Barthes dissects is that of the Latin grammar exercise, the sentence the schoolboy is supposed to learn (1972:117–21). Like literature itself, Barthes constantly rebels against imposed meanings, and he sees good literature as that which can construct artificial myths, as Flaubert does in *Bouvard and Pécuchet* or Baudelaire in *Les Fleurs du mal.*

And yet, when the possibility of a *non-intellectual* liberation from imposed meanings appears—as when Benveniste faces Peirce and a world where everything is a sign (subject/object/*and* interpreter)—there is hesitation, a stopping on the edge of an abyss. Benveniste (1969b), in a move that really reverses the trend toward the primacy of the signifier (although it does not announce itself as such), demands of any semiotic system that it have a *meaningful* unit of analysis. Language is the master of semiology *because* its smallest units are *meaningful signs* (11–12), whereas in music, for example, the note is but a meaningless mark, except in relation to other notes. Like Barthes's, Benveniste's overall aim is to *save* the *Understanding,* if not the Reason.

The abyss of semiosis here is not so much that of the endless possibilities for meaning-generation, but the loss of *levels,* or hierarchies, to establish meanings, provisionally or legislatively. At stake is the masterful consciousness, the capacity to control meaning by intellectual integration. Even though control is to be accomplished in a sophisticated and enlighted fashion, even though it is understood that meanings are neither essential nor eternal, but volatile and open to change, Benveniste leads us away from semiotics and in the direction of philology, or evolutionary linguistics.

It is precisely this Benvenistian desire for clearly understanding meanings that is threatened by the semiotic revolution. For the sign presents itself first as some sort of a 'meaning', but a 'meaning' that is not understood, misinterpreted. To see the sign as ultimately 'meaningless', as Barthes does, is already an interpretation in defense of Understanding. Post-structural semiotics' romance with Freud is the first systematic attempt to deal with neither Reason nor Understanding, but Misunderstanding.*

---

*Here Paul de Man's work straddles the two camps.

Julia Kristeva sees the desire for synthetic integrative understanding as a weakness, an appeal, in effect, to transcendence (1975a:19). Her work is still well within the limits of a semioanalysis that regards the signifier as primary and the signified as a mystification; but her position dethrones the importance of the intellect, or the critic, as the means of decomposing the sign. For her, the sign is subject to dissolution through a process of its own. As with the archetypal human composition—ego identity—the sign is prey to loss of composure; it can decompose under the pressure of eruption of expressions from an unconscious level. "La sémiotique" (1975c:17), whose most notable example is poetic language, disrupts the symbolic order, that falsifying set of social contracts or shared meanings that has served to disguise desires and drives. Desires derived from the drives, that is, are totally heterogeneous to the sign: signs are, in effect, the sign of desire's exclusion from expression. Here Kristeva expands upon Lacan's hypothesis that it is the acquisition of language, the entrance into the symbolic order during the "mirror stage," that cuts the subject in two and relegates the drives to the unconscious or the inexpressible. Yet these same drives continue to operate to reconstruct the subject and to cross over the line: they appear in the form of psychopathologies or partially expressed feelings the totality of which Kristeva terms *the semiotic* (1975c:15–17). The apparent lack of motivation of the sign in de Saussure (it is arbitrary, but so is all of language—recall the remark, "It has no reasonable basis") is radically rejected in the Kristevan analysis because for her the semiotic is essentially the space of unconscious "reasons," motivations by desires and drives viewed from the existential point of view of the signifier.[25] The difference between desires (and drives) and rational reasons is that the desires can never appear in the pseudo-totality that is the sign. In a sense, Kristeva's work attempts to correct the incipient transcendentalism we have witnessed in Benveniste and the Barthes of the sixties. It might be added that Barthes himself had begun to acknowledge the importance of unconscious desires in literary expression ("logothesis") and that he had turned to the search for the basic signifier of this desire in literature—what Steven Ungar has called an *erotheme* to correspond to the *phoneme* (1977:64).

Why retain the notion of the sign? The great work has been the liberation of the signifier from any link to the mystification of the signified, to the pretentious and "scientific" concept. Even though this liberation has tended to hypostatize the signifier and to inflate, ever so slightly, the role of the critical intellect, surely Lacan's and Kristeva's correctives are beneficial, and retaining the sign appears to be a regression. In some instances it is. However, two major figures who retain the sign will allow us to see the very different directions in which the sign (as distinct from the signifier) can lead semiotics.

The Meaningful Sign and the Indicative Sign

One conception of the sign is that it is an *essence,* of a Husserlian type—a monad, basically immaterial and spiritual—that its manifestation is clearest in the work of art, and that its semiotic system is the totality of artistic achievement.

Gilles Deleuze's book *Proust and Signs* comes as close as any work one can think of to epitomizing the idealization (some would say the ideologization) of the sign:

> Essence is incarnated in the work of art. . . . Art therefore has an absolute privilege, which is expressed in several ways. In art, substances are spiritualized, media dematerialized. The work of art is therefore a world of signs, but they are immaterial and no longer have anything opaque about them: at least to the artist's eye, the artist's ear. In the second place the meaning of these signs is an essence, an essence affirmed in all its power. In the third place, sign and meaning, essence and transmuted substance are identified or united in a perfect adequation. [1972:46–49]

Deleuze, of course, implies that this is a rendering of Proust's own theses; we shall not take time to argue with this debatable hypothesis. No matter who is promulgating the postulates here, Proust or Deleuze, the voice that addresses us aims at anonymity, at transcending personality. As such, it is legitimate to treat the work as an essay on signs, not on Proust, and to consider the semiotic it proffers.

Here is a semiotic in which the sign remains intact: at least nominally. But any sign that seems to have a worldly element in it is rated inferior to the spiritual sign: "worldly signs," the "signs of love," and the "sensuous signs" are a waste of time (20). Yet we know that in order to be a sign there must be a manifestation: this is the work of art in the first citation. In order for the work of art to be a superior sign, it must be spiritual:

> What is the superiority of the signs of art over all the others? It is that the others are material. Material, first of all, by their emission: they are half sheathed in the object bearing them. Sensuous qualities, loved faces, are still matter. . . . *Only the signs of art are immaterial.* [Deleuze's emphasis]

Delineations of spiritual ascent to the truth, the meaning of signs, appear in Deleuze's text (pp. 85–87). He gives the spiritual disproportionate attention, even though many of Proust's citations belie this emphasis, and even though Deleuze admits that the body involuntarily betrays material truth (the body is for him another "kind" of intelligence). The sign appears to be the essence of truth, true meaning, and it also appears as a kind of monad, unity, existing by its distinction from the degraded forms of other signs. Deleuze/Proust recognizes, however, that to be a sign it must address someone, it must communicate, but not in the degenerate form of interpersonal communication. The work of art is a "formal structure" and self-sufficient, inventing a code of its own (149; Deleuze relies on Umberto Eco's terms here) and yet it could remain a mere structure with no formal *unity* between its parts. The capacity of one part of a structure to communicate (and form a "unit") with another Deleuze calls "transversality" (a term borrowed from the psychoanalyst Félix Guattari): the structure can be unified and totalized by the intercommunication of its parts. This intercommunication has two other parallels: the transversality that articulates a single work of art to other works by the same artist; and the transversality that links the work to the public and to all other works of art (150). At all times the notions of address, communication, and codes are given a non-empirical interpretation—texts can influence each other in the absence of empirical or demonstrable activity. (We use the word "influence" advisedly here, because of the suggestion of spirituality it has always carried.)

Kristeva calls Deleuze and Guattari's analyses *"lacanisme de droite"* (1975a:33), and if there is any correctness at all to this characterization, it stems from the hypostatizing of the sign that is effected in their analyses. The materiality of the sign is either left out or totally swallowed up, so that the body itself becomes only its essence—desire. In later texts Deleuze and his colleagues will extend this essentialism and make of desire the motive force for all meanings and systems: identities, groups, institutions, economies.[26] Once the essence has been perceived, like the Cusan God, as being everywhere and nowhere, one can redescend to the worldly and discover traces of the essence in its signs (Deleuze and Guattari 1977a:88).

The spirituality of this version of the sign, the sign as embodiment of an essence or spiritual meaning, has a curious outcome politically. Jean-Marie Benoist (1970:15–17) accuses the Rebels of 1968 of having been mesmerized by signs, and signs of a very Deleuzian sort—signs imbued with essence, transsubstantiated signs, in which the God has become the demon, Descartes's *malin génie.*[27] This type of spiritual reading of the sign is only possible if one makes the essentializing move; taking the sign to be meaning*ful* and its meaning available only to those prepared to hear it speak. And although we must disagree with Benoist's interpretation of the events of May 1968, it is clear that the politics of the sign have been taken by many in exactly the way he has defined them: even the book of *graffiti* on the events is entitled *"Les murs ont eu la parole"* (Besançon 1968). The Deleuzian *sign* is, in fact, hardly a sign in semiotic terms: the weight is all on the signified. Gone is the material aspect of the sign, Saussure's insistence on the *mutual determination* of image and concept (both are chaotic outside their relationship to each other [Saussure 1966:112]); gone is the limited and finite aspect of the sign that distinguishes it from the abstract *concept,* which is capable of infinite transformations, like a god, the contrast between sign and concept pictured so vividly by Lévi-Strauss in *The Savage Mind* (1966:18). The impulse toward meaning that does not depend radically upon its sign character (signifier and signified)—and *a* meaning at that, one meaning, desire—is in every way counter to the semiotic revolution.[28]

But there is another approach to the sign, the one made by Derrida that releases its revolutionary potential. In his early critique of Husserl's theory of signs Derrida was able to discover the alternative to the meaningful sign in and alongside of the "central" hypothesis of meaningful signs. In an aside, in the margins of his discourse, Husserl provides a theory that signs, though signs, do not mean by being filled with meaning. The sign as mere mark *(Anzeichen),* whose essence is not meaning but only potential readability, avoids both the impasse for the critics of the signifier (its tendency toward transcendentalism) and the Deleuzian hypostasis of meaning described above. Marks, notations (even the musical notes expelled from semiology by Benveniste), have all the attributes Saussure gave to the sign: they have *value* (1966:114) by virtue of their differential position vis-à-vis other such signs in the finite system in which they occur; and they acquire meaning by a different sort of *difference,* that of deferred interpretation after the fact of their presentation. On the margins of Husserl, Derrida discovers this theory of signs that are not-yet-full of meaning; and he goes on to draw out the latent radicalism of Saussure's sign on the basis of his discovery.

Derrida takes Saussure literally when the Swiss writes of the absolute implication of the concept in the signifier and vice versa. In a move quite distinct from the Barthesian/Kristevan et al. move, Derrida does not decompose the sign into signifier and signified and eliminate the latter from semioanalysis. The splitting of the sign—salutary when the signifier retains primacy, suspect when the signified does—limits one to Discourse on the one hand (no matter how broadly conceived by Barthes, Kristeva, Foucault) and to ineffable spiritual meaning on the other.

> All terms which semiotically condense a whole process elude definition; only that which has no history can be defined. [Nietzsche (1887) 1956:212]

Conclusion

We have seen how the splitting of the sign has been in part occasioned by an incapacity to control the concept or signified, which has, according to Lévi-Strauss, an unlimited capacity for transformations. The vision of meaning running unchecked or uncontrolled has tended to lend prestige to the signifier (as material image) as counterweight, ballast. But this resort to the imagination as opposition to the rational "concept" remains within the limits of Romantic Idealism's appeal to the imagination, falling short of Saussure's overcoming this particular concept/image opposition in his definitions of the sign. For Derrida, such a move is unnecessary if the sign is taken literally enough: the concept is enmeshed in its signifier, there is no concept without its signifier. But more than this, the concept is not single or unique. For Derrida, every signifier in a sense is *overdetermined.* Its signified is multiple, though not infinite. Meaning does not run uncontrolled because of this multiplicity in Derrida's disseminational view: those meanings (signifieds) that are most manifest are always potentially eroded by the latent meanings their manifestation has provisionally repressed. For Derrida signs are dis-unities, as in Peirce and Saussure; they are ambiguities (a term, oddly enough, with which Barthes will almost never deal). The latent meanings repressed by the most manifest one are prior readings or interpretations of the sign. Moreover, it is when a sign appears to be insignificant that its latency can be uncovered. It is for this reason that Derrida, a la Freud, tracks the margins, the "asides," the signatures.

We can illustrate the revolutionary implications of Derrida's model of the sign, by again taking up an issue that has produced a great deal of confusion within semiotics: namely, Derrida's alleged failure to comment on Marx or to relate his grammatology to Marxism. Derrida's replies to critical inquiries on this point have always rung with ironic ambiguity.[29] We think this is because Derrida knows his *Grammatology* to be something more than a footnote to Marx. It is a radical re-reading that pulls out Marx's semiotic. Recall that Marx, like Nietzsche, discovered the sign in modern culture: the original equivalency character (metaphor) of the commodity and its secondary capacity for endless substitution (metonymy). Once the reading of Marx is reframed in this way, his analysis of money appears to deviate from the overall plan of *Capital.* Money, according to Marx, is a double abstraction: the representation of a representation,[30] or the sign of a value which is itself already a sign of equivalences. In short, Marx failed to do a Marxist analysis of money, that is, money as a commodity produced under material conditions.

A Marxist analysis of money would lead to the discovery of the merely representational character of the stock exchange, against which Marxists have directed so much criticism to no avail. The stock exchange is a dramatization, a spectacle, a diversion. The real work of making money at the mint controls the course of economic life. Engraving, printing, writing the money, increasing the "money supply," are the moves that give the central government its legitimation, creating "authority" out of "authorship."

To our knowledge, no Marxist has studied the making of money itself —indeed, such a study would make no sense outside a semiotic re-reading of Marx, even though its salutary implications for revolutionary praxis are easy enough to see, once stated. Derrida is clearly trying to pull us in this direction. He has titled the first chapter of *Grammatology* *"exergue,"* a term that means "hors d'oeuvre," *ex-ergos,* outside the main work. It also means *the mark on a coin or engraved medal that gives the signature or sign of the engraver and/or the date and place of its having been struck.* Derrida's first chapter is framed as an implicitly Marxist semiotic wherein he treats the "circulation" of signs, "values," and the "inflation" of the sign, fully integrating these with an advanced concern for the exploitation of man by man. (Althusser's works conflate Lacan and Marxian semiotic terms.[31] For example, see the chapter in *For Marx* (1977:89–127) on "Contradiction and Over-determination," which is in effect a reading of the Russian revolution as a mixed historical sign of the Derridean sort.)

Close attention to the bounded multiplicity of meanings that a signifier can have and *has already acquired* prevents the radical sign from participating in the a-historical tendencies in the bourgeois hypostasis of the sign. Ironically, it is the mixed and thoroughly historical sign that is rejected by the "New French Philosophers," the darlings of *Time* magazine—Glucksmann, Lévy, and Lardreau[32]—even though the leading academic followers of Derrida in America have claimed them to be Derridists (Spivak and Ryan 1978). This new non-philosophy is little more than a series of melodramatic pronouncements aimed at obfuscating the discrimination of signs: "Marx is dead"; "Russian bombs and U.S. B-52's are all the same"; "the camps, Gulag, the camps!" The most overworked term in the writings of this group is: 'pure and simple'. If there is any single feasible characterization of a semiotic, it is that it is neither of these.

8

A Community
without Definite Limits

What we have learned from Saussure is that, taken
singly, signs do not signify anything, and that each one
of them does not so much express a meaning as mask
a divergence of meaning between itself and other signs
... [L]anguage is made of differences....

—M. Merleau-Ponty, *Signs* (39)

We might say that an entire cultural movement is like a
sentence.... Now, there is much in human discussion
throughout the ages which is like this shifting of a
metaphor, as men have ever approached ultimate
concerns from out the given vocabularies of their day,
such vocabularies being not words alone, but the social
textures, the local psychoses, the purposes and
practices that lie behind these words.

—Kenneth Burke, *Permanence and Change* (182)

Scientific communities that are based on a desire for unity think
themselves to be destroyed by internal differences. In the last chapter
we tried to show that modern semiotics, which is technically post-
logical, advances by differentiating. As sharp as the differences are,
they are rarely expressed as such. They ferment beneath the surface.
Here we want to reflect on semiotics itself from the perspective developed in this book.

The Beginning of Semiotics and the End of Science

In the preface to *Sight, Sound, and Sense,* Thomas A. Sebeok
(1978:viii) reminds us that semiotics is "an ancient discipline, stemming
from pre-Socratic clinical roots." Sebeok and others have traced semiotics back to the earliest arts of diagnosis and prognosis, which still
haunt rational scientific attempts at observation and prediction.[1] Semiotics' antiquity usually appears under a positive sign, as a rallying point,
a flag, designed to convey a sense of pride and solidarity with an
ancient community, a community without definite limits. We wish to

suggest the contrary, that semiotics' antiquity properly belongs under a negative sign. Consider the alternative hypothesis that semiotics has existed for so long in the same form as we know it today because it has been suppressed. It exists everywhere *in hiding:* in Rousseau, Locke, Poinsot, Dante, Augustine, on the walls of caves, etc.[2] Access to the history of semiotics is accomplished not so much by a process of discovery as by liberation. The obstacles in the way of semiotic understanding are alliances of intellectual tradition formed to preserve dying scientific, religious, literary-historical and political systems.

Systems in decay set as their first and final task that of protecting their basic framework of values from critical examination. This is something more than Parsonian "boundary maintenance." Protective mechanisms operate at the level of consciousness to prevent thought from returning to its own source. Two main strategies have been used. (1) The framework of core values is screened or masked, as when a group's real values are systematically violated in all its public acts. This describes the political program of the hard sciences, for example, when they pretend that their language is not metaphorical until a new theory replaces an old one at which time all the old terms suddenly "become" metaphors—aether, phlogiston, neutron, particle. (2) Or, values can be fully exposed but always qualified with the claim that they are not values at all but real and true parts of the actual constitution of the universe, for which claim there is a second claim of ample proof. This strategy is also found in science but it is most developed in religious thought and in other systems which run on blind faith.*

Semiotics, originally designed, perhaps, for more limited purposes, inevitably collides with these and all other forms of self-imposed cultural despotism. This was the most painful lesson of C. S. Peirce's intellectual life, interestingly centering on his disagreement with his father about the definition of mathematics.[3] To Charles, it was eventually not logical to assert, as his father had, that mathematics is restricted to drawing conclusions from "known" hypotheses:

> Mathematics may be defined as the study of the substance of exact hypotheses. It comprehends 1st, the *framing* of hypotheses, and 2nd, the deduction of their consequences . . . [T]he definition I here propose differs from that of my father only in making mathematics to comprehend the *framing* of the hypotheses as well as the deductions from them. [Fisch 1978:45, our emphasis]

---

*It seems ironically apparent that today it is science itself that seems a system based on faith, a faith that is on the verge of fading.

It is the essence of semiotics to put a system's frame or generative principles into question first, prior to any examination of deductions from them. Properly followed through, this operation has the potential to liberate thought and action in ways foreclosed even in Marx's crude semiotic of material values.[4] As the great Peirce scholar Max Fisch (1978:36) has stated: "There are no uninferred premisses and no inference-terminating conclusions."

The advance of semiotics is blocked when there is placed in its path an aspect of culture that is protected by science, for example, or a religious belief or a political or economic system, that has developed to the point where it exists 'without question'. In other words, science purports to ask questions about economic systems, for example, but close examination reveals that the questions it asks are *off to the side* of certain features of our system. These are also the conditions under which academic freedom may be directly opposed to intellectual freedom—semiotic questioning of basic frameworks is sufficient grounds for its exclusion from the 'established' disciplines.

Now we face an even more interesting possibility, namely that semiotics has sufficient power to 'establish itself', to transform itself into a barrier to semiotic understanding. There is evidence of a desire within semiotics to forget the origin of meaning in difference, to consolidate and unify the semiotic community, to define it and give it definite limits. This is still a minor theme, expressed openly in only a few essays (see, for example, Umberto Eco 1978:74 and Alain Rey 1978:99) and opposed by others. It is this opposition of a unified semiotics to a semiotics of difference that is destined to become more important as the deep structural contradiction at the heart of the semiotic revolution, as the basis for the revolution within the revolution.

Critique of the Semiotics of Unity

There is nothing morally or aesthetically wrong with unity in and of itself, nor can there be. Unity is often understood as a positive aesthetic value, as the opposite of alienation, or as referring to an instant of peaceful completeness. As such, unity attracts powerfully. Plato, then Freud, claimed we all wish for it. It is possible, even desirable within certain frameworks, to undertake a quest for unity in a state of innocent ignorance.

The quest for semiotic unity usually appears as a scientific effort to annihilate ambiguity. If a communication system is working properly, according to this view, a message links a receiver to the intention of its sender. What at first appears to be a simple communication model is something more: a logocentric one-way communication model, an extension of the will. Thus, for example, Alain Rey (1978:108) proposes to restrict a branch of "unified semiotics" to the study of "voluntary messages," and Eco (1978:74) writes of "pseudo-communication between an unintentional sender and an unintentional receiver." These statements are easily recognized by semiotic insiders as based on a literal reading of Saussure, a reading that suggests semantic unification of the diadic signifier/signified relationship. The opposition is with more figural readings of Saussure, such as the one provided by Merleau-Ponty, and with Peircian triadic semiotics, which locates interpretation on the same plane with signifier and signified, automatically producing a counter-tendency toward ambiguity and differentiation.[5]

In the semiotics of unity, language becomes a communication device —albeit usually not a very good one. Eco (1978:78) writes: "it is not possible to conceive the reason for the institution of such signifying relationships if not for communicative purposes." From the standpoint of theories of figural language (for example, Peirce or Rousseau), this statement constitutes a radical reduction of linguistic possibility. Within the semiotics of unity, however, it is a valorization of language to define it by its role in conscious or willed *communication*, which is an ultimate value for those who seek comm*unity*.

It is possible to arrive at the same destination from either an ideological or a theoretical starting point. A commitment to unity is built into semiological theory that presupposes a unified language community and an ideal two-person speaker:hearer relationship.[6] It was by means of these originally harmless fictions that Saussure cleared the ground for modern linguistics. But these same ideas can have a negative influence if they intrude into general semiotics and foreclose access to the individual and the community. The semiotics of unity shares with the discipline social sciences the best strategy yet devised for suppressing understanding of individuals and communities, specifically their promotion to the status of *units* of analysis.

Assumptions of unity at the level of the individual or the community are based on a desire to return to a state of nature. Nature, which has no knowledge of itself, is not alienated. Within nature there is no deviation and ambiguity. Nature can be seen as approaching the ideal of pure communication. Some ethologists, already operating within a semiotic frame, subscribe to a semiotics of unity and locate humanity in the nature-culture, pure communication model. For example, Paul Ekman

(1978:141) has written: "My discussion of emotion has argued that the linkage between facial movement (sign) and emotions (significant) is natural, with an evolutionary basis, rather than a conventional or arbitrary association."[7] Beginning with Saussurian assumptions, Ekman (this is also characteristic of Birdwhistell and others) eventually contradicts Saussure's principle of the arbitrariness of the link between signifier and signified. Other ethologists, already operating within a semiotic frame, subscribe to a semiotics of differences and locate animals in culture. For example, Peter Marler (1978:115) describes the monkeys he studied as intersemiotic beings, operating between systems of signs, constructing and deconstructing meaning by movement, pitch, tone, utterance, and relationship, in short, beings already at a considerable remove from a state of nature.[8] The semiotics of unity produces some of the same results produced by disciplined social science. Ekman's men are presented as natural objects which produce meaning-for-scientists. His men seem more like monkeys, while Peter Marler's monkeys seem more like men.[9]

The method of unified semiotics is *unidirectional interpretation,* a scientific praxis designed to determine, in the sense of "fix," *proper* meanings within semantic fields, that is, to forge consensus. This method is in alignment with the moral programs of the un-thought-through discipline social sciences in which everyone is supposed to have a clear message to send and a fine reason to send it; in which verbal communication is held to be good for mind and body.[10] The urgent communicative requirement of a semantic "fix" creates a situation in which no sign is trans-systemic. As a modern Californian might express it, "it is impossible to know where I am coming from unless you have been there yourself." Position, stance, particular perspectives, become sacred. The semantic meaning of a sign's position in its system becomes the meaning sought by science, and science when its work is done becomes scripture. No one has spoken more eloquently than William Stokoe of the human consequences of the moral programs implicit in unidirectional interpretation:

> [J]ust as Sebeok finds *nonverbal* given unclear and conflicting interpretations, the term *verbal* is used as badly or worse. . . . In the jargon of educators and counselors and interpreters who work with the deaf, *verbal* represents one end of a bi-polar opposition, and their term *low-verbal deaf* both mislabels and condemns. . . . A deaf person's competence in English is likely to be much less than his competence in sign language. But no person's competence should be judged solely

on performance in a second language to which he can have little or no direct exposure, and the competence in sign language is completely ignored ... by those ... who go on to infer deficits in language competence, cognitive skills, and intellect. ... What is more disturbing about those who bandy about the term *verbal* is not so much their ignorance of Peirce's semiotic as the vicious assumption their usage conceals. By their use of the terms *verbal, low-verbal* and *nonverbal* they reveal perhaps their unconscious fear of the primitive, animal side of human nature.

The postulate of unity is the starting point for a retrogressive moment: humanity is sent back to nature, animals are demoted to the realm of the pre-natural or mechanical.[11] It is a reflex of the Cartesian scientific mind to hold itself above its subject matter, to pretend that *its* thoughts, at least, are not signs. Descartes claimed that he could think without signs or metaphors and Charles Peirce criticized Descartes for making this claim. Within the framework of unified semiotics, the scientific investigator claims all the important work of differentiating and classifying. Alain Rey (1978:105), who interestingly remarks that he would have preferred a Husserlian or Heideggerian starting point, writes:

> I would like to classify the basic types of relationships between the scientist, the scholar—man in his own historical and cultural situation, with all his psychological motives, including the unconscious ones— and the objects, considered here as signs, systems of signs ... and so forth.

It would be interesting indeed if science truly arrogated to itself absolutely the right to divide up the world. But it appears at crucial moments that this "science" demands the right to classify only in order to align itself with existing categories powerfully enforced by conventional social structural arrangements (subject/object, male/female, public/private, individual/group, man/animal, East/West, etc., etc.) including existing arrangements within the university. Note, for example, that Rey is trying to open the back door of semiotics to all the academic categories (in just one sentence he uses the words "scientist," "scholar," "historical," "cultural," "psychological," "motives," "unconscious") which semiotics is currently in the process of reevaluating. This is the way that conventional social arrangements arm themselves with science and become "second nature."[12] The image of man that emerges from the semiotics of unity is, to our mind, one of the least attractive we have ever devised for ourselves, exactly that of a political animal.

THE SECOND SEMIOTIC: THE SEMIOTIC OF DIFFERENCE

As should by now be clear, semiotics contains its own internal critique of the semiotics of unity. This critique operates, for the most part, implicitly at the level of the way decisions are made in semiotic analyses.[13] Now it is possible to assess the positive contribution of this other mode. This contribution falls mainly into three areas: Further refinement of (1) an approach to communication that does not necessarily involve human individuals as senders and/or receivers, (2) an integrated semiotics of communication and structure, and (3) applications of semiotics to diverse fields of inquiry, a diversity that ought to recast the divisions of knowledge—from veterinary medicine to comparative literature, from the practice of translation to the psychoanalysis of philosophy.

From the standpoint of this second semiotic of difference, assumptions of unity are separated from questions having to do with the *appearance* of unity. All cultural systems (religions, languages, normatively governed face-to-face behavior, etc.) project unified imagery that attracts support in the form of faith or belief. This imagery is the domain of general semiotic research. Such research, however, attacks its own roots if it aligns itself politically with conserving unity, not as image but as 'reality'. Of course, it is possible that by falling in line with rigidified cultural categories, the semiotics of unity might be contributing to its downfall (culture's, its own) by amplifying redundant convention to the point where it becomes just noise.

Along these lines, Paul Bouissac re-writes the term *nonsense* in much the same way that Stokoe re-writes the term *nonverbal*. Specifically, Bouissac (1978:250) suggests that clowns function to remind us of the arbitrariness of conventions, that nonsense is meta-sense:

> The semiotic operation of the clown act enunciates negatively the fragile balance of culture always threatened on the one end by the seduction of nature and on the other end by its own excesses. Something can be overdone to the extent that it disappears; this, in turn, can disrupt the system to the extent that the most basic cultural categories are overturned.

We are not entirely convinced that cultural revolution works exactly in this way, but we are certain that Bouissac's study of clowns and limericks is written on the side of a semiotic of difference. This is expressed not merely in his willingness to question conventional unities, but in his still more radical move to discover tendencies within culture itself to question its own conventions, to differentiate itself internally.

As we suggested above, the semiotics of difference is based on two related principles:

I. The Ends of a Communication Relationship Are Not Necessarily Individuals

The structure Bouissac has described, in which a semiotic subsystem (nonsense) questions the other (modern culture) of which it is a part radically opens the definition of communication. Here we have two systems communicating through clown acts. The individual in this arrangement, like Marler's monkeys, is an intersemiotic being. And, while he would not necessarily think of himself this way, his communications with other individuals are by-products of his activities as an operator between semiotic/cultural systems. Communication is both less willed and more important from the standpoint of the living community than it is in the semiotics of unity.

We could be on the verge of a new era of freedom in intersemiotic studies, the opening of direct analytical relations between semiotic systems.[15] Until recently, intersemiotic analysis was restrictively bound to a linguistic core. It proceeded by the rather cumbersome process of translating all systems of meaning into languages or language-like devices, after which operation their comparison became either unnecessary or impossible. This is the reason why the monuments of social and critical thought remain more sophisticated than their discipline followers. Marx moved freely between economic and political systems, Durkheim between social organization and religion, and Weber between religion and economy. They uncovered differentiation, class, value, etc., in institutional arrangements directly. The important point for semiotics is that they did not first have to show the elegant phonological analogues of these concepts. Recent advances of the Tartu school, the *Tel Quel* group in Paris, and the Bloomington Center have made it possible to move beyond the one-way relationship of language to other systems of meaning. Boguslaw Lawendowski (1978:280–81) criticizes Jakobson's restriction of the meaning and method of "intersemiotics," but he might just as well have mentioned Benveniste or anyone else writing on the subject ten years ago:

[L]et us not confuse the relatively narrow concept of 'intersemiotic' processes introduced by Jakobson (1959) with the much broader framework of semiotics known to us today. He indicated the interactions between nonverbal signs and language in a particular way. Things such as traffic signs, for example, carry conventional messages adopted by members of a given community but if a sign turns out to be easily interpretable in more than one way attempts are made to replace it with a univocal, as it were, message. Therefore even though formally such signs are not verbal they are strictly an offshoot of language. In our understanding, the Jakobsonian 'intersemiotic' processes are not really intersemiotic since they automatically involve language. They are, for want of a better term, 'semio-linguistic' processes, as is the case with all instances when non-verbal messages are processed into verbal, regardless of whether it means vocal or graphic externalization or what we know as 'inner speech.'

A process closer to intersemiotic exchange should embrace direct interaction of non-verbal elements, without the go-between of language.[14].

How the Semiotics of Difference Changes Priorities in the Disciplines

The decentering of linguistics within semiotics has potentially far-reaching implications for the structure of the disciplines in the college of liberal arts. So long as semiotics maintained one of the academic disciplines as central, it could be classified under that discipline and incorporated into the academy piecemeal without its having much effect on existing structures, hierarchies, and priorities between and among the disciplines. This is no longer possible. Now that semiotics is moving off to the side of linguistics, it urges upon us the need to rebuild completely the disciplinary structure of the academy. Everyone is in a classic double-bind: semiotics needs a home which it cannot have; the academic disciplines need new ideas that only semiotics can provide.

There have been several notable recent efforts to pressure disciplinary structures through the development of semiolinguistics and semiolinguistic criticism. The model provided by Benveniste has found more readily than most some acceptance in the avant-garde of academic fields. But there are difficulties with the model, a model that makes language the master-pattern of semiotics. Benveniste argues quite persuasively that language is only a member of a class of cultural systems of meaning. His argument breaks down, however, into a series of unsupported assertions about the privileged position of language over the other semiotic systems, of natural language over literary language, and the impossibility of translating one semiotic system into another (e.g., music into language). These assertions, if believed, would tend to maintain university departments exactly as they are now defined, with literary, history, and language studies at the core. Fredric Jameson, who has given a great deal of careful consideration to these matters echoes Benveniste (1978b) in terms of the initial challenge to rethink traditional studies. But he does so with a note of worried concern, using such phrases as "the more mindless forms of the fetishism of language" and stating that the idea of "the primacy of language . . . is in so much of today's critical practice little more than a received idea or unexamined presupposition" (508). As we have suggested, the weakness of the claim of semiotic priority of "natural" languages has not gone unnoticed in Bloomington, Paris, and Tartu. In the mode of error, an error which Jameson is repeating, Benveniste liberated structuralism from the prison-house of language. Post-disciplinary thought is composing itself very rapidly of *direct* semiotic studies of non-linguistic cultural productions: ritual, film, economic exchange, behavior, etc. and these studies are the most fruitful when, as we have suggested in the introduction, they give us the power to reflect *on* language, and show it (and us) its own image. It follows that criticism and all other forms of interpretation should not be a specialized department of culture, but should be evenly distributed throughout culture and society, perhaps even throughout the university. Professor Jameson has a mastery of structuralist concepts and vocabulary and he is committed to the positions of the New Left. But these features of his style could not eventually deflect the conservative direction of an intellectual program organized around maintaining the autonomy of language and its transcendence over all other systems of meaning. This larger program is based on a hierarchy of values that elevates literature over other aspects of culture (510); text over history (511); unity over difference (513); motive over act (514); theory over practice (515); subject over object (516); and the unconscious over the conscious (521).

There would be no reason to decry this program if the hierarchization of values did not also imply certain political and institutional hierarchizations that we feel sure Professor Jameson would personally deplore. For so long as language's transcendent position remains ultimately unquestioned then the critic alone is priest:

> [T]he heightened appreciation of the inner logic and autonomy of language itself thus makes for a situation in which the temperament of the individual critic—if the latter is not too self-indulgently aware of that fact—can serve as a revealing medium for the textual and formal phenomena to be examined. [508]

Or a rabbi:

> The art and practice of virtuoso reading does not seem to me to be
> the noblest function, the most urgent mission of the literary and cul-
> tural critic of our time. In a society like ours, not stricken with aphasia
> so much as with amnesia, there is a higher priority than reading and
> that is history itself: so the very greatest critics of our time—a Lukács,
> for example, or, to a lesser degree, a Leavis—are those who have
> construed their role as the teaching of history, as the telling of the tale
> to the tribe, the most important story any of us will ever have to listen
> to. . . . [523]

There is an unmistakable elegiac tone here, a tone that should probably
not be indulged. History is indeed the most important text we will ever
have to *read,* but its significance extends beyond narrative, as Marx
and Lukács knew. 'History' only emerges through its difference from
what appears to be 'new' or 'modern', a difference that finds its most
powerful expression in literary form. Literature is where we learn to read
the signs of history and literary studies have no need of a nostalgic
defense based on the hypostasis of the term 'history', as in Roger
Shattuck's recent defense (1980:29–36) of the Spanish professor who
taught by reading *Don Quixote* aloud to his classes. Literature is where
we learn to read signs, the most important skill the modern world, like
the traditional one, has ever needed.

   The current effort to restore (essentially historicist) priorities in the
discipline humanities finds many parallels in the social sciences. Linguistics, sociology, anthropology, etc. are undergoing their own defensive changes. The typical pattern here is a revival of interest in British
empiricism and a simultaneous effort to sweep under the rug the obvious displacement of subjectivity produced by the semiotics of difference. Intersemiotics is intersubjectivity. Or, as Peirce (*Collected
Papers,* vol. 5, p. 289, n.1; cited in Fisch 1978:36) put it, "just as we say
that a body is in motion, and not that motion is in a body, we ought to
say that we are in thought and not that thoughts are in us." John Deely
(1978:10) makes the same point: "a given relation, formed once by
nature, another time by mind, is equivalent for signifying precisely because the relation is in either case an intersubjective mode of being,
having its proper reality in the union of two (or more) otherwise distinct
objects." As we have suggested above, a proto-semiotic version of this
idea is found in Marx's or Durkheim's analyses of religion. Setting aside,
for the moment, the rather different conclusions which they drew from
their findings, both Marx and Durkheim showed the ways religion acts

as an interpreter of economic and social organization, an interpreter that coordinates the activities of individuals without necessarily requiring of any of them full consciousness of the range of problems they are solving: in fact, quite the opposite—the religion is more sophisticated than its adherents. Durkheim (1965a:21–33) eventually suggested that the categories of science and logic, what he called our "priceless instruments of thought," "time, space, class, number, cause, substance, personality, etc.," originated in the structure of the human community, first appearing as normatively governed social relations.

No idea has been more strongly resisted than this one. Sometimes we suspect that students are attracted to the social sciences as missionaries to fight this idea from within, to make the social sciences the final resting place of conventional Western religious and economic thought, specifically to continue to promote the individual, now in the name of science, to the status of a being who is both spiritually and physically independent and autonomous, a being with an unalienable right to pray to his own god and sell his own labor. We think it therefore highly unlikely that the discipline social sciences will accept Peirce's formulation of these matters which, from a conventional standpoint, is more radical still, standing Durkheim and Marx on their heads:

> [T]he very origin of the conception of reality shows that this conception essentially involves the notion of a COMMUNITY, without definite limits, and capable of an indefinite increase in knowledge. So the social principle is rooted intrinsically in logic.[15]

II. Semiotics Integrates Communication and Structure

The problem of the relationship of communication and structure (the latter variously conceived as *interaction* and/or *exchange*) has been the major limiting factor in the development of the conventional, discipline social sciences since the writings of Durkheim and Marx. It is politely disattended by most students. The braver ones write about it. For example, Marcel Mauss (1967:1) begins his study of *The Gift* with a bold statement, perhaps a challenge to his famous uncle's ideas, to the effect that the *exchange* of gifts is an alternate form of social *structural* differentiation: "We shall note the various principles behind this necessary form of exchange (which is nothing less than the division of labor itself)." Similarly, Erving Goffman (1961:7) comments: "The study of every unit of social organization must eventually lead to an analysis of the interaction of its elements. The analytical distinction between units of organization and processes of interaction is, therefore, not destined to divide up our work for us."

The promise of these statements is realized for the first time in the semiotics of difference with its decentered (that is, inter-) subjectivity and its admission of other than human interlocutors. (Even Marx's claim that commodities enter into social relations with each other has been difficult for his otherwise radical followers to accept.) Now it is possible to state that communication equals form or structure without having to deny everything we intuitively know about culture: namely, that culture can interpret, although, turned against itself, sometimes it refuses to do so. The following simple illustrations indicate that social group formation (for example) can be both product and source of communication.

   A. Communication forms a group:
      "Everyone with last names beginning with the letters A through D
      line up on the right."
   B. Group forms a communication:
      "Five thousand hostiles are camped in the valley of the Little
      Bighorn River."

Any semiotic/cultural system capable of producing interpretative consciousness (for example, a school of art, a political movement, a person) either within or without, communicates. A cobra communicates by sitting on the veranda in a way that is understood by all men and other animals. Interpretation transforms communication into something more than messages sent. Even if the so-called "content" of the message is impoverished by interpretation, it is still a message that has been interpreted. It has become a part of the community without definite limits that is "capable of an indefinite increase in knowledge."

Until quite recently, it has not been possible to advance beyond the disciplines in the construction of new models of culture and subjectivity. We have suggested that the second semiotics, the semiotics of difference, provides both programs and examples to get the humanities and social sciences moving again. It also provides the logical basis for an as yet unwritten post-individualistic political economy.

Notes

INTRODUCTION: THE SEMIOTIC REVOLUTION

1. Gerald Graff (1979) has argued in no uncertain terms for a reversion to "mimetic" literature (and criticism) and has expressed suspicion not only of critics engaged in "deconstructing" literary fiction, but of primary literary works, like Robbe-Grillet's *nouveaux romans,* which are anti-mimetic. A more sophisticated meditation on mimesis occurs in the recent writings of René Girard and his defense of the Judaeo-Christian tradition against modernism.

2. In the academy, semiotics has the most direct relevance for the institutional "reforms" which began in the 1960s: those tentative experiments (begun at great social cost) in recognizing, intellectualizing and accommodating non Anglo-Saxon, even non-Western cultures into our curriculum, to say nothing of our awareness. Many new fields are appearing on this horizon: American studies, ethnic studies, women's studies, community studies, international studies, communication. These reforms have, for the most part, failed because presemiotic paradigms for the interpretation of culture made absolute distinctions between modes of analysis of art, music, drama, politics, etc., on the one hand, and ethnicity on the other. We are trying to fit new peoples and ideas into old institutional frameworks and they do not fit. A few scholars in the new disciplines have managed to break free of stereotypes and produce some excellent writings, but there has been very little institutionalization of excellence in the post-disciplinary *avant-garde.* This has been due, for the most part, to a healthy hesitation and uncertainty about the best direction to take. The growth of ethnic studies programs and applied and interdisciplinary social sciences and humanities has not produced intellectual prestige necessary for leadership. We do not think that the lack of prestige of the new programs reflects any real differences in the quality of the research between the new programs and the old, which is the conventional view held on campus. Rather, it reflects difficulty in articulating, staging, and framing the post-disciplinary setting.

There comes a point, and we think we have reached that point, where indecision is more destructive than any decision at all, even one that is based on half-knowledge. We are suggesting that semiotics offers the strongest, indeed the proper, vocabulary and methodology for institutionalizing post-disciplinary understanding. It is a coherent framework that has the power to transcend old disciplinary boundaries. Viewed from this standpoint, it has no competitors.

3. Modern physicists freely admit the constructions they put on physical matter may be less appropriate as far as real matter is concerned than they are as projections of mind: see for example Gary Zukav's (1979) popularization of current speculations in quantum physics in *The Dancing Wu Li Masters.* Yet here, no less than in Descartes himself, we find projections taking the form of metaphor.

4. A recent book that makes this tendency in semiotics explicit is Marc Eli

Blanchard's *Description: Sign, Self, Desire* (1980). Here he calls for a return to the subject (conscious or unconscious) that produces signs—a return from sociolinguistics and narratology. "[S]igns are used to communicate not only a finished product, the message, but also the processes which make the ongoing production of that message possible . . ." (1980:2). This statement falls short of Jakobson's work on the sender and receiver and offers little specific advice on how to gain access to the subject. Blanchard's work is basically itself a return to a venerable critical method, stylistics, which traditionally deals with the psychological, subjective processes underlying literary structure. It is a relative more of hermeneutics than of semiotics.

5. Thomas A. and Jean Sebeok (1980) have offered us what must surely be the definitive critique of the logocentric attempt to make animals talk to us in their recent book, *Speaking of Apes.*

6. A superior study of the rebirth of Satanism in religion is William Bainbridge's (1978) *Satan's Power.*

7. Jonathan Culler's (1975) lucid guide, *Saussure,* offers an excellent summary of the excited speculation about language in the seventeenth and eighteenth centuries in continental Europe, especially as it paved the way for Saussure's groundbreaking work.

8. Certainly the major philosophies of Heidegger and Wittgenstein privilege language, as does the extreme linguistic bias of A. J. Ayer, for example. Even local, regional disciplines, such as psychoanalysis (Lacan), anthropology (Cassirer, Langer), and history (Foucault), exhibit an extraordinary degree of linguistic self-awareness. Now it is precisely this (painful) self-consciousness that prompts at this time a critical turn toward finding alternatives to linguistic primacy. Speech act and performative (Searle, Austin) theses in philosophy reattach language to its (latent) communicative function; one realizes the seductive, desiring aspect of language-as-discourse, i,e., as addressed by a subject to other subjects, personal or transpersonal, in the work of Foucault, Kristeva, Barthes, sociolinguistics, etc. In this respect we must note that it is semiotics that most often serves as a point of departure for breaking out of the prisonhouse of language as far as recent theorists are concerned: one could cite, for example, Milton Singer's address to the 1980 American Anthropological Association, "Signs of the Self: An Exploration in Semiotic Anthropology;" Clifford Geertz's *Interpretation of Culture* (1973); Paul de Man's (1973) "Semiology and Rhetoric;" Geoffrey Broadbent's (1977) semiotic for architecture and design; the essays in the 1976 *Modern Language Notes* symposium on semiotics; the new journal *Poetics Today;* the growing acceptance of Lacan's semiotic psychoanalysis; the movement toward semiotics in ethology, expressed openly by Sebeok (1978) and Medawar and Medawar (1977); the *Drama Review's* issue devoted to "Structuralist Theatre" (vol. 23, no. 3, September 1979). See also recent writings by Clifford Geertz, Erving Goffman, David Schneider, Victor Turner, Jacques Derrida, Christian Metz, etc.

In short, what seems to be happening is that systems of signification that rival language or compete with it for attention as meaning-bearing are, as Saussure predicted, being discovered and analyzed with semiotic methods. Sex, politics, manners, kin relations, clothing styles, etc., as systems of signs are beginning to serve us as much-needed "mirrors" for, or reflections upon, the nature of language itself.

9. Lionel Gossman (1976) gives a calm, detached assessment: "The startling scope of semiotics may in itself give pause and cause us to reflect on the

assumptions of such a wide-ranging enterprise, on the significance of its ambition to be a science, and even on the reasons for its growing institutional acceptance. There is a hint of self-questioning that is already under way among semioticians in the preoccupation shown by some of the speakers at the symposium ... with the theoretical foundations of semiotics."

1. A GENERAL SEMIOTIC OF CULTURAL CHANGE

1. Any cultural production can serve the function of exemplarity, as a 'condensation point' (to use Freud's term for metaphor) which then reopens culture to speculation. Modern instances are Freud's *dreamworks* (1965:311ff; the emphasis is on the dream as artful production), Dean MacCannell's *monuments* (1976a), Goffman's *selves* (1959:252–55), which are staged. A follower of Emile Durkheim, the American structuralist Frank W. Young, writes of social *movements* as symbolic structures in "Reactive Subsystems" (1970).

2. Dean MacCannell's "Making Space" (1978) makes extended use of these concepts.

3. See Lotman's essay in Lucid (1977:99–100), where he distinguishes between I/he communication and I/I (external vs. internal speech). In this model, external speech is syntagmatic, the code is constant, and the message is a variable text, usually decreasing in information in transmission. Internal speech, on the other hand, is seen as iconic and associative, accompanied by a transformation of the text from one code into another. In this case it is the code that is variable, and the system is oriented toward receiving codes not messages.

4. Mary Douglas's (1970:11) viewpoint is neo-Durkheimian. Her position is that "the social relations of men provide the prototype for the logical relations between things," i.e., symbolic systems or patterns. This seems to us one-sided, for it is indeed possible that symbolic systems can operate to shape the social relations of men and women.

5. An important essay for the current debate on the 'subject' is Walter Benn Michaels's cogent essay (1977): he finds that Peirce specifically developed his semiotics in the light of the Cartesian subject, in a kind of replaying of the seventeenth-century empiricist/rationalist debate.

6. Jacques Derrida's book (1967a) on Rousseau's *Essai sur l'origine des langues* put the radical question to Rousseau and Saussurian semiotics— whether one could find an exit from the semiotic world. He ascribed to both these Swiss a nostalgia for a pre-semiotic or a-semiotic world. Whether this ascription is a correct reading of their attitudes or not, the question is entirely valid. Derrida's work is of interest in its attempt to find in differentiation and writing exits from metaphorization (1972:261–69).

7. In the *Essai* ([1747]1968:197–99), Rousseau describes how sign can devolve from a richly associative rhetorical matrix into a mere system of directives:

> Ces progrès ne sont ni fortuits ni arbitraires, ils tiennent aux vicissitudes des choses. Les langues se forment naturellement sur les besoins des hommes: elles changent et s'alterent selon les changements de ces mêmes besoins. Dan les anciens temps où la persuasion tenoit lieu de force publique l'éloquence étoit nécessaire. A quoi serviroit-elle aujourd'hui que la force publique supplée à la persuasion? L'on n'a besoin ni d'art ni de figure pour dire, *tel est mon plaisir.* ... Les sociétés ont pris leur dernière forme; on n'y change plus rien qu'avec du canon et des écus, et comme on n'a plus rien à dire au peuple sinon, *donnez*

de l'argent, on le dit avec des placards au coin des rues ou des soldats dans les maisons. . . .

These developments are neither fortuitous nor arbitrary, they belong to the vicissitudes of things. Languages form themselves naturally around the needs of men: they change and are altered accordingly as these needs change. In ancient times where persuasion took the place of public force, eloquence was necessary. What use would it be now that public force supplements persuasion? One needs neither art nor figure to say 'Such is my pleasure'. . . . Societies have reached their final form; one effects change only with cannons and coins, and since one has nothing to say to the people except 'Give money' one says it with posters on street corners and soldiers posted in houses. . . .

8. E. C. Hughes, chief architect of the Chicago School of Sociology's later phase (1971:ix) writes, "Men constantly make and break norms, there is never a moment when norms are fixed and unchanging." Similarly his student Erving Goffman notes (1959:12–13), "the initial definition of the situation projected by an individual tends to provide a plan for the co-operative activity that follòws. . . . Any prójected definition of the situation also has a distinctive moral character." The importance of 'definitional disruptions' (13) in this view of human interaction is their revelation of interaction as a pure socio-cultural production, subject to change. In Goffman's work these disruptions, like Freud's psychopathologies (escaped feelings, *pathos* taken in the etymological sense), are not willed changes in the situation but are a part of the semiotic mechanism. See also David Schneider (1968:6–8). On this point, then, the Hughes/Goffman studies differ entirely from American 'ethnomethodology', wherein only an effort of will (Garfinkel 1972:29–31) can disrupt the defined situation and uncover its unconscious norms.

9. Rousseau (1968:45–47) writes that the first language must have been figurative and that "proper meaning" was found afterwards by an act of "transposition." See also pp. 64–67 on "De l'écriture," where writing accomplishes the fixing of values. Writing, the apparent 'dead letter', is however, a supplementary origin of semiosis: as Jacques Derrida has shown (1972:375), the essence of writing is to be readable, and Rousseau writes that language passes from written books into discourse; "En disant tout comme on l'écriroit on ne fais plus que lire en parlant" (p. 69). ["By saying everything as one would write it one no longer does anything but read by speaking."]

10. Jean-Joseph Goux (1968:65) writes:

Dans 'la dérive indéfinie des signes comme errance et changement de scène, enchaînement de représentations les unes aux autres, sans commencement ni fin' [Derrida], dans cette dérive des objets de valeur, des pièces de rechange, une hiérarchie (des valeurs) s'institue. Un principe d'ordre et de subordination par lequel la grande majorité (complexe et multiforme) des 'signes' (produits, faits et gestes, sujets, objets) se trouve placés sous le *commandement sacré* de quelques-un d'entre eux. En certains points de condensation la valeur semble se réserver, se capitaliser, se centraliser, investissant certains éléments d'une représentativité privilégiée, et même du *monopole de la représentativité* dans l'ensemble diversifié dont ils sont éléments.

In the "indefinite drift of signs as wandering and change of scene, linking representations one to another, without beginning, without end" [Derrida], in this drift of objects of value, pieces of re-exchange, a hierarchy (of values) is instituted. A principle of order and subordination by which the great majority (complex and multiform) of 'signs' (products, facts and gestures, subjects, objects) is found placed under the *sacred command* of one among them. In certain condensation points value seems to reserve itself, to capitalize itself, centralize itself, investing certain elements with a privileged representativity, and *even with the monopoly of representativity* within the diversified totality of which they are elements.

See also the literary critic Paul de Man (1973). De Man's insights are consistent with those explored here, though he seems committed to a Benvenistian position, assigning primacy to language over other semiotic systems. This is a move, one suspects, based on the central organizing principles of 'literary studies', which assign ontological primacy to certain representative figures in order to distinguish themselves from the semiotic study of culture. Literature, the sign-system *par excellence,* could be defined as the attempt to create the illusion of mastery over semiotic production. See also Derrida (1972:267).

11. A striking example of the revolution of value scales around an axis that acquires the allure of being compelling and central is the figure of Manon in Prevost's *Manon Lescaut.* Des Grieux blends fraternal (lateral) and paternal (hierarchical) versions of Heavenly Love in his descriptions of the amoral girl, and she seems to take on a supreme value (she is *"L'Amour Même"*) at the moment of and because of the displacement.

12. Kant (1952:50 and 57–64). Kant investigates the relative priority in a judgment of taste of "the feeling of pleasure and the estimating of the object." In other words, the two value scales are the foundation of a second-order evaluative act, taste or 'aesthetic judgment'.

2. PHALLACIOUS THEORIES OF THE SUBJECT: ON THE FREUDIAN MARXIST SYNTHESIS

1. Lacan's secret seminar was attended by the *Tel Quel* group (Sollers, Kristeva, Barthes) and by Foucault, Derrida, Lévi-Strauss, and Althusser (see Wilden 1968:xiv and Turkle 1979:21–22). Lacan participated in the original introduction of Freudian theories into France and was a friend of Princess Marie Bonaparte and the surrealist André Breton. He trained analysts for years but had a falling out with Nacht in the early nineteen fifties when the attempt was made to legitimate psychoanalysis in France by making it a medical subspecialty. Lacan resigned from the Paris Analytic Society and helped found the French Analytic Society. Splitting from the original society caused the dissidents' exclusion from the International Analytic Society. The International Society eventually made Lacan's removal as a training analyst the *sine qua non* of reinstatement for the entire French Society. The French agreed to this stipulation, and Lacan, with much anguish, moved from the medical setting of Saint Anne's Hospital to the *Ecole Normale Supérieure.* He founded the *Ecole Freudienne* in 1962. (See Turkle 1979:101–18 for a vivid narrative of these events.) The *Discourse of Rome* was an address to a group of French psychiatrists that occurred during the first phase of the political difficulties with the Paris and International Societies. It is a text that shows the force of feeling translated into text.

2. Laplanche (1976:136–37) also notes how Freud constantly transmutes his categories in an attempt to keep up with the psyche's own revisionism: at times the Unconscious is the source of discontinuity, at other times, of continuity; sometimes it is metaphoric, sometimes metonymic: just so *any* form of reproduction implies the problems of sameness and difference. See also Jeff-

rey Mehlmann (1970:382) who reviews the duality-become-multiplicity of the ego, at times *fort,* at other times *faible.* In his introduction to his translation of the Laplanche book (original French edition 1970), Mehlmann (1976:ix–x) describes Freud as delineating the "processes whereby a bizarre form of culture or intersubjective exchange—'unconscious sexuality'—is generated in humans entirely through a movement of deviation from (natural) instinctual processes." It is the way of understanding this deviation that creates theoretical divisions between those psychoanalysts who see the process of repression of nature in ego formation as maturational or developmental and those who see it as recurring at different levels and at different moments of psychic life.

3. For some last-ditch efforts to save those lifeless forms, see Sennett (1976), Shils (1974), and Jameson (1978:338).

4. See Althusser, "Freud et Lacan" (1965:91), and Coward and Ellis (1977), who document a shift toward materialism and the primacy of the material signifier in the work of Roland Barthes.

5. In *Language and Materialism* (1977) Coward and Ellis present their effort to form, forge—at times, just to force—a synthesis of the three figures. Linking them has much heuristic value and is theoretically correct for our current cultural situation. Coward and Ellis rely heavily on Lacan's connection of Saussure and Freud.

6. Judith Adler (1976) discusses the counterculture (American hippie and French '68ers) in these terms. She also gives an interesting interpretation of how Herbert Marcuse, *philosopher,* became a *figure*—the prophet (419).

7. This process is clearly set forth in Benveniste (1966:3–13). In his exposition, language remains an empty form until it is linked to the subjective experiencing of it as an 'event', in the speech act—like the existential foreknowledge that structures but cannot capture experience. Conversely, subjective relation to the event appears to be autonomous and 'free', while it is thoroughly positioned by the (pre)form(ations) of language structure. Thus, for example, in Benveniste's argument, the 'I' is a mere lexical, like any other, yet when it is used in a speech event it "means" one's own subjective life; and it will "mean" the same to whoever uses it.

8. We must recommend Anthony Wilden's *System and Structure* (1972:30–62), especially the chapter on Freud's semiotic and on entropy (155–78) for the cybernetic versus thermodynamic (or even hydraulic) interpretation of Freud. It is an important book and ought to have had somewhat better luck in Anglo-America, inasmuch as it tries to link our philosophies to Continental ones. Much that Coward and Ellis have to say has in fact been done by Wilden. Many writers cite Wilden's work, but few engage him or even acknowledge his actual contributions—or when they do it is in the mode of (unjustified) attack. Jameson (1978:352), for example, attributes 'confusion between penis and phallus' to Wilden when, indeed, the very pages he cites in Wilden's work contain the same insight (see Wilden 1978:286).

9. Mehlmann (1976:viii–ix) writes a brief history of the secrecy and influence of Lacan; so does Wilden (1972:1–30). Turkle's (1979) book sets the stage better than these do, but hers is not a conceptual account.

10. Lacan uses Benveniste's "it," as in "It is raining," as an example of the subject of the unconscious (1970:188). Samuel Weber also resorts to the metaphor of a grammar, seeing the id as a "third person neuter . . . beyond volition and consciousness" (1977:25–26). It is this third person that is in a sense the hero of discourse, the ultimate addressee and the ultimate respon-

dent. (Weber appears to be critical of Lacan on this point; we fail to see the differences.) Voloshinov/M. M. Bakhtin (1976) offers a social, rhetorical rather than grammatical model for the 'it'.

11. Marjorie Grene (1973:185–202) examines Sartre's "Marxism" in the *Critique.* From Lacan to Kristeva it is clear that the concern for matter and praxis in semioanalysis has been filtered through Sartre's concerns, in particular that of the ironic unleashing of the negative object of human activity by activity: the "fall" of "individual praxis" into the collective "practico-inert."

12. Few of those who try to relate Freud to materialism via Lacan and semiotics refer to the work of Maurice Merleau-Ponty. Coward and Ellis never cite him. Not only does he stress the kind of corporeality and existential viewpoint often found in Lacan, but he also prepared the way for his successor in French philosophy, Jacques Derrida, by means of his work on Husserl and signs.

13. See Eugenio Donato's reading of the Unconscious as the experience of alienated subjectivity (1978:575–76)—like Benveniste's reading (1971:65–67), this is close to Hegel.

14. Emma is the obverse of Balzac's Vautrin, who not only sees a spirit in all social institutions but rises above them to equal or excel them in subjective power. Emma's "dropping out" before making anything of her various situations reminds us of this aspect of Guattari/Deleuze, but Vautrin's mobility and mastery remind us of their underlying interest in *power*. See Deleuze and Foucault (1977).

15. Benveniste's interpretation (1971:66) is that symbols are substitutes for unnameable desires; they are motivated by desire, but this desire cannot be formulated as such. Donato (1978:575) interprets the Unconscious as the murderer of desire, its ruination. For Kristeva it is the Symbolic Order as the Unconscious in the broadest sense that demands the sacrifice of desire (1975b). These theses presuppose that desire knows itself originally but loses, radically and forever, the capacity for self-knowledge by entry into the "Symbolic Order," or *langue:* only discourse *(parole)* can begin to retrieve desire. Other models for desire are available, for example Girard's famous triangle, in which desire is originally mimetic, the desire of the other (See Girard 1965 and Lacoue-Labarthe 1978:12). What we have been trying to explore in this chapter is the possibility that it is the unmotivated sign (the arbitrary association between signifiers and signifieds) which is also the structure of desire and affect, at the same time that this desire is repressed.

16. Freud's analyses are aimed at uncovering blockages or obstacles to the direct expression of desire or wish. These blockages are what he terms "monuments" to the original semiosis—the bestowing of a sexual or erotic meaning upon an object (1936:14–15). One treads upon the earth and links this treading to sexual transgression of the mother (Mother Earth); one sees one's setting pen to paper as a sexual image (stylus, cutting into, etc.) These associations, free semiosis, the desire itself, are not pathological: it is the fear of the freedom that is. Thus the association made is consciously and conscientiously denied —but the path linking the signifiers to the signifieds has already been traced while consciously erased. The *symptom* is generated when these denied signs discharge their affect into substitutes: one begins to have a hysterical limp, one suddenly has "writer's block." As Freud wrote, one has a symptom in order not to have anxiety—the anxiety of free-wheeling semiosis, free-wheeling sexuality —for Freud anything can be eroticized. Thomas A. Sebeok (1976a) has desig-

nated Freud's anxiety signal as equivalent to Peirce's index. These monuments to past loves that have been denied appear as the totality of cultural productions, metaphors, social relations, etc.

17. Lyotard (1977:13–15) describes the free flows of desire and Kapital.

18. Rousseau speaks in the *Social Contract* of the entrance into culture as evidenced by the creation of "needs" for the mind: "The mind has its needs as does the body . . ." (1964:111).

19. Freud's great critique of the notion that the aim of all life is survival in *Beyond the Pleasure Principle* clearly brings what had first seemed to be a purely psychic model to the understanding of biological development. Freud used development against a continuum model of evolution: entities, biological and psychical, develop not via a series of forward progressions whose beneficial by-product is the will to survive handed on to succeeding generations and mature psychic states. Development occurs, rather, as a series of halting movements, painfully contradicting the lower levels of existence toward which all life ironically tends (lower psychic tension; lower material organization).

20. Rousseau claims in the *Confessions, III* (1964:I:114–15) and the *Dialogues, II* (1964:I,807–8) that neither interpersonal nor personal events had any meaning for him in the present: he always had to understand social situations after the fact; and no sensation remained in his memory were it not associated with a "distinct feeling of pleasure or pain that accompanied it." This *"sentiment distinct"* is an interpretation (conscious or no), which charges the groove made by an empirical experience with affect. Emotions are blockages (figures, interpretations, signs) independent of sense experience.

21. Even the "gap" has been masculinized: see the recent essay by Guy Hocquenghem on male homosexuality, in which the male anus is shown to have attractive power superior to that of the female anus (1977:150–51). Lacan sees the void or lack as the source of subjective desire, as in note 15 above: the other is the final cause of the subject, just as the phallus is only a signifier or the presence of another who is the object/source of desire (this is an ultra social model). The difficulty, as Derrida tries to show, lies not only in subjectifying the structure of desire and overorganizing semiosis into oppositional categories that quickly become structural hierarchies, but also in the fact that the choice of the phallus as the prime example of the signifier is no more neutral in Lacan's theory than it has been in human society. Derrida has of course vaginalized phallic discourse wherever possible.

22. A striking example is the devotion of a recent issue of *Yale French Studies* (1978) to this kind of staging of Lacan for Americans. Two earlier issues of the same journal (1967 and 1974) had placed Lacan within the matrix of Freud's French Revolution, though they had not brought out clearly any of the major theoretical conflicts that have arisen between Lacan and some of the students who attended his crucial seminars in the 1960s—Derrida and Foucault, for example. It would have been possible in the 1978 issue to bring into focus the theoretical and historical positioning of Lacan; instead, we have an apostolic Lacan, useful for our own moral and political end of saving literature by admitting sexuality into it. Not a sexuality of satisfaction, *à la* N. O. Brown, W. Reich, or H. Marcuse, but a sexuality that fits into our puritanical ethics. See for example Fredric Jameson's essay, which develops his earlier understanding of Lacan (1972:172). In *The Prison-House of Language* (1972) Jameson read Lacan's theory of *béance* and the introduction of the phallus as supplementary signifier of a lack. He then claims that Lacan teaches us that we must submit

to lack of satisfaction if we are to keep desire alive: "Genuine desire ... is a consent to incompleteness, to time and to the repetition of desire in time; whereas the disorders of desire result from an attempt to keep alive the delusion of and the fiction of an ultimate satisfaction. Lacan's stoicism is the antithesis of the sexual optimism of a Wilhelm Reich. ..." This elegiac moral, so easy for the descendants of Puritans to grasp, results from a grave misreading of both Lacan and Freud: it is *not* the separation from the mother, her loss, that creates the anxiety of *béance:* it is satisfaction itself, the very satisfaction that the mother provides that is the source of anxiety. *For in satisfaction, desire loses its object,* and it is the loss of its *object* (desire's whole reason for being is to have an object) that is the source of anxiety *and* of semiosis (metonymization of the object; metaphorization of the aim; i.e., breast is substituted for milk; pleasure is substituted for the satiation of hunger). On anxiety, see Freud (1936:114ff); on anaclisis, Lacan (1966:691) and Laplanche (1976:13–24). The point here is that we are often too avid to see the moral and political implications of someone's writing practice. We fail to read the theory correctly. Sherry Turkle's excellent book (1979) on psychoanalysis in France (though it fails to cover all the theoretical disagreements) has to present itself in the mode of a political analysis, prepared in the current version of the acceptable role for the academic female: interviewer/reporter.

23. This 'call' is heard in the recent issue of *Modern Language Notes* (1978), in Fredric Jameson's essay (1978), and in Coward and Ellis's (1977) book. The 'call' may be more politically than conceptually motivated: after all, if the leading French Marxist (Althusser 1965:91) and the non-Marxist power analysts like Foucault demand an end to the subject as a humanist ideological construct, then we would "of course" have to oppose them. Kristeva's handling of the death of the subject is, like Althusser's, the analytic demystification of individual "identity" and is much less sweeping than Foucault's historical pronouncements about the end of man. Brenkman (1978:445,n.43) gives a good summary of the current anti-ego, anti-imaginary trend.

4. ETHNOSEMIOTICS: BEYOND STRUCTURAL ANTHROPOLOGY

1. Western economic thought and its extension into the Third World operates as a kind of mirror image of anthropology, but it contains a similar lapsus. Alain de Janvry (1975a and 1975b) suggests that the application of the "Western Paradigm" to peripheral regions, which is believed to lead to their economic development, may have an opposite result:

> a number of essential determining factors that prevailed through the eighteenth and nineteenth centuries—when today's more-developed countries including the United States, Russia, and Japan went through their economic takeoffs— simply do not exist anymore. Patterns of development followed in this context cannot be repeated. To the contrary, transposition of the Western Paradigm into today's structural conditions of the periphery—largely characterized by the nature of the international division of labor—leads to the development of underdevelopment. [de Janvry 1975b:5–6]

2. For an example of ethnographic writing that is aware of itself as an extension of Western values, see Paul Rabinow's sensitive autobiographical introduction to his *Uncommonplaces* (1975b). The same theme is treated analytically in a recent essay by Vincent Crapanzano (1977).

3. There are openings now that may lead to important changes in this situa-

tion: for example, the recent opening in the anthropology department at Berkeley of a faculty position in "theory" with no specific culture area designation. Also, in this regard, David Schneider's (1968) trailblazing study of American culture should be seen as a noteworthy exception.

4. Another exception is Laura Nader's (1964 and 1974) persistent criticism of anthropology for falling short of its promise to be a "*mirror* for man."

5. This same interpretation was proffered by Michel Leiris in an exceptional paper, "*L'ethnographe devant le colonialisme,*" written in the early fifties but published much later. Leiris (1966:131) wrote:

> Or, dès l'instant que toute culture apparaît comme en perpetuel devenir et faisant objet de dépassements constants à mesure que le groupe humain qui en est le support se renouvelle, la volonté de conserver les particularismes culturels d'une société colonisée n'a plus aucune espèce de signification. Ou plutôt une telle volonté signifie, pratiquement, que c'est à la vie même d'une culture qu'on cherche à s'opposer.

> Now, from the moment that culture appears as if in a state of becoming and of constantly being overcome, insofar as the human group that supports it renews itself, the will to conserve the cultural particularity and specificity of a colonized society has no longer any kind of meaning. Or, rather, such a will signifies, practically speaking, that it is the life itself of a culture that is being opposed.

6. This point has been made many times, often in less polite language, by historians, anthropologists, and other analysts who originally came from the Third World. See, for example, Howard Adams's (1975) touching and angry account of the life of half-breeds on the Canadian prairie. See also Jack Forbes's (forthcoming) well-documented critique of the policy changes affecting Indians under the Nixon administration. There is also Malinowski's (1929) paper on the importance of anthropology for colonial administrators. The best analytical summary of this type of literature is found in Bastide's (1974) *Applied Anthropology*.

7. For a more complete treatment of current macrostructural change affecting modern society, see D. MacCannell's articles "Negative Solidarity" (1977a) and "Pseudo-Espionage" (1978).

8. This term was used suggestively but not developed in the same way we have developed it here in a recent article by Donna Jean Umiker (1974). Jacques Derrida has also used it as an adjective to describe Rousseau's anthropology.

9. D. MacCannell has begun to develop this theme elsewhere. See his reports, 1976a, b, c, d, and 1977b and c.

10. We have borrowed the term "Fourth World" from Nelson Graburn (1976).

11. The best review of the recent development of semiotics in the field of anthropology that we have read is Milton Singer's (1978) "For a Semiotic Anthropology."

12. Here, and elsewhere, we are benefiting from a recent radical reinterpretation of Rousseau by philosophers and literary critics in Europe and America. See, for example, Juliet Flower MacCannell (1977a and b), Paul de Man (1976), and Jacques Derrida (1967a).

13. Rousseau's use of methods of argumentation which he devised to maximize their unacceptability should not prejudice us against the correctness of his ideas.

14. Dumont's fieldwork among the Panare is also reported in his (1976) ethnography *Under the Rainbow.*

15. Rabinow's interpretation appears to us to be a macro-level variant of the double-bind theory of mental disorder first advanced by Gregory Bateson et al. (1956) and eventually elaborated at the level of face-to-face interaction by Erving Goffman (1971:355–90; 1974:7 and passim), R. D. Laing (1965), and others.

16. The last of Marx's (1967:402) epigrammatic "Theses on Feuerbach," the one that appears on his headstone in Highgate Cemetery, reads: "The philosophers have only interpreted the world in various ways; the point is to change it." Rabinow's reflections on his field experience (1975b) reveal the strain of attempting to do new ethnography within the rules of classical ethnography, which rigorously holds to pre-Marxist principles: interpretation and description are the only goals; the point is not to change the culture that is studied.

17. This research, which was based on several years of field observations in Eastern and Western Europe and North America, is reported in D. MacCannell 1973, 1976a, and 1977b.

18. Some of this research is reported in Valene L. Smith, ed. (1977). On the Eskimo see Smith's own contribution to her volume: "Eskimo Tourism: Micro-Models and Marginal Men." Specifically on Eskimo arts and tourism, see Graburn (1976). The Basque case is reported in Greenwood (1976). On the transformation of the Amish into a tourist attraction see Roy C. Buck (1977) and D. MacCannell and J. Hostetler (1974).

19. There are other examples of the new ethnography that would have served as well as the ones discussed here for purposes of illustration. Some of these are beginning to find their way into mainstream anthropological journals. In a recent issue of the *American Anthropologist,* for example, we can read in the biographical sketch of Lee Drummond (1977:842): "Several years of thinking about this subject have left me with a commitment to social anthropology conceived as the study of what people think about other people, and therefore about themselves."

20. It is noteworthy that European students, especially those working within the semiotic frame, have been quick to use the United States as an ethnographic field area. See the recent issue of *Tel Quel* on the United States and Julia Kristeva's (1977) study of the Chinese in Manhattan.

21. For a helpful recent discussion of the expansion of the structural linguistic paradigm to cover other cultural domains, see Winner and Winner (1976:128 and *passim*).

22. For a more thorough review of recent anthropological theory that arrives at the same conclusion, see Peter K. Manning (in press).

23. Lévi-Strauss owes future students a technical manual containing scoring protocols for the myths and step-by-step explanations of how they were set up for machine analysis. Such a manual could build upon and make operational his (1958:104–5) remarks in his 1955 American Folklore Society paper:

> The task of analyzing mythological literature, which is extremely bulky, and of breaking it down into its constituent units, requires teamwork and secretarial help. A variant of average length needs several hundred cards to be properly analyzed. To discover a suitable pattern of rows and columns for those cards, special devices are needed, consisting of vertical boards about two meters long and one and one-half meters high, where cards can be pigeon-holed and moved at will; in order to build up three-dimensional models enabling one to compare

the variants, several such boards are necessary. . . . Furthermore, as soon as the frame of reference becomes multi-dimensional (which occurs at an early stage . . .) the board system has to be replaced by perforated cards which in turn require I.B.M. equipment, etc.

Reanalysis and continued development of the *Mythologiques* by others will be greatly impeded if we must reconstruct these procedures at the level of the division of the myths into their "constituent units."

24. Paul Ricoeur (1970, 1971) has begun the important task of describing the theoretical and methodological (as opposed to the political) differences between semiotics and phenomenology as they apply to the "sciences of man." Much of the difference, according to Ricoeur, can be traced to simple terminological confusion and to the fact that important questions remain unexplored by both groups. A good discussion of these issues and Ricoeur's contribution to understanding them is found in Winner and Winner (1976).

25. D. MacCannell first presented this argument in a paper at the Eastern Meetings of the American Sociological Society in 1975.

26. Apparently, this structure operates even on a philosophical level. Husserl criticized non-Western thought for being incapable of arriving at critical self-understanding. In so doing, he ignored his own insight into Western thought; that it often hides from itself; that philosophical language as well as ordinary language can simultaneously obscure and reveal. Paul de Man (1967:52–53) comments:

> As a European, it seems that Husserl escapes from the necessary self-criticism that is prior to all philosophical truth about the self. He is committing precisely the mistake that Rousseau did not commit when he carefully avoided giving his concept of natural man, the basis of his anthropology, any empirical status whatever. Husserl's claim to European supremacy hardly stands in need of criticism today. Since we are speaking of a man of superior good will, it suffices to point to the pathos of such a claim at a moment when Europe was about to destroy itself as center in the name of its unwarranted claim to be the center.

27. In a remarkable series of recent papers and addresses, Thomas A. Sebeok (1977, in press) has advanced the more radical suggestion that we should examine the systems of communication between *species* as well as between cultures and individuals for clues about the ultimate structures of meaning.

28. Peter Manning (1976) has undertaken what we cannot do here, namely, a thorough review of Goffman's published writings. Manning's thoughtful and sympathetic article is unique, as far as we know, in its effort to link Goffman's writings to the wider socio-historical context in which they appeared.

29. As a discipline, American sociology lacks the theoretical vocabulary to discuss Goffman's works in these terms. For a recent "in house" analysis, see Gonos (1977) who suggests that Goffman has been miscast as a "symbolic interactionist" and should be labeled a "structuralist." This argument is correct, as far as it goes, but from an ethnosemiotic standpoint both structuralism and symbolic interactionism would be seen as "first drafts" of a semiotic of social relations. The Gonos paper can be criticized for not attending to Goffman's phenomenology.

30. For a recent demonstration of Goffman's skill at interpreting interpretations, see his (1976) presentation, "Picture Frames."

31. Much of the Third-World community research done by the Youngs and their students at Cornell is summarized in Young and Young 1973. The analysis of movements is reported in Young 1970 and elsewhere.

32. For a discussion of the technical aspects of using aerial photographic data for a semiotic of community structure, see Young and D. MacCannell 1967, especially p. 345.

5. THE SECOND ETHNOMETHODOLOGY

1. Consider the complex, illustrative case of Erving Goffman who was type-cast by sociology as an ethnomethodologist, but never accepted into the ranks of ethnomethodology, nor apparently desirous of such acceptance. Even though Goffman was trained at Chicago in the most prestigious sociology program of his day, and tenured by the Berkeley sociology department during its brief apogee, he abandoned the field completely at mid-career. After arriving at the University of Pennsylvania in 1967, he used the anthropology department as his mailing address, did not participate in the training of graduate sociologists, and never again published in a sociology journal.

2. Although he is not self-identified as such, for reasons of overlapping theoretical antecedents and empirical domain (everyday life), we shall consider Peter Berger a classificatory cousin of the ethnomethodologists. Nicolas C. Mullins (1973) also groups Berger with the ethnomethodologists.

3. See Aflred Schutz's essay on the "Problem of Rationality in the Social World" (1964:x,64–88).

4. Heap and Roth (1973) have written a helpful article that is explicitly critical of the naive adaptation of phenomenological concepts by discipline sociologists. They correctly point out, for example, that "intentionality" and other borrowed terms are often misused by sociologists as if their technical meaning corresponds to their folk-psychological meaning.

5. See, for example, Victor Turner's proto-semiotic studies of ritual in primitive societies or Dean MacCannell's forthcoming study of modern ritual.

6. It is worthwhile to mention here that in its struggle for life in the infertile soil of American sociology, much of the excellent work that has been accomplished has been forced to deny its own historical basis. Sudnow, for example, does a fairly straightforward re-test of several of Sartre's ideas about the glance, but nowhere in his writing does he give any sign of awareness of his own substantial existential ancestors. This is only one of the ways in which the location of ethnomethodological studies within sociology effectively prevents them from becoming cumulative.

6. ON THE NATURE OF THE LITERARY SIGN

1. We refer of course to theorists such as Wolfgang Iser (1974), Paul de Man (1972 and 1979), and those interested in reception theory. In an earlier study of Rousseau (1974), Juliet MacCannell attempted to describe the narcissistic structure involved when the author moves from a public-audience orientation to discovering him or herself as the reader or receiver of the written message. Jacques Derrida's essay in *Marges* (1972: especially 372–75) is an intricate but important scrutiny of the notion of reading as communication. Recently Umberto Eco (1979) has underscored the importance of a theory of reading in

semiotics. His analysis is extremely idealized, positing Model Readers and authors as each purely "textual strategies." Overall the separation of author-function and reader-function remains in Eco's work. In this paper we tend to see author and reader not as textual strategies—a natural consequence of *parole* orientation—but rather as both implicated in the *sign,* which for us still remains the focus of the literary attention.

2. See in particular Paul de Man's essay on "Semiology and Rhetoric" (1979:8–9) in *Allegories of Reading.* Décio Pignatari (1978) has taken the logocentric bias in Saussurian semiotics as the exaltation of the verbal and syntagmatic over the iconic, and he turns to Peircian definitions as the proper alternative to neo-Saussurian terminology for literary criticism.

As a brief aside, one could characterize several tendencies in critical theory as presuming literary analysis divided between a pictorial or iconic emphasis and a verbal or narrative emphasis. Wayne Booth's (1961:3–20) early *Rhetoric of Fiction* sets forth this paradigm and attacks the image bias in literature (the showing over the telling) as a Romantic heritage. Pignatari's essay mentioned above sees a similar division, while demanding attention to the pictorial or imaged elements. It is interesting to note that the title of one of the most influential treatises in American criticism—*The Verbal Icon* (1954) by W. K. Wimsatt, Jr.—is literally a collation of these two elements. Our essay here shows, we hope, that the verbal and iconic are not mutually exclusive but mutually determinant, especially in the work of Saussure. Thomas A. Sebeok (1976) provides an invaluable guide to the structure of iconicity both historically and in the work of Peirce. Paul de Man's early essay (1960) on the intentional· structure of the Romantic image is indispensable for those wishing to trace the genealogy of the Saussurian literary sign.

3. Here we refer the reader to our analysis of the splitting of the Saussurian sign into analyzable parts in "On the Discriminations of Signs," chapter 7. In it we track the sign in Barthes, Jakobson, Benveniste, Deleuze, Kristeva, Lacan and Derrida as well as in Lévi-Strauss, relating all these writings of Saussure to the story of post-rationalism.

4. Anglo-American debates on modernism and referentiality, as in W. B. Michaels (1978) and Gerald Graff (1979), with political battle lines drawn between anti- and pro-mimeticists are uncalled for from a semiotic standpoint. Language as nomenclature does not exist as a problem in Saussure, nor for that matter in Peirce, whose liberties with terminology are infamous. The tendency to identify *words* as semiostructural units (as in the Todorov passage cited later) and then to concentrate on the question of reference rather than meaning (as in Todorov's adoption of Frege's tripartite division of the sign) is a pattern in structural literary criticism. In a sense, the potential explosion of meaning generated by the differential sign-machine is controlled by the structuralist poetics and should thus find a sympathetic audience in the proponents of "referentiality."

5. This issue of stability is most seriously raised and also undermined in Saussure's work on the "language-state," the "synchronic," which like any other "state" in human affairs is fictional. In the "language-state" one of the elementary forms of relationship is the "association," which is, however, not "free-wheeling." This type of relationship, which post-Saussurian semioticians have assumed to be the same as the paradigmatic (Culler 1976:48–49), has been neglected, particularly because of its overtones of idiosyncratic psychologizing, even though it is structural for Saussure. First Emile Benveniste

(1971:4ff.), then Jameson (1972:22ff), and now Lentricchia (1980:112ff.) argue against the antihistorical bias in Saussure's scheme, particularly when the "language-state" is taken as a set of categories that determine historical speech events. Both the charge of idiosyncrasy and the accusation that Saussure overstructuralizes seem to us irrelevant if one views his "language-state" as we have here. Saussure's "association" is not merely an individual and local question of psychology; nor is the "synchronic" devoid of a temporal dimension, e.g., *the* temporality of culture, memory, the contemporary use of the past.

6. Lévi-Strauss's chapter on the "Science of the Concrete" in *The Savage Mind* contains the absolutely indispensable discussion of the differences between the material signifier, imbedded in a finite context, and the concept—detachable, transportable, and flexible, the Cartesian "universal instrument."

7. Lucien Goldmann's thesis on Kant presents the clearest discussion we know of this relationship. Goldmann still sees Kant as a "rationalist," however, without noting the "post-rational" influence of Rousseau on Kant's thought. See Goldmann 1971.

8. Jonathan Culler (1976:56–59) gives a concise and very useful sketch of the language theories of seventeenth- and eighteenth-century continental thinkers. See also Roman Jakobson 1975.

9. W. B. Michaels (1978) has recently attacked members of the "New Yale School" for their elision of 'reference', and he has pronounced them to be as formalist as the "Old Yale School" of Wimsatt, Warren, and Wellek. Michaels cites a recent text by Paul de Man ("The Purloined Ribbon," 1977) as typical of the difficulty of formalism. Interestingly enough, the essay by de Man, also the target of an attack by Gail Wade (1978), is one of the few of his essays that deal with literature as a performative speech act, contextually conditioned or 'situated' by the implicit operations of desire. It is ironic that an essay of this type, rather than, say, the more 'purely cognitive' ones such as his work on the epistemology of metaphor (1978) should have excited charges of formalism.

10. We are indebted to Jacques Derrida's essay on the trope, "La mythologic blanche," in *Marges* (1972) and Paul de Man's essay mentioned above on the history of tropes and the epistemology of metaphor (1978), each of which pinpoints in its own fashion the keys or turning points in transition between the hermeneutic and post-structural approaches to reading metaphors. The recent essay by Derrida in *Enclitic* (1978), written in response to Paul Ricoeur's *La métaphore vive* (1975), is an example of the clash we are talking about. The disagreement is over the interpretation of a line from Heidegger linking the fate of metaphor with that of metaphysics. The recent book by Daniel Giovannangeli (1979) should be useful to those interested specifically in the transitions between phenomenology, hermeneutics, and post-structuralism in relation to literary aesthetics.

11. Lionel Gossman's (1976) division of comparative literature from the study of national literatures on the basis of a synchronic versus a diachronic approach is particularly apt and politically correct. One must not, however, neglect the important dimension of what Saussure calls here "mnemonic history" in the comparative literature methodology. In fact, the implications for a methodology that would deal with 'value' and 'significance' in literature (differences) without dependence upon oppositional structures, such as a comparative literature methodology would be, are profound, and it is our hope to see them worked out over the next decade.

7. ON THE DISCRIMINATIONS OF SIGNS

1. Probably the best possible description of the spirit of Cartesian science is contained in Michel Foucault's *The Order of Things* (1970:50–58).

2. Edward Wilson (1978:13) states the challenge succinctly:

> Reduction is the traditional instrument of scientific analysis, but it is feared and resented. If human behavior can be reduced and determined to any considerable degree by the laws of biology, then mankind might appear to be less than unique and to that extent dehumanized. Few social scientists and scholars in the humanities are prepared to enter such a conspiracy, let alone surrender any of their territory. But this perception, which equates the method of reduction with the philosophy of diminution, is entirely in error. The laws of a subject are necessary to the discipline above it, they challenge and force a mentally more efficient restructuring, but they are not sufficient for the purposes of the discipline. Biology is the key to human nature.

3. Romanowski (1974) finds that Descartes's use of the address *(je/vous)* in his scientific writing opened the breach for the sign (communicative) to enter the Cartesian attitude and undermine it: he moves from science to philosophic *discourse.* It is interesting to note that Descartes' great twentieth-century *malin génie,* Michel Foucault, has opted for Discourse as his counter to rationalism. Anti-rationalism is the basis for his rhetorical (tropological) discourse analyses. Foucault's is, in a way, a truncated hermeneutics, the interpretation of the world made by langauge not only as instrument but agent, and without Understanding as the key component.

4. Kenneth Burke (1957:157–58) writes of the fundamental differences between James and Peirce,

> ... differences that led Peirce to call his own philosophy by the slightly altered name, "pragmaticism."
>
> James said that efficacy was the test of truth. And then, as a humanitarian afterthought, he expressed the hope that we would apply this test only to 'good' efficacy. Peirce resented this mere annexing of a corrective. He sought a test of truth whereby the moral evaluation would be an integral part of the test. . . . Dewey's instrumentalism brings out James' problem even more clearly, in so far as instrumentalism becomes the philosophy of technology. . . . Technology as the coefficient of power. A power is something in itself 'neutral', that can be used for either 'good' or 'evil'. . . . Dewey's job was the 'humanitarian' task of saying 'Power is the test of truth', and then furtively annexing, 'But let us mean *good* power'.

5. *The New York Review of Books* (1967) helped reawaken and widen interest in Peirce; it seems as if academia had to lose some of its exclusive rights to sanctifying writers before Peirce could come most fully into his own. The story of Peirce's mistreatment by the moral structure of the university still shocks us, evoking the passionate discourse of one of our most eminent scholars and leading semioticians: Thomas A. Sebeok (1976b:1430) remarked in his keynote address to the C. S. Peirce Symposium on Semiotics and the Arts at the Johns Hopkins University: "The harsh facts are that Peirce, who 'remains the most original, versatile, and comprehensive philosophic mind this country has yet produced,' was dismissed by your university after five years of sterling service and he never again succeeded in holding any academic post."

6. See Juliet Flower MacCannell (1977) on the conceptual problems of pity and self-love in the eighteenth century.

7. In the mid-twentieth century there appeared some exquisite literary criticism based on phenomenology's reassessment of the Cartesian *cogito*. The work of Georges Poulet is an example of literature's benefiting from phenomenology: for the first time certain Romantic and pre-Romantic texts were adequately analyzed. Poulet's former colleague at the University of Zürich, Paul de Man, also successfully employed phenomenological methods at the beginning of his literary career. The benefits have flowed in more than one direction: Heidegger's existential analysis of Being claimed that "Being-a-sign-for" was a universal relationship of "showing" such that the "sign-structure itself provides an ontological clue for characterizing any entity whatsoever" (1967[1927]:108). Thenceforth the "world" has had the same "being" as the literary work—composed of signs; it became perfectly legitimate for literary critics to apply their analytic methods to culture outside of printed texts, as Roland Barthes and Walter Benjamin have done.

8. Jacques Derrida devotes a long essay to his teacher in his 1967 book, *L'Ecriture et la différence*. Lévinas was most instrumental in bringing Husserl and Heidegger to a French audience, through his many important articles and books on German phenomenology and existentialism, including his and Pfeiffer's French translation of Husserl's *Cartesian Meditations*. His 1930 work on Husserl's theory of intuition (1973) was made available to Americans through the series on Continental philosophy published by Northwestern University Press. It is Lévinas's theory of the *trace* that sets off Derrida's own meditation, a meditation he collates with Freud's notion of *frayage (Bahnung)* to make the transition to his post-structural psychoanalysis of philosophy.

9. Heidegger's comments on ethnography are interesting because although he decides *against* empirical social investigation (it would "fail to recognize the real problem. . . . the genuine knowledge of essences" [1962:77]), his version of the 'primitive' is true to the Romantic equation of primitive with genuine (and in Heidegger's case the pre-Socratic Greeks, perhaps?):*

> To orient the analysis of Dasein towards the 'life of primitive peoples' can have positive significance as a method because 'primitive phenomena' are often less concealed and less complicated by extensive self-interpretation on the part of the Dasein in question.
> Primitive Dasein often speaks to us more directly in terms of a primordial absorption in 'phenomena' (taken in the pre-phenomenological sense). A way of conceiving things which seems, perhaps, rather clumsy and crude from our standpoint, can be positively helpful in bringing out the ontological structures of phenomena in a genuine way. [1962:76]

Heidegger's anti-Semitism may well be an embarrassing consequence of an old Romantic (syntagmatic) opposition between naive and complex souls (naive, spontaneous, Greek/complex, interior, Judaeo-Christian).

10. Paul Ricoeur's (1967) outstandingly clear exposition of Husserl's transcendental self, together with Husserl's own descriptions have formed the basis of our seeing culture as the "first *epochē*" in chapter 3. Of course, this is our own derivation; Ricoeur himself has characterized Lévi-Strauss's work as "Kantism without a transcendental subject," which implies that the transcen-

*Romanticism and anti-self-consciousness. . . .

dental subject is modeled on the superior Cartesian *cogito,* an inference that is often made (see Milton Singer, 1978:218). See Paul de Man's essay (1971:10ff.) on the crisis in criticism in the late 1960s when the lack of central subjectivity was perceived as a crucial issue for literature. See also Donato 1974:160–62, where Donato sets up the question of the self (as subject or shifter) as a kind of either/or question for literature. This should be read in the light of his later (1978) decision for the subject discussed here in chapter 2. T. S. Eliot's "stock exchange" metaphor for literary tastes is as appropriate as ever for the representatives of American literary scholarship.

11. Benveniste (1966) demonstrates that subjective time, oriented toward the present, depends absolutely on linguistic time, whose only mode is the present. Past and future are situated in relation to it.

12. Barthes and Lévi-Strauss concur that myths are good to think with, though Barthes decries them when they constitute the mythology of the bourgeoisie foisting off its representations on others as well as on itself. Lévi-Strauss does not moralize, and we are immensely indebted to him for characterizing mythic thought so explicitly and without the adulation of the primitive, a common form of condescension evident even in Heidegger. Moreover, Lévi-Strauss's vision of the mythic totality provides us with a wonderful sense of the 'totality' of Western culture and establishes 'savage thought' as appropriate for culture studies.

13. Saussure distinguishes between two types of semiotic *relations* at the level of language: syntagmatic and associative. Semioticians have restricted themselves almost exclusively to the syntagmatic. (For discussion, see chapter 6, "On the Nature of the Literary Sign.") The similiarities in associations are neither purely arbitrary nor rationally necessary. They are constellations, pluralities of like signifiers *and* signifieds. Barthes declares in his *Système de la mode* (1967a) that associations are impossible in fashion and sticks to syntagms. Paradigm classes are accumulations of syntagms, *not* associations. Perhaps the renewed interest in Freud's ideas of condensation, displacement, and overdetermination will help us to understand Saussure's association relation more completely.

14. Lévi-Strauss in the *Scope of Anthropology* (1967) uses the Oedipus and the Christian quest myths as his 'sources' for typological insight into Amerindian myths.

15. Nietzsche (1956:189): "Oblivion . . . is an active screening device." For him forgetting is a necessary component of memory and of the present itself.

16. This blindness to the sign-character of scientific representation is evident today in a recent popular book by an eminent American ethologist, Edward Wilson's *On Human Nature* (1978). The ineffable is also given many nods, in the form of "touchstone" quotations from indisputable "great" writers, throughout the book. Wilson reserves almost all his openly expressed antagonisms for post-rational thinkers, from Kant to Camus: recall that his most famous work, *Sociobiology,* opens with an attack on Camus's statement that suicide is the central question of philosophy. This is natural in a scientist. Sociobiology does have its right and left wings, that is, its division between those who cannot see the representation-character or sign mechanism of the objects they study and those whose inquiries are compatible with semiotics, such as Tynbergen, Dawkins, and the Medawars (see Sebeok 1972).

The rapid invasion of culture studies by biologists ought to give rise to some reflection on the part of those in the humanities; it should at least compel them to ask whether the rationalist versus the post-rationalist positions on culture may not give them a good handle on where they themselves may be divided. Some philosophers, historians, and literary critics will hold to a rational stance, honoring reason in the face of irrationality, and will feel a kinship of purpose with science. But it should also be recalled that "rationality" has its applied behavioral science, as Max Weber taught us: bureaucracy, hierarchy, the decision against "irrational" bonds (e.g., family, love) for organizing our relationships. (Family or 'genetic' ties are considered by Edward Wilson to be one example of the 'biological' forces against which reason must fight.)

There are also adherents of the anti-rational or irrational positions—Michel Foucault is the great doer of battle with the Cartesian *cogito*. It may well be that he is still controlled by the rationalist position, even in the way he operates his antitheses. He refuses the signified and decides for Discourse analysis (rather than separating language and speech as Saussure did). But in essence that is what Descartes did, though he was blind to the significance of his own moves, when he moved from science to philosophy (and method). Baudrillard's work consistently criticizes the hypostasis of the signifier and takes a tack opposing Foucault.

17. See Dean MacCannell on "Marx's Semiotic" in *The Tourist* (1976a).

18. Singer (1978) and de Man (1973) characterize "semiology" as Saussurian-linguistic and "semiotic" as Peircian and broader (usually less verbal and more visual in orientation).

John Deely (1978:21) gives a lucid philosophical review of the difficulty of identifying signs with representations. He distinguishes between signs that represent objects and signs that serve "only to found relations to what they themselves are not, namely the objects of which we are directly aware." It is clear that the next important issue for semiotics will be shaped around the problem of representation: are there objects of which we *are* "directly aware"? This coming debate (if it ever comes) will have to consider the possibility of even these foundational signs as "representation," as in the recent works on mimesis by Philippe Lacoue-Labarthe (1978) and the neo-Nietzschean interpretation of Freud's unconscious in this way. (In this version "consciousness" is an original hypothesis: the hypothesis that consciousness represents an elsewhere, an 'it' heterogeneous to itself. See Lacoue-Labarthe 1977. Consciousness presents itself as a "representation.") Also pertinent will be Derrida's "White Mythology" (1974). The varieties of the Unconscious would be an excellent central organizing topic.

19. Derrida 1973: Part I, "Sign and Signs," refers to the ambiguous construction Husserl noted in the sign, which is both expression *(Ausdruck)* and indication *(Anzeichen)*. The latter are signs "that express nothing because they convey nothing" one could ever call meaning *(Sinn)* (17). Considering one of the etymologies of metaphor as that which conveys or transports meaning we have here the beginning of what will grow to be a non-metaphoric or differently metaphoric sign in Derrida and deconstruction, the open trope.

20. This literature is carefully reviewed by Jonathan Culler in his books on *Structuralist Poetics* (1975a) and on Saussure (1976). Derrida's definitive review, "Linguistics and Phonology," in *Grammatology* (1976:27–73) cannot be ignored by scholars and critics.

Culler's judicious book is a painstaking analysis of structuralism-for-literature. His conclusion that linguistics is to language as poetics is to literature seems to us an example of the kind of Lévi-Straussian mythic accommodation which would allow the disciplines to continue to function, especially without having to challenge the concept of literature as narrative. Culler's *The Pursuit of Signs* (1981) appeared too late for us to comment on it.

21. S. Saumjan (Benveniste 1966:136–52) criticizes the work of Chomsky and the generative grammarians for remaining solely within the limits of the *syntagm* in their analysis of language. The paradigmatic axis is left out.

22. The important contribution to communication theory made by the great structural linguist Roman Jakobson in effect weds Peirce and Saussure. See Jakobson (1960:253) for a communication model that accommodates both. Wilden (1968:184) speaks of this in Freud. The entire section on the "Cogito and the 'True' Subject" (177–84) is worth reading. See also Daniel Laferriere's attempt to calibrate Freud and Chomsky in his recent (1979) book.

23. A. J. Greimas (1970:13) relegates "meaning" to the question of levels:

> Signification is thus nothing but such a transposition from one level of language to another and from one language to a different language, and meaning is nothing but the possibility of such *transcoding*.

Barthes claims that semiolinguistics has never gone beyond the level of the sentence and that Discourse lies beyond the analytic scope of grammar:

> Because it lies beyond the sentence, and though consisting of nothing but sentences, discourse must naturally be the object of a second linguistics. The linguistics of discourse has for a very long time has a famous name: rhetoric. But as a result of an intricate historical process, rhetoric was switched over to the humanities that had become separated from the study of language. [1975:240]

This might have been seen as a challenge to departments of rhetoric to study the semiotic mechanics of language; however, this is not the trend. (Seymour Chatman is a noteworthy and rather unusual exception.) One might also note that Barthes, like Lacan, sees the acquisition of speech as that which shapes *human* personality (in the form of the Oedipal situation), but he does not take this amiss (1974:271; also 1975:47): "Death of the Father would deprive literature of many of its pleasures. . . . Doesn't every narrative lead back to Oedipus? . . . Oedipus was at least good for something: to make good novels." Deleuze has an anti-Oedipal stance (1978). He opposes Oedipus as narrative, full of the signifier, fictional to the point of schizophrenia, the sign divided by itself.

There has also been a critique of semiolinguists for not doing the semiotic of language, by Christian Metz in his *Essais Sémiotiques* (1977).

24. See Michel Foucault (1977:81–82): according to Lacanian theory, the terrifying fact that the signifier signifies nothing generates psychosis. Michel Foucault, despite his disagreement with psychoanalysis, gives a good summary:

> Lacan, following Melanie Klein, has shown that the father, as the third party in the Oedipal situation, is not only the hated and feared rival, but the agent whose presence limits the unlimited relationship between the mother and child. . . . Consequently, the father separates, that is, he is the one who protects when, in his proclamation of the Law, he links space, rules, and language within a single major experience. At a stroke he creates the distance along which will develop the scansion of presences and absences, and the speech whose initial form is based on constraints, and finally the relationship of the signifier to the signified

> which gives rise to not only the structure of language but also the exclusion and symbolic transformation of repressed material. . . . The "no" through which this gap is created does not imply the absence of a real individual who bears the father's name; rather, it implies that the father and . . . the position of the signifier has remained vacant.

This "catastrophe of the signifier," its failure to mean anything beyond itself or to signify anything more than a lack, is best illustrated in Lacanian theory by the phallus.

25. The signifiers precede the imposition of the symbolic order by the mirror-stage and the acquisition of language. The point is that language always conceals as it reveals—a very Heideggerian notion, or even Hegelian.

26. See their essays in *Anti-Oedipe* and articles by and about them in *Sémiotext(e)*, especially their collaborative essay on the desiring machine, and the replay of Freud's wolfman in "One or Several Wolves."

27. Foucault's theses on madness as Reason's disowned alter ego (Descartes's *malin génie*) are well known.

28. Here one might compare the vogue for the young Lukács's aesthetic theories in the later 1960s (see Paul de Man 1971;36–50). Some saw the same kind of transversality there as a way of retaining the formal and phenomenological sign-character of the work of art without having it tied to empirical conditions of social communication. For an opposing Marxist viewpoint, see the very lucid exposition by V. N. Voloshinov (1977:96–108). Voloshinov opens the work of art to discourse analysis and attacks the notion of essence. See also Mukarovsky 1976:3–10.

29. For example, Jean Houdebine's open letter to Derrida, which specifically questions his position on Marx (1973:57). See also the 1980 conference at Cérisy, especially the talk by Joel Rogozinski on Derrida and Marx.

30. Most analysts of the value and meaning of 'money' refer to its metaphoric status, as in Foucault's *The Order of Things* (1970:168–82), in which Foucault speaks of money as a representation of a representation, whose legitimation derives from its reproduction of the image of the ruling authority (prince, president, etc). As the age of mechanical reproduction cedes to the age of electronic reproduction, however, questions such as these must be re-thought. Clearly Derrida has found in another of Rousseau's themes, counterfeiting, a clue at least to money's 'legitimation'—and the source of its *value* in the work of the laborer who produces it.

31. Althusser attended Lacan's seminars on Freud.

32. The "New Philosophers" include André Glucksmann, Guy Lardreau, and Jean-Marie Benoist as well as Bernard Lévy, who actually studied with Derrida. This group has adopted a post-semiotic vocabulary for their anarchical withdrawal into individualism. Benoist, for example, expresses this tendency toward isolation and purity when he proclaims that Marx is dead, but he has been killed only to be "at last" purified of Lenin, Stalin:

> C'est, marchant sur les décombres de tous ces faux dieux, sur les débris fracassés des sédiments léninistes, maoïstes, castristes ou trotskistes, qui s'y trouvent mêlés, se frayer *enfin* une voie vers le texte de Marx, vers son écriture qu'il faut scruter comme écriture, pas seulement du regard, mais en y mettant la main, pour pratiquer des incisions, de coupûres, des actes de violence. . . .

> It is, in walking on the ruins of all these false gods, the shattered debris—Leninist, Maoist, Castroist, or Trotskyist—that are found mixed therein, to carve

> *at last* a pathway toward the text of Marx, toward his writing, not just by looking at it, but by digging into it, cutting into it, making incisions, acts of violence. . . .

Etc. The overt hostility to a Marx reduced to a single text in order to be cut apart is unfortunate; but it is also pernicious in its pretence to be a part of "the structural revolution": for if there is anything that structuralism and post-structuralism has taught us, it is the lession of intertextuality, the critical role of the *(hi)story of its readings* as constitutive of the *text.*

Glucksmann's book *Les Maîtres penseurs* (1977) is a decadent exercise: it denounces the right and the left in the name of their common resort to "the camps" to oppress the "plebe" (whose paradigm is—ironically, neo-romantically—the European peasant [291]). According to Glucksmann, the peasant has always been the butt of the modern bourgeoisie's scorn. But let us make no mistake: this is not Sartre or Merleau-Ponty denouncing Stalinism in the name of a commitment to a Eurocommunism that attempts to correct the Soviet excesses (bureaucracy and terror), it is an appeal to an ideal type that perhaps never existed.

Lardreau (1973) also appeals to a purposely vague "people" to support his anarchism, whose method is that of removing differences and distinctions: Freud's repression is the "same as" oppression; the social contract (which actually constitutes the sovereignty of the people in Rousseau—see J. MacCannell 1978) ought to be "suppressed" (142); the body itself abolished (229). It is clear these are not adherents of Derrida, no more than of Marx—nor of any other *philosophy* at all.

8. A COMMUNITY WITHOUT DEFINITE LIMITS

1. John Deely (178:18) extends semiotics even further back into antiquity, before the Greeks: "The terms of Poinsot's theory enable us to grasp the origin of the human world in a semiotic act—the act of insight into the mind-dependent status of certain signs." Boguslaw Lawendowski (1978:266) echoes Deely's radical claim that the origin of semiotics is the same as the origin of culture.

2. Augustine's and Rousseau's contributions to the doctrine of signs have been discussed in the previous chapters. For a helpful comment on Dante's contribution, see Thomas A. Sebeok (1975:233). Locke's contribution to semiotics is well-known and was acknowledged by Peirce to be the single greatest influence on Peirce's own work. John Deely (1978) has reintroduced a formerly obscure text, Poinsot's *Tractatus de Signis* (first published in 1932), which anticipates many of Peirce's ideas in much the same way that Dante's *De vulgari eloquentia* anticipates Peirce. One of the best general treatments of the history of the idea of *sign* is Erich Auerbach's (1959:11–78) classic essay "Figura."

3. Here we are following Max Fisch's (1978:31–70) sensitive handling of Peirce's ideas and life.

4. For more detail on "Marx's Semiotic," see D. MacCannell 1976a:19ff.

5. See Milton Singer's (1978:214) parallel contrast of Peirce's *semiotic* versus Saussure's *semiology.* See also J. Lotman in Lucid 1977.

6. This structure is made explicit in Neil Bruss's (1977:131–47) *Semiotica* essay in which he combines Freud and Chomsky in a semiotic frame.

7. This version of the sign is also the one found in Edward Wilson's sociobiology.

8. Making the same point for humans, Goffman (1967:7–10) has written: "[T]he person's face clearly is something that is not lodged in or on his body, but rather something that is diffusely located in the flow of events . . . [I]t is only on loan to him from society. . . ."

And later in the same essay: "Universal human nature is not a very human thing" (45).

9. Peter Marler's work (1978:115) has many nice empirical observations, for example, that monkeys sometimes use the same expression, with different inflections, to mean "man" and "snake."

10. For an excellent critique of these assumptions, see Harley Shands's (1978:175–201) report on his work with disabled arthritics and their different capacities to express themselves.

11. Peter Marler (1978:114) argues strongly against those who are "convinced of the inflexible automaticity of the animal as an unthinking machine."

12. On this point, see also Juliet Flower MacCannell (1978:477):

> Rousseau cannot therefore . . . terminate his analysis with the happy accession of man to the state (or language or culture). For the state, in becoming a "second nature" begins a process of dynamic conflict with its own will to freedom even above the level of individual desire, since by definition the will is opposition to "nature."

13. We do not wish to carry the critique of the semiotics of unity to the point of destruction, for now that the forces opposing semiotics are operating from within, they can be put to good use as an effective impetus to clarify basic issues.

14. Lawendowski (1978) further suggests that the production and interpretation of signs has

> always been taking place at several levels: (1) Personal; (2) Interpersonal, which falls into (2a) Intra-tribal or Intra-societal and (2b) Inter-tribal or Inter-societal. A parallel set of terms could be (3a) Intra-cultural and (3b) Inter-cultural. [267]

In chapter 5 we have called Lawendowski's type 3b "ethnosemiotics." The best example of ethnosemiotics we have seen is Lee Drummond's (1977) study of ethnic stereotyping among Carib Indians. See also Gary Stonum's (1977:947) essay on noise as form of escape or Anthony Wilden's treatment of similar issues (1972).

15. See also Peirce (1955:162ff) on the indefinite, limitless community. It is noteworthy both that Peirce appears to have been disturbed that his theory of consciousness did not involve a psychological subject necessarily and that Fisch singles out this concern for special attention. In a letter to Lady Welby reproduced by Fisch (1978:55) Peirce wrote:

> I define a Sign as anything which is so determined by something else, called its object, and so determines an effect upon a person, which effect I call its Interpretant, that the latter is thereby mediately determined by the former. My insertion of "upon a person" is a sop to Cerberus, because I despair of making my own broader conception understood. . . . [S]igns require at least two *Quasi-minds*; a *Quasi-utterer* and a *Quasi-Interpreter*; and although these two are at one (i.e. *are* one mind) in the sign itself, they must nevertheless be distinct. [55]

Bibliography

Adams, Howard
 1975   *Prison of Grass: Canada From a Native Point of View.* Toronto: New Press.

Adler, Judith
 1976   " 'Revolutionary' Art and the Art of Revolution: Aesthetic Work in a Millenarian Period." *Theory and Society* 3 (Spring): 417–35.

Adorno, Theodor
 1967   *Prisms.* Tr. S. Weber. London: Neville Spearman.

Althusser, Louis
 1964–65   "Freud et Lacan." *La Nouvelle Critique,* nos. 161–62 (December–January), 91–97.
 1977   *For Marx.* Tr. B. Brewster. Surrey: Unwin/Schocken. (Original French edition 1965).

Arnold, Matthew
 1961   "Hebraism and Hellenism." *Poetry and Criticism of Matthew Arnold,* ed. A. D. Culler. Boston: Houghton Mifflin.

Auerbach, Erich
 1959   "Figura." *Scenes From the Drama of European Literature.* Tr. W. Trask. New York: Meridian.

Bainbridge, William Sims
 1978   *Satan's Power: A Deviant Psychotherapy Cult.* Berkeley and Los Angeles: University of California Press.

Barthes, Roland
 1967a   *Système de la mode.* Paris: Seuil.
 1967b   *Elements of Semiology.* Tr. A. Lavers and C. Smith. Boston: Beacon.
 1972   *Mythologies.* Tr. A. Lavers. New York: Hill and Wang.
 1974   *S/Z.* Tr. R. Miller. London: Cape. (Original French edition 1970).
 1975a   "Introduction to the Structural Study of Narrative." *New Literary History* 6: 2 (Winter), 237–71.
 1975b   *The Pleasure of the Text.* Tr. R. Miller. New York: Hill and Wang.

Bastide, Roger
 1974   *Applied Anthropology.* Tr. Alice Morton. New York: Harper and Row.

Bateson, Gregory
 1972   *Steps to an Ecology of Mind.* New York: Ballantine Books.

Bateson, G.; Jackson, D. D.; Haley, J.; and Weakland, J.
 1956   "Toward a Theory of Schizophrenia." *Behavioral Science* 1, 251ff.

Baudrillard, Jean
 1972   *Pour une critique de l'économie politique du signe.* Paris: Gallimard TEL.

Benjamin, Walter
1969   *Illuminations.* Tr. H. Zohn. New York: Schocken.
Benoist, Jean-Marie
1970   *Marx est mort.* Paris: Gallimard NRF.
Benveniste, Emile
1966a   ed. *Problèmes du Langage.* Paris: Gallimard.
1966b   "Le Langage et l'expérience humaine." In Benveniste 1966a, pp. 3–13.
1969a   "Sémiologie de la langue." *Semiotica* 1:1, 1–12.
1969b   "Sémiologie de la langue." *Semiotica* 1:2, 127–35.
1971a   *Problems in General Linguistics.* Tr. E. Meek. Miami: University of Miami Press.
1971b   "Language in Freudian Theory," In *Problems in General Linguistics.*
Berger, Peter, and Luckmann, Thomas
1966   *The Social Construction of Reality.* Garden City, N.Y.: Doubleday.
Besançon, Julien
1968   *Les Murs ont eu la parole: Journal Mural, Mai 68.* Paris: Tchou.
Birdwhistell, Ray L.
1952   *Introduction to Kinesics.* Washington, D.C.: Foreign Service Institute.
Blanchard, Marc Eli
1980   *Description: Sign, Self, Desire.* The Hague: Mouton.
Bogatyrev, Peter
1976   "Costume as a Sign." In Matejka and Titunik 1976, pp. 13–19.
Booth, Wayne C.
1961   *The Rhetoric of Fiction.* Chicago: University of Chicago Press.
Bouissac, Paul
1978   "A Semiotic Approach to Nonsense: Clowns and Limericks." In Sebeok 1978a, pp. 244–63.
Brenkman, John
1978   "The Other and the One: Psychoanalysis, Reading, *The Symposium.*" *Yale French Studies* 55/56, 396–456.
Broadbent, Geoffrey
1978   "A Plain Man's Guide to The Theory of Signs in Architecture." *Architectural Design* 7/8, 474–82.
Bruss, Neal H.
1977   "The Freudian Practitioner as 'an Ideal Speaker-Listener.'" *Semiotica* 19:1/2, 131–47.
Buck, Roy C.
1977   "The Ubiquitous Tourist Brochure: Explorations in its Intended and Unintended Use." *Annals of Tourism Research* 4:4 (March/April), 195–207.
Buckley, Walter
1967   *Sociology and Modern Systems Theory.* Englewood Cliffs, N.J.: Prentice-Hall.
Burke, Kenneth
1957   *The Philosophy of Literary Form: Studies in Symbolic Action.* New York: Vintage.

1965   *Permanence and Change: An Anatomy of Purpose.* Indianapolis: Bobbs-Merrill.

Carontini, Enrico, and Peraya, Daniel
1975   *Le Projet Sémiotique.* Paris: Jean-Pierre Delarge.

Cassirer, Ernst
1946   *Language and Myth.* New York: Harper and Brothers Publishers.
1955   *The Philosophy of the Enlightenment.* Tr. F. C. A. Koelln and J. P. Pettigrew. Boston: Beacon.

Chabrol, Claude
1973   *Sémiotique narrative et textuelle.* Paris: Larousse.

Chapple, Eliot
1978   "Letter to the Editor." *Anthropology Newsletter* 19:9 (November), 2.

Charles, Michel
1977   *Rhétorique de la lecture.* Paris: Seuil.

Cherry, Colin
1966   *On Human Communication.* Cambridge, Mass.: M.I.T. Press.

Chomsky, Noam
1966   *Cartesian Linguistics: A Chapter in the History of Rationalist Thought.* New York: Harper and Row.
1968   *Language and Mind.* New York: Harcourt, Brace, and World.
1977   *Language and Materialism.* London: Routledge and Kegan Paul.

Communications
(This journal is devoted to the semiotic analysis of culture.)
1969   No. 14, "La Bande dessineé." (On comics)
1970   No. 15, "L'Analyse des images."
1973   No. 20, "Le Sociologique et le linguistique."

Coward, Rosalind, and Ellis, John
1977   *Language and Materialism.* London: Routledge and Kegan Paul.

Crapanzano, Vincent
1977   "On the Writing of Ethnography." *Dialectical Anthropology* 2:1 (February), 69–73.

Culler, Jonathan
1974   "Commentary." *New Literary History* VI, 219.
1975a   *Structuralist Poetics.* Ithaca: Cornell University Press.
1975b   "In Pursuit of Signs." *Daedalus* (Fall), 95–111.
1976   *Saussure.* Sussex: Harvester.
1981   *The Pursuit of Signs.* Ithaca: Cornell University Press.

Darwin, Charles
1965   *The Expression of the Emotions in Man and Animals.* Chicago: University of Chicago Press.

Dawkins, Richard
1976   *The Selfish Gene.* New York: Oxford University Press.

Deely, John N.
1978   "Toward the Origin of Semiotic." In Sebeok 1978a, pp. 1–30.

DeJean, Joan
1977   "In Search of the Artistic Text, Recent Works by Lotman and Uspensky." *Sub-stance* 17, 149–58.

Deleuze, Gilles
1972   *Proust and Signs.* Tr. R. Howard. New York: Braziller.

Deleuze, Gilles, and Foucault, Michel
1977   "Intellectuals and Power," In *Language, Counter-Memory, Prac-
              tice,* ed. D. F. Bouchard, tr. D. F. Bouchard and S. Simon, pp.
              205–17. Ithaca: Cornell University Press.
Deleuze, Gilles, and Guttari, Félix
1977a   "Balance-Sheet Program for Desiring Machines." *Semiotext(e)*
              II:3, 117–35.
1977b   *Anti-Oedipus: Capitalism and Schizophrenia.* Tr. R. Hurley, M.
              Seem, H. R. Lane. New York: Viking Press.
De Man, Paul
1960   "La structure intentionnelle de l'image romantique." *Revue In-
              ternationale de Philosophie* 14 (1960), 68–84.
1967   "The Crisis of Contemporary Criticism." *Arion* (Spring), 38–57.
1971   *Blindness and Insight.* New York: Oxford University Press.
1972   "Literature and Language: A Commentary." *New Literary His-
              tory* 4:1 (Autumn), 181–91.
1972   "Commentary." *New Literary History* 6:1 (Autumn), 181–91.
1973a   "Semiology and Rhetoric." *Diacritics* (Fall), 27–33.
1973b   "Theory of Metaphor in Rousseau's *Second Discourse.*" *Stud-
              ies in Romanticism* 12, 475–98.
1977   "The Purloined Ribbon." *Glyph* 1, 28–49.
1978   "The Epistemology of Metaphor." *Critical Inquiry* 5:1 (Autumn),
              13–30.
1979   *Allegories of Reading.* New Haven: Yale University Press.
Derrida, Jacques
1967a   *De la grammatologie.* Paris: Minuit.
1967b   *L'Ecriture et la différence.* Paris: Editions du Seuil.
1970   "Structure, Sign, and Play." In Macksey and Donato 1970.
1971   "Sémiologie et Grammatologie." In Kristeva, Rey-Debove, and
              Umiker 1971, pp. 11–27.
1972a   *La Dissémination.* Paris: Seuil. (Reading of Saussure's notion of
              difference)
1972b   *Marges.* Paris: Minuit.
1973   *Speech and Phenomena and Other Essays on Husserl's Theory
              of Signs.* Tr. D. B. Allison. Evanston: Northwestern University
              Press.
1974a   "Freud and the Scene of Writing." *Yale French Studies.*
1974b   "White Mythology." *New Literary History* 6:1 (Autumn), 5–74.
1975   "The Purveyor of Truth." *Yale French Studies* 52, 31–115.
1976   *Of Grammatology.* Tr. G. Spivak. Baltimore: Johns Hopkins Uni-
              versity Press. (Part I: "Writing Before the Letter," pp. 1–95.)
1978   "The Retrait of Metaphor." *Enclitic* 2:2 (Fall), 5–33.
1978   *Writing and Difference.* Tr. A. Bass. Chicago: University of
              Chicago Press.
1979   *Spurs: Nietzsche's Styles.* Tr. B. Harlow. Chicago: University of
              Chicago Press.
Descartes, René
1956   *Discourse on Method.* Tr. L. J. Lafleur. Indianapolis: Bobbs-
              Merrill.
Dodds, E. R.
1951   *The Greeks and the Irrational.* Berkeley and Los Angeles: Uni-

versity of California Press. (Especially pp. 207–235, "Plato and the Irrational Soul")

Donato, Eugenio
1974   "Structuralism in Literature." In Macksey 1974. Baltimore: Johns Hopkins University Press.
1977   "The Idioms of the Text: Notes on the Language of Philosophy and the Fictions of Literature." *Glyph* 2, 1–13.
1978   "The Ruins of Memory: Archaeological Fragments and Textual Artifacts." *Modern Language Notes* 93:4, 575–96.

Douglas, Mary
1970   *Natural Symbols.* New York: Vintage.

Drummond, Lee
1977   "Structure and Process in the Interpretations of South American Myth: The Dog Spirit People." *American Anthropologist* 79:4 (December), 842–68.

Dumont, Jean-Paul
Forthcoming *The Headman and I.* Austin: University of Texas Press.
1976   *Under the Rainbow.* Austin: University of Texas Press.

Durkheim, Emile
1965a   *The Elementary Forms of the Religious Life.* New York: Free Press.
1965b   *Montesquieu and Rousseau.* Tr. R. Manheim. Ann Arbor: University of Michigan.

Eco, Umberto
1976   *A Theory of Semiotics.* Bloomington: Indiana University Press.
1978   "Semiotics: A Discipline or an Interdisciplinary Method?" In Sebeok 1978, pp. 73–83.
1979   *The Role of the Reader.* Bloomington: Indiana University Press.

Ekman, Paul
1978   "Facial Signs: Facts, Fantasies and Possibilities." In Sebeok 1978a, pp. 124–56.

Felman, Shoshana, ed.
1978   "Psychoanalysis and Literature." *Yale French Studies* 55/56.

Fisch, Max
1978   "Peirce's General Theory of Signs." In Sebeok 1978a, pp. 31–72.

Flaubert, Gustave
1965   *Madame Bovary.* Tr. P. de Man. New York: Norton.

Foucault, Michel
1970   *The Order of Things.* New York: Vintage.
1971   *L'ordre du discours.* Paris: Gallimard.

Fresnault-Deruelle
1975   "L'Espace interpersonnel dans les comics." In Helbo 1975.

Freud, Sigmund
1929   *Essais de psychanalyse.* Tr. S. Jankelevitch. Paris: Payot. (Especially "*Psychologie collective et analyse du moi*")
1936   *The Problem of Anxiety.* Tr. A. Bunker. New York: Norton.
1965   *The Interpretation of Dreams.* Tr. J. Strachey. New York: Avon.
1967   *Beyond the Pleasure Principle.* Tr. J. Strachey. New York: Bantam.

Gadamer, Hans-Georg
1975 *Truth and Method.* Tr. G. Barden and J. Cumming. New York: Seabury.
Garfinkel, Harold
1967 *Studies in Ethnomethodology.* Englewood Cliffs, N.J.: Prentice-Hall.
1972 "Studies of the Routine Grounds of Everyday Activities." In Sudnow 1972a, pp. 1–30.
Gasché, Rodolphe
1978 ed. "Autobiography and the Problem of the Subject." *Modern Language Notes* 93:4 (May).
Geertz, Clifford
1973 *The Interpretation of Cultures.* New York: Basic Books.
Genette, Gérard
1966 *Figures: Essais.* Paris: Editions du Seuil (collection *Tel Quel*).
1971 "Langage poétique, poétique du langage." In Kristeva, Rey-Debove, and Umiker 1971, pp. 423–46.
Giovannangeli, Daniel
1979 *Ecriture et répétition: Approche de Derrida.* Paris: Grasset.
Girard, René
1965 *Deceit, Desire and the Novel.* Tr. Yvonne Freccero. Baltimore: Johns Hopkins University Press.
1977 *Violence and the Sacred.* Tr. P. Gregory. Baltimore: Johns Hopkins University Press. (Original French edition 1972. Paris: Grasset.)
Glaser, Barney G., and Strauss, Anselm L.
1964 "Awareness Contexts and Social Interaction." *American Sociological Review* 29, 669–79.
Glucksmann, André
1977 *Les Maîtres penseurs.* Paris: Grasset.
Goffman, Erving
1961 *Encounters.* New York: Bobbs-Merrill.
1963 *Stigma: Notes on the Management of a Spoiled Identity.* Englewood Cliffs, N.J.: Prentice-Hall.
1967 *Interaction Ritual.* Chicago: Aldine.
1974 *Frame Analysis: An Essay on the Organization of Experience.* New York: Harper and Row.
1976a "Picture Frames." Slide and paper presentation to the Department of Applied Behavioral Sciences, University of California at Davis (April), aspects of which are incorporated in his monographs.
1976b *Gender Advertisements.* Cambridge, Mass.: Harvard University Press.
Goldmann, Lucien
1969 *The Human Sciences and Philosophy.* Tr. Hayden White and Robert Anchor. London: Jonathan Cape.
1971 *Immanuel Kant.* Tr. R. Black. London: New Left Books.
Gonos, George
1977 "Situation Versus Frame: The 'Interactionist' and the 'Structuralist' Analysis of Everyday Life." *American Sociological Review* 42 (December), 854–67.

Gossman, Lionel
"Introduction." *Modern Language Notes* 91 (Symposium on Semiotics), 1424–26.
Goux, Jean-Joseph
1968   "Numismatiques I." *Tel Quel* 35 (Automne), 64–89.
Graburn, Nelson
1976   *Ethnic and Tourist Arts: Cultural Expressions from the Fourth World.* Berkeley and Los Angeles: University of California Press.
Graff, Gerald
1979   *Literature Against Itself.* Chicago: University of Chicago Press.
Greenwood, Davydd
1976   "Tourism as an Agent of Change: A Spanish Basque Case." *Annals of Tourism Research* 5:3 (Jan/Feb), 128–42.
Greimas, A. J.
1970   *Du sens.* Paris: Seuil.
Grene, Marjorie
1973   *Sartre.* New York: New Viewpoints.
1076   "Life, Death and Language: Some Thoughts on Wittgenstein and Derrida." *Partisan Review* 43:2, 265–79.
Guattari, Félix
1977   "Psychoanalysis and Schizoanalysis." *Sémiotext(e)* 2:3, 76–86.
Hawkes, Terence
1977   *Structuralism and Semiotics.* Berkeley and Los Angeles: University of California Press.
Hazlitt, William
1902   "On the Character of Rousseau." *The Collected Works of William Hazlitt in Twelve Volumes.* Vol. 1, pp. 88–93. London: J. M. Dent.
Heap, James A., and Roth, Phillip A.
1973   "On Phenomenological Sociology." *American Sociological Review* 38:3 (June), 354–67.
Heath, Stephen
1977   "Language, Literature, Materialism." *Sub-stance* 17, 67–74.
Heidegger, Martin
1962   *Being and Time.* Tr. John Macquarrie and Edward Robinson. New York: Harper and Row.
Helbo, André
1975   ed. *Sémiologie de la représentation.* Paris: Complexe.
Hocquenghem, Guy
1977   "Family, Capitalism, Anus." *Semiotext(e)* 2:3, 148–58.
Hölderlin, Friedrich
1965   *Hyperion.* Tr. W. R. Trask. New York: Ungar.
Houdebine, Jean
1973   "Réponse." *Diacritics* 3:2 (Summer), 57.
Hughes, Everett C.
1971   *The Sociological Eye: Selected Papers on Work, Self, and the Study of Society.* Chicago: Aldine.
Husserl, Edmund
1962   *Ideas: General Introduction to Pure Phenomenology.* Tr. W. R. Boyce Gibson. New York: Collins.

1966   *Méditations Cartésiennes: Introduction à la phénoménologie.*
              Tr. (from the German) Gabrielle Pfeiffer et Emmanuel Levinas.
              Paris: Librairie Philosophique. J. Vrin.
Iser, Wolfgang
1974   *The Implied Reader.* Baltimore: Johns Hopkins University Press.
Jakobson, Roman
1960   "Closing Statement: Linguistics and Poetics." In Sebeok 1960,
              pp. 350–77.
1974   *Main Trends in the Science of Language.* New York: Harper and
              Row.
1975   *Coup d'oeil sur le développement de la sémiotique.* Blooming-
              ton, Ind.: Research Center for Language and Semiotic Studies.
              (Distributed by Humanities Press, N.Y.)
Jameson, Fredric
1972   *The Prison-House of Language.* Princeton: Princeton University
              Press.
1978a   "Imaginary and Symbolic in Lacan: Marxism, Psychoanalytic
              Criticism, and the Problem of the Subject." *Yale French Studies*
              55/56, 338–95.
1978b   "The Symbolic Inference; or Kenneth Burke and Ideological
              Analysis." *Critical Inquiry* 5:2, 417–22.
de Janvry, Alain
1975a   "The Political Economy of Rural Development in Latin America:
              An Interpretation." *American Journal of Agricultural Economics*
              57:3 (August), 490–99.
1975b   "The Importance of a Small Farmer Technology for Rural Devel-
              opment." Paper for the seminar on *Economic Analysis in the
              Design of New Technologies for the Small Farmer,* ComitéInter-
              nationale d'Agriculture et Technologie, Columbia University (No-
              vember).
Kant, Immanuel
1952   *Critique of Judgment.* Tr. J. C. Meredith. Oxford: Clarendon.
Kristeva, Julia
1969   *Sémiotikē: Recherches pour une Sémanalyse.* Paris: Seuil.
1971   "L'expansion de la Sémiologie." In Kristeva, Rey-Debove, and
              Umiker 1971, pp. 30–45.
1974   *La Révolution du langage poétique.* Paris: Seuil ("Sémiotique et
              symbolique").
1975a   "The Subject in Signifying Practice." *Semiotext(e)* 1:3, 19–34.
1975b   "La fonction prédicative et le sujet parlant." In *Langue, discours,
              société: Pour Emile Benveniste,* ed. Kristeva, Milner, and
              Ruwet, pp. 229–59. Paris: Seuil.
1975c   "Pratique signifiante et mode de production." In *La Traversée
              des signes.* Paris: Seuil, pp. 11–30.
1977   "Des Chinoises à Manhattan," *Tel Quel* 69 (Printemps), 11–17.
Kristeva, Julia; Rey-Debove, Josette; and Umiker, Donna Jean
1971   ed. *Essays in Semiotics.* The Hague: Mouton.
Labov, William
1972   "Rules for Ritual Insults." In Sudnow 1972a, pp. 120–69.
Lacan, Jacques
1966   *Ecrits.* Paris: Seuil.

1967	"The Insistence of the Letter in the Unconscious." *Yale French Studies* 39, 112–47.
1968	"The Function of Language in Psychoanalysis" [Original 1953, the "Discours de Rome"]. In Wilden 1968, pp. 3–87.
1970	"Of Structure as an Inmixing of the Otherness Prerequisite to any Subject Whatever." In Macksey and Donato 1970, pp. 186–95.

Lacoue-Labarthe, Philippe

1977	"Theatrum Analyticum." *Glyph* 2, 122–43.
1978	"Mimesis and Truth" (review of the work of René Girard). *Diacritics* 8:1 (Spring 1978), 10–23.

Laferrière, Daniel

1978	*Sign and Subject.* The Hague: De Ridder.

Laing, R. D.

1965	*The Divided Self: An Existential Study in Saints and Madness.* London: Pelican.

Laplanche, Jean

1974	"Postscript." *Yale French Studies* 48, 176–78.
1976	*Life and Death in Psychoanalysis.* Tr. J. Mehlmann. Baltimore: Johns Hopkins University Press.

Lardreau, Guy

1973	*Le singe d'or: essai sur le concept d'étape du marxisme.* Paris: Mercure de France.

Lawendowski, Boguslaw P.

1978	"On the Semiotic Aspect of Translations." In Sebeok 1978a, pp. 264–282.

Leiris, Michael

1966	*Brisées.* Paris: Mercure de France.

Lentricchia, Frank

1980	*After the New Criticism.* Chicago: University of Chicago Press.

Levinas, Emmanuel

1973	*The Theory of Intuition in Husserl's Phenomenology.* Tr. A. Orianne. Evanston: Northwestern University Press.

Lévi-Strauss, Claude

1950	"Introduction à l'oeuvre de Marcel Mauss." In Mauss, *Sociologie et Anthropologie,* ed. C. Lévi-Strauss. Paris: P.U.F.
1958	"The Structural Study of Myth." In *Myth: A Symposium,* ed. T. A. Sebeok, pp. 81–106. Bloomington: Indiana University Press.
1963	*Structural Anthropology.* Tr. C. Jacobsen. Garden City, N.Y.: Anchor Doubleday.
1966	*The Savage Mind.* Chicago: University of Chicago Press
1967	*The Scope of Anthropology.* Tr. Sherry O. Paul and Robert A. Paul. London: Jonathan Cape.
1968	*Tristes Tropiques.* New York: Atheneum.
1970	*The Raw and the Cooked.* Introduction to a Science of Mythology. Vol. 1. New York: Harper and Row.
1973	*From Honey to Ashes.* Introduction to a Science of Mythology. Vol. 2. New York: Harper and Row.
1979	*Myth and Meaning.* New York: Schocken.

Locke, John

	Essay Concerning Human Understanding. Ed. B. Rand. Cam-

bridge, Mass.: Harvard University Press. In Book IV, chap. 21, Locke marks out the domain of semiotic and identifies ideas as signs. (See Deely's excellent analysis in Sebeok 1978a, p. 21.)

Logan, Rose-Marie
1977   ed. *Yale French Studies* 52. "Graphesis: Perspectives in Literature and Philosophy."

Lotman, Yuri
1974   "The Sign Mechanism of Culture." *Semiotica* 12:4, 301–5.
1975   "The Discrete Text and the Iconic Text: Remarks on the Structure of Narrative." *New Literary History* 6 (Winter), 333–38.

Lotman, Yuri, and Uspenskiy, B. A.
1978   "On the Semiotic Mechanism of Culture." *New Literary History* 9:2, 211–32.

Lotman, Ju; Uspenskij, B.; Ivanov, V. V.; Toporov, V. N.; and Pjatigorskij, A. M.
1975   *Theses on the Semiotic Study of Culture.* Lisse: Peter de Ridder.

Lotringer, Sylvrère
1977   ed. *Sémiotext(e)* 2:3. "Anti-Oedipus."

Lovejoy, Arthur O.
1948   "On the Discrimination of Romanticisms." *Essays in the History of Ideas,* pp. 228–53. New York: Capricorn.

Lucid, Daniel P.
1977   ed. *Soviet Semiotics.* Baltimore: Johns Hopkins University Press. (Introduction by Lucid, pp. 1–23).

Lyotard, Jean-François
1971   *Discours, Figure.* Paris: Klincksieck.
1977   "Energumen Capital." *Sémiotext(e)* 2:3, 11–27.

MacCannell, Dean
1973   "Staged Authenticity: Arrangements of Social Space in Tourist Settings." *American Journal of Sociology* 79:3 (November), 589–603.
1975   "The Second Ethnomethodology." Paper read at the Southern meetings of the American Sociological Association, Washington, D.C. (April).
1976a   *The Tourist: A New Theory of the Leisure Class.* New York: Schocken.
1976b   "The Past and Future of Symbolic Interactionism." *Semiotica* 16:2, 99–114.
1976c   "On Social Meaning." Paper presented in the session on *Phenomenological Sociology* at the National Meetings of the American Sociological Association, New York (September).
1976d   "The Anthropology of Modern Culture." Paper presented at the University of California at Berkeley (November).
1977a   "Negative Solidarity." *Human Organization* 36:3 (Fall), 301–4.
1977b   "The Tourist and the New Community." *Annals of Tourism Research* (March/April), 208–15.
1977c   "Ritual in Face-to-Face Interaction in Modern Society." Paper presented to the Chicago Seminar in Symbolic Anthropology in Palo Alto (February).
1978a   "Making Space." Address delivered at the University of Pennsylvania (March).

1978b	"Pseudo-Espionage: An Interpretation of Modern Spying." *Sociological Quarterly* 19:1, 152–60.
1980	"A Community Without Definite Limits." *Semiotica* 31: 1/2, 87–98.

MacCannell, Dean, and Hostetler, John

1974	"Tourism and Tradition Among the Pennsylvania Amish." Proposal submitted to the National Science Foundation (not funded).

MacCannell, Juliet Flower

1974	"The Post-Fictional Self." *Modern Language Notes* 89 (Winter), 580–99.
1975	"Fiction and the Social Order." *Diacritics* (Spring), 7–16.
1977a	"The Self and Modern Culture." Invited paper, Fifth Annual Conference on Sociology and the Arts, Pomona, New Jersey (April).
1977b	"Nature and Self-Love: A Reinterpretation of Rousseau's Passion Primitive." *PMLA* 92:5 (October), 890–902.
1978a	"Ms. MacCannell Replies," *PMLA* 93:4 (May), 477–78.
1978b	"The General Self: Liberation by Text." Invited paper, International Association for Philosophy and Literature, Cleveland (May).
1979a	"Phallacious Theories of the Subject" (Review of Coward and Ellis: *Language and Materialism*). *Semiotica* 30:3/4, 359–74.
1979b	"The Semiotic of Modern Culture." *Semiotica* 35:3/4.
1980	"On the Nature of the Literary Sign." Seminar presented at the International Association for Philosophy and Literature Meetings. University of Maine, Orono (May).

Macksey, Richard

1974	ed. *Velocities of Change*. Baltimore: Johns Hopkins University Press.

Macksey, Richard and Donato, Eugenio

1970	ed. *The Structuralist Controversy*. Baltimore: Johns Hopkins University Press.
1976	ed. *Modern Language Notes* 91: Symposium on Semiotics.

Malinowski, Bronislaw

1929	"Practical Anthropology," *Africa* 2, 22–38.

Manning, Peter K.

1976	"The Decline of Civility: A Comment on Erving Goffman's Sociology." *The Canadian Review of Sociology and Anthropology* 13, 13–25.
In press	"Structuralism." *Contemporary Sociology*.

Marcuse, Herbert

1962	*Eros and Civilization*. New York: Vintage.
1968	*Negations: Essays in Critical Theory,* chap. 5 "On Hedonism." Tr. Jeremy J. Shapiro. Boston: Beacon Press, pp. 159–201.

Marler, Peter

1978	"Affective and Symbolic Meaning: Some Zoosemiotic Speculations." In Sebeok 1978a, pp. 113–123.

Marx, Karl

1965	*Capital*. Vol. 1. Moscow: Progress Publishers.
1967	"Theses on Feuerbach" (From the notebooks of 1844–45). In

Writings of the Young Marx on Philosophy, ed. D. Easton, tr. K. Gudat, pp. 400–402. Garden City, N.Y.: Anchor Doubleday.

Matejka, L. and Titunik, I. R., ed.
1976   *Semiotics of Art: Prague School Contributions.* Cambridge, Mass.: M.I.T. ["Costume as a Sign," pp. 13–19, by Peter Bogaty-rev.].

Mauss, Marcel
1967   *The Gift.* New York: Norton.

Mead, George H.
1934   *Mind, Self, and Society,* ed. Charles W. Morris. Chicago: University of Chicago Press.

Medawar, P. B., and Medawar, J.
1977   *The Life Sciences.* New York: Harper and Row.

Mehlmann, Jeffrey
1970   "Entre psychanalyse et psychocritique." *Poétique* 3, 365–83.
1974   ed. "French Freud." *Yale French Studies*

Merleau-Ponty, Maurice
1962   *Phenomenology of Perception.* Tr. Colin Smith. London: Routledge and Kegan Paul.
1963   *The Structure of Behavior.* Tr. A. L. Fisher. Boston: Beacon Press. (Original French edition 1942)
1964   *Signs.* Tr. R. C. McCleary. Evanston: Northwestern University Press.

Metz, Christian
1968–73   *Essais sur la signification au cinéma.* Vols. 1–2. Paris: Klincksieck.
1971   "Propositions méthodologiques pour l'analyse du film." In Kristeva, Rey-Debove, and Umiker 1971, pp. 502–15.
1977   *Essais Sémiotiques.* Paris: Klincksieck.

Michaels, Walter Benn
1977   "The Interpreter's Self: Peirce on the Cartesian 'Subject.' " *The Georgia Review* 31 (1977), 383–402.
1978   "Saving the Text: Reference and Belief." *Modern Language Notes* 93, 771–93.

Morris, Charles W.
1946   *Signs, Language and Behavior.* New York: Prentice-Hall.
1964   *Signification and Significance: A Study of the Relations of Signs and Values.* Cambridge, Mass.: M.I.T. Press.

Mukarovsky, Jan
1976   "Art as Semiotic Fact." In Matejka and Titunik 1976, pp. 3–10.

Mullins, Nicholas C., and Mullins, Carolyn J.
1973   *Theories and Theory Groups in Contemporary American Sociology.* New York: Harper and Row.

Nader, Laura
1964   "Perspectives Gained from Field Work." In *Horizons of Anthropology,* ed. Sol Tax, pp. 148–59.
1974   "Up the Anthropologist—Perspectives Gained from Studying Up." In *Reinventing Anthropology,* ed. Dell Hymes, pp. 284–311. New York: Vintage.

Nerval, Gérard de
1958   "Sylvie." *Oeuvres Complètes,* Vol. 1, pp. 589–626. Paris: Garnier.

Nietzsche, Friedrich
1956   *The Birth of Tragedy and the Genealogy of Morals.* Tr. F. Golffing. Garden City, N.Y.: Anchor Doubleday.
Ogden, D. K., and Richards, I. A.
1946   *The Meaning of Meaning.* New York: Harcourt Brace.
Ostwald, Peter
1971   "Symptoms, Diagnosis, and Concepts of Disease." In Kristeva, Rey-Debove, and Umiker 1971, pp. 239–50.
Parsons, Talcott
1977   *The Evolution of Societies.* Englewood Cliffs, N.J.: Prentice-Hall.
Peirce, Charles Saunders
1930–35
and 1958   *Collected Papers* Vols. 1–6, ed. Hawthorne and Weiss; Vols. 7–8, ed. Burks. Cambridge, Mass.: Harvard University Press.
1955   *The Philosophical Writings of Peirce.* Ed. Justus Buchler. New York: Dover.
Pottit, Philip
1975   *The Concept of Structuralism.* Berkeley and Los Angeles: University of California Press.
Pignatari, Décio
1978   "The Contiguity Illusion." In Sebeok 1978, pp. 84–97.
Pjatigorskij, A. M. and Uspenskij, B. A.
1978   "The Classification of Personality as a Semiotic Problem." In Lucid 1978, pp. 137–56.
Poulet, Georges
1949   *Etudes sur le temps humain.* Edinburg: At the University Press.
Rabinow, Paul
1975a   *Symbolic Domination: Cultural Form and Historical Changes in Morocco.* Chicago: University of Chicago Press.
1975b   *Uncommonplaces: Field Work Situations.* Berkeley and Los Angeles: University of California Press.
Redfield, Robert
1941   *The Folk Culture of Yucatán.* Chicago: University of Chicago Press.
1953   *The Primitive World and Its Transformations.* Ithaca: Cornell University Press.
Rey, Alain
1973–76   ed. *Théories du signe et du sens.* 2 vols. Paris: Klincksieck.
1978   "Communication vs. Semiosis: Two Conceptions of Semiotics." In Sebeok 1978, pp. 98–110.
Ricoeur, Paul
1967   *Husserl: An Analysis of His Phenomenology.* Evanston: Northwestern University Press. Especially: "Husserl and the Sense of History," pp. 143–74; "Kant and Husserl," pp. 175–201; "Existential Phenomenology," pp. 202–12.
1970   *Freud and Philosophy.* New Haven: Yale University Press.
1971   "What is a Text? Explanation and Interpretation." In *Mythic Symbols, Language, and Philosophic Anthropology,* ed. David M. Rasmussen, pp. 135–50. The Hague: Martinus Nijhoff.
1975   *La métaphore vive.* Paris: Seuil.

Romanowski, Sylvie
  1974   "Descartes: From Science to Discourse." *Yale French Studies*
              49:96–110.
Rousseau, Jean Jacques
  1964a.   *The First and Second Discourses.* Tr. R. and J. Masters. New
              York: St. Martin's Press.
  1964b   *Oeuvres Complètes.* Vols. 1–5, Ed. B. Gagnebin and M. Ray-
              mond. Paris: Gallimard.
  1966   "Essay on the Origin of Language." In *On the Origin of Lan-
              guage,* ed. John H. Moran and Alexander Gode. New York:
              Frederick Ungar.
Sartre, Jean-Paul
  1940   *L'Imaginaire.* Paris: Gallimard NRF.
  1957   *The Transcendence of the Ego.* Tr. F. Williams and R. Kirkpa-
              trick. New York: Noonday Press.
  1976   *Critique of Dialectical Reason.* Tr. A. Sheridan-Smith. Atlantic
  v   Highland, N.J.: Humanities Press. (Original French edition 1960)
Saumjan, Sebastian K.
  1966   "La cybernétique et la langue." In Benveniste 1966a, pp. 137–
              52.
Saussure, Ferdinand de
  1966   *Course in General Linguistics.* Tr. W. Baskin. New York:
              McGraw-Hill.
Schneider, David
  1968   *American Kinship: A Cultural Account.* Englewood Cliffs, N.J.:
              Prentice-Hall.
Schneider, David M., and Smith, Raymond T.
  1973   *Class Differences and Sex Roles in American Kinship and Fam-
              ily Structure.* Englewood Cliffs, N.J.: Prentice-Hall.
Scholes, Robert
  1974   *Structuralism in Literature.* New Haven: Yale University Press.
Scholes, Robert, and Kellogg, Robert
  1966   *The Nature of Narrative.* New York: Oxford University Press.
Schutz, Alfred
  1964   *Collected Papers. Volume II: Studies in Social Theory.* The Ha-
              gue: Martinus Nijhoff.
Sebeok, Thomas A.
  1960   *Style in Language.* Cambridge, Mass.: The M.I.T. Press.
  1975   "Six Species of Signs: Some Propositions and Strictures."
              Semiotica 13:3, 233–60.
  1972   ed. *Perspectives in Zoosemiotics, Janua Linguarum,* no. 122.
              The Hague and Paris: Mouton.
  1976a   "The Semiotic Self" (working draft).
  1976b   "Iconicity." Keynote Address to the *Charles S. Peirce Sym-
              posium on Semiotics. Modern Language Notes* 91, 1427–56.
  1976c   *Zoosemiotics.* The Hague: Mouton.
  1977   "Natural Semiotics." Paper read at the 76th Annual Meeting of
              the American Anthropological Association, Houston (Decem-
              ber).
  1978a   ed. *Sight, Sound, and Sense.* Bloomington: Indiana University
              Press.

1978b   "Looking for in the Destination What Should Have Been Sought in the Source." In *Language and Psychotherapy,* ed. L. Horowitz, A. Orenstein, R. Stern. New York: Haven Publishing Corp.

1979   *The Sign and its Masters.* Austin: University of Texas Press. (Especially chapters 1 and 9).

Sebeok, Thomas A., and Sebeok, Donna Jean Umiker

1979   "You Know My Method: Charles S. Peirce and Sherlock Holmes." *Semiotica* 26:3/4, 203–50.

1980   ed. *Speaking of Apes: A Critical Anthology of Two-Way Communication with Man.* New York: Plenum.

Sennett, Richard

1977   *The Fall of Public Man.* New York: Alfred A. Knopf.

Shands, Harley

1978   "Verbal Patterns and Medical Disease: Prophylactic Implications of Learning," In Sebeok 1978, pp. 175–201.

1979   "Body, Mind and Third World Object: A Dyadic Theory of Meaning." *Semiotic Scene* 3:1–23 (especially pp. 22–23, "The Golem and the Virus").

Shapiro, Michael, and Shapiro, Marianne

1976   *Hierarchy and the Structure of Tropes.* Bloomington, Ind.: Research Center for Language and Semiotic Studies.

Shattuck, Roger

1980   "How to Rescue Literature." *New York Review of Books 27:6* (April 17), 29–36.

Shils, Edward A.

1956   *The Torment of Secrecy: The Background and Consequences of American Security Policies.* New York: The Free Press. (Reprinted 1974 Arcturus Paperbacks. Carbondale: Southern Illinois University Press).

Singer, Milton

1978a   "For a Semiotic Anthropology." In Sebeok 1978, pp. 202–31.

1978b   "Signs of the Self." Address to the National Meeting of the American Anthropological Association, Los Angeles (November).

Smith, Valene L.

1977   ed. *Hosts and Guests: The Anthropology of Tourism.* Philadelphia: The University of Pennsylvania Press.

Spitzer, Leo

1962   "American Advertising Explained as Popular Art." *Essays on English and American Literature.* Princeton: Princeton University, pp. 248–77. (Spitzer was a 'stylistics' critic and follower of Heidegger.)

Spivak, Gayatry Chakravortry, and Ryan, Michael

1978   "Anarchism Revisited: A New Philosophy." *Diacritics* 8:2 (Summer), 66–79.

Stendhal (Marie Henri Beyle's pseudonym)

n.d.   *Racine et Shakespeare.* Paris: Le Divan.

1961   *La Chartreuse de Parme.* Paris: Garnier.

Stokoe, William C.

1978a   "Sign Languages and the Verbal/Nonverbal Distinction." In Sebeok 1978a, pp. 157–72.

Stonum, Gary Lee
1977   "For a Cybernetics of Reading." *Modern Language Notes* 92:944–68.

Sudnow, David
1972a   ed. *Studies in Social Interaction.* New York: The Free Press.
1972b   "Temporal Parameters of Interpersonal Observation." In Sudnow 1972a, pp. 259–79.

Sturrock, John.
1979   ed. *Structuralism and Since.* New York: Oxford University Press.

Todorov, Tzvetan
1967   *Littérature et signification.* Paris: Larousse.
1971   *La poétique de la prose.* Paris: Seuil.
1977   *Poetics of Prose.* Ithaca: Cornell University Press.

Turkle, Sherry
1979   *Psychoanalytic Politics.* New York: Basic Books.

Turner, Victor
1967   *The Forest of Symbols: Aspects of Ndembu Ritual.* Ithaca: Cornell University Press.

Umiker (Sebeok), D. Jean
1974   "Speech Surrogates: Drum and Whistle Systems." In *Current Trends in Linguistics* 12, ed. T. A. Sebeok, pp. 497–536.

Ungar, Steven
1977   "RB: The Third Degree." *Diacritics* 8:1, 67–77.

von Uexkull, Thure
1979   *Terminological Problems of Medical Semiotics.* Munich: Fink.

Voloshinov, V. N.
1976   *Freudianism: A Marxist Critique.* Tr. I. R. Titunik. New York: Academic Press.

Wade, Gail
1979   "A Lacunian Study: De Man and Rousseau," *Eighteenth Century Studies* 12:4 (Summer), 504–12.

Weber, Samuel
1977   "The Divaricator: On Freud's *Witz.*" *Glyph* 1, 1–28.

Wellek, René, and Warren, Austin
1942   *The Theory of Literature.* New York: Harcourt Brace.

White, Leslie
1949   *Science of Culture.* New York: Farrar, Straus, and Giroux.

Wilden, Anthony
1968   *The Language of the Self.* New York: Dell. (Comment on Lacan's "The Function of Language in Psychoanalysis")
1972a   *Essays in Communication and Exchange: System and Structure.* London: Tavistock. (Freud's semiotic, pp. 155–78; pattern encoding, pp. 351–412).

Wilson, Edward
1975   *Sociobiology.* Cambridge, Mass.: Harvard University Press.
1978   *On Human Nature.* Cambridge, Mass.: Harvard University Press.

Wimsatt, William K., Jr.
1954   *The Verbal Icon: Studies in the Meaning of Poetry.* Lexington: University of Kentucky Press.

Wimsatt, W. K., Jr., and Beardsley, Monroe C.
1960   "The Intentional Fallacy." In *The Study of Literature,* ed. S. Barnet, M. Berman, and W. Burto. *et al.* Boston: Little, Brown.
Winner, Irene P., and Winner, Thomas G.
1976   "The Semiotics of Cultural Texts." *Semiotica* 18:2, 101–56.
Wordsworth, William
1961   "The Preface to the *Lyrical Ballads"* [Original 1802]. *The Prelude: Selected Poems,* ed. C. Baker. New York: Holt, Rinehart and Winston.
Young, Frank W.
1964   "Location and Reputation in a Mexican Intervillage Network." *Human Organization* 23 (Spring): 36–41.
1966   "A Proposal for Cooperative Cross Cultural Research on Intervillage Systems." *Human Organization* 25 (Spring), 46–50.
1970   "Reactive Subsystems." *American Sociological Review* 35:2 (April), 297–307.
1976   "Communities as Symbolic Structures." Paper presented to the Dept. of Applied Behavioral Sciences, University of California at Davis (March)
Young, Frank W., and Young, Ruth C.
1960   "Social Integration and Change in Twenty-Four Mexican Villages." *Economic Development and Cultural Change* 8 (July), 366–70.
1973   *Comparative Studies of Community Growth.* Rural Sociological Society Monograph Number 2. Morgantown: West Virginia University Press.
Zukav, Gary
1979   *The Dancing Wu Li Masters: An Overview of the New Physics.* New York: William Morrow.

Index